# KINGDOM

Haroldson Lafayette Hunt

# KINGDOM

The Story of the Hunt Family
of Texas

Jerome Tuccille

Jameson Books
Ottawa, Illinois

Copies of this book may be purchased from the publisher for $16.95. All inquiries and catalogue requests should be addressed to Jameson Books, Inc., 722 Columbus St., Ottawa, IL 61350. (815) 434-7905.

ISBN: 0-915463-00-8

**Library of Congress Cataloguing in Publication Data**

Tuccille, Jerome.
    Kingdom: the story of the Hunt family of Texas.

    Bibliography: p.
    Includes index.
    1. Businessmen—United States—Biography.
2. Capitalists and financiers—United States—Biography.
3. Hunt family.   I. Title.
HC102.5.A2T83   1984      338.092'2 [B]      83-26747
ISBN 0-915463-00-8

With love to
Marie, Christine, and Jerry

# Contents

# Contents

# Prologue

IN 1960 JOHN F. KENNEDY was elected president of the United States. That was also the year the richest man in the world, H. L. Hunt, was asked about his relationship with the famous French soprano Lily Pons.

"I admire her and we're just friends," Hunt replied to a gaggle of reporters who had been hounding him for weeks on the subject. Stories about a romantic liaison between the American oil billionaire and France's most illustrious opera star had been circulating ever since Pons had taken up residence at Hunt's home in Dallas. Why else would he have shown a sudden interest in opera? the reporters asked one another. Why else would Hunt, a man who had never been known for his generosity or for his interest in cultural affairs, be staging a performance of *The Barber of Seville* at the Music Hall in the Dallas Fair Grounds? His libido had to be involved. The old man, at seventy-one, was still said to have an eye for a well-turned ankle by those who knew him well. And the famous French soprano, at fifty-six, was just the sort of spirited voluptuary Hunt had always fancied.

But, despite appearances, H. L. Hunt insisted that the opera singer's presence in his home was strictly professional. Love of opera was the only bond they shared. When the big night finally arrived, the crowds came flooding into the Music Hall in their best Texas finery. It was not often that anyone had a chance to enjoy a night of entertainment at H. L. Hunt's expense. It was a glorious evening and the performance went smoothly. The enthusiastic audience demonstrated its appreciation with cries of "Bravo!" and "Brava!" after every aria. Then, during intermission, the entire cast came out on stage and spoke as one. Overwhelmed by the great success of the evening, which of course was made possible by the uncharacteristic generosity of Mr. Hunt, the cast asked the great man to come up on stage and take a bow—perhaps even say a word or two to the audience.

A hush fell over the Music Hall as every head turned toward the figure rising in the front row. He smiled down at his wife and children, then walked tall and erect to the stage. The audience applauded loudly as he strode to center stage. The bright spotlight played on the thin tufts of white hair surrounding his bald head and his bowtie wagged beneath his chin. He seemed to be carrying a carton or a small box under one of his arms. After a moment or two the applause subsided, and H. L. Hunt looked out across the audience. He reached into the carton, removed an object from within, and held it high over his head.

"Hello, I'm H. L. Hunt," he said, "who some people think is the world's richest man. And this here is Gastro-Majic, which I take every day, so it must be good."

The audience, speechless with gratitude a brief moment before, sat dumbfounded as its benefactor proceeded to use up the entire intermission reading from an anticommunist tract he sponsored on the radio every Sunday morning. While he recited his exotic message, which combined Christian fundamentalism and ultraright politics, several of his aides dispensed samples of Gastro-Majic—the elixir Hunt believed to be nothing less than the divine Fountain of Youth—among the multitudes. The crowd sat quietly through the impromptu performance, too stunned to utter a sound.

H. L. Hunt was paying for this night at the opera, you see. But nobody ever said it would be a commercial-free evening.

When H. L. Hunt died on November 29, 1974, just three months shy of his eighty-sixth birthday, the world remembered him as a stingy oil billionaire, as well as a right-wing bigot, something of a racist and an anti-Semite, a religious fanatic, and a health-food faddist who dined on nuts, fruit, and strange elixirs every day.

Yet, most people would have been surprised to hear that Hunt was, more than anything else, a man of paradox, and of larger-than-life contradictions. In his youth he had been a reckless wanderer, a roughneck, a professional gambler who bet on everything from poker games and crap games to horses and baseball, a bigamist who sired two families simultaneously and fathered four illegitimate children while he was still living with his first wife, a failed cotton farmer and real estate speculator who went broke half a dozen times before he was forty, and a consummate con artist who acquired the most productive oil leases in the country with other people's money.

The story of Hunt is the story of one of the most towering figures in American history. It is the story of a self-made man, a man who was above all a successful gambler and womanizer and who became, ironically enough, a puritanical political and religious fanatic relatively late in life. Despite his quixotic crusades on behalf of Christian fundamentalism, he himself was not converted to the faith until the sprightly age of seventy. His political association with Senator Joseph McCarthy and his championship of General Douglas MacArthur for president of the United States read more like comic opera than anything else. The story of Hunt lives on today in his sons

Bunker and Herbert, who rocked the financial world with the silver crash of 1980.

To understand this unique American, whose life intertwined with so many leading figures of the forties, fifties, and sixties, and whose family continues to dominate the financial world of the eighties, we have to go back in time. Back to the roots. Back to a small town in Illinois right after the Civil War.

# Book I

# The Wanderer

# 1.

YOU KNOW HOW IT USED to be in Carson Township, Illinois, during the years right after the Civil War. One road came east out of Ramsey and the other one, the main road, ran north from Vandalia. Where they crossed two churches stood, and in the morning the early sun shone white against their steeples.

Up there in southern Illinois the farmland held greater promise than it did in Arkansas following the Civil War. Waddy Thorpe Hunt had originally moved his family from Georgia to the foothills of the Ozark Mountains in Arkansas, and when the great war broke out between the states he formed a cavalry company to fight for the Confederacy. Captain Hunt headed up the outfit and his son, Haroldson Lafayette, served under him as a trooper. When Captain Hunt was shot to death near his farm by northern raiders, H. L., or Hash as he was called, was prematurely thrust into his father's role as head of the family.

Hash decided to move the family north after taking an oath of allegiance to the Union in 1864. The southern cause was lost and Lee's surrender at Appomattox drove the final nail into the coffin of the Confederacy. The Plan of Reconstruction would soon begin, and carpetbaggers and northern businessmen were already streaming south into the ravaged and defeated countryside, introducing their alien style of commerce and trampling underfoot the traditions of a once proud and venerated people. Up north was where the money was, Hash told his family. The South, as they had known it all their lives, was finished. It would not rise again for fifty years at least.

So north they went. Abandoning their farm in Arkansas and loading what possessions they could on their backs and on a rickety makeshift wagon, they took to the road on foot. Trudging along past idle and deserted farms in southern Missouri, they headed northeast toward St. Louis. Everywhere they traveled they could see evidence of the recent war. The land around Lynchburg, then farther northeast in Salem and Cherryville, Missouri, was cut and laid open by the machines of destruction. Fallow farmlands were scarred and untended. They continued farther north where the countryside and the people looked more promising.

Crossing into Illinois, they suddenly knew they had arrived. The scene before them seemed in every way transformed, as though a Great Divide had been bridged and they had crossed safely into a new land where people breathed a different kind of air, where they seemed a little less defeated as they went about their daily business of wrenching a living out of the rich and fertile soil, and where the land itself was healthy and unravaged by the brutalizing war. Hash Hunt may have been a Confederate veteran, but he was determined to survive and prosper as a Yankee farmer.

When the family came to the farming country where the two churches stood at the crossroads north of Vandalia, Hash Hunt was a strapping young man nearly six feet tall. Rugged and handsome, he had a full head of sandy hair, light penetrating eyes, which he fixed directly on those he spoke to, and a reddish-blond beard and mustache covering his broad jaw. His body was hard from years of tough physical labor.

Fully determined as he was to become a northerner as quickly as possible, it was not too surprising that he soon took up with a pretty young girl, two weeks older than himself, who was the daughter of a Union army chaplain. Ella Rose Myers Henderson was descended from an old Huguenot line, and she deported herself with a certain aristocratic air not unworthy of her birthline. She was pretty in a rather pinched, prim sort of way, having dark-brown hair that fell in a thin curtain of twisting curls to her shoulders and pale-blue eyes a shade lighter than Hash's. Ella Rose married Hash and the two set up housekeeping on a five-hundred-acre farm a few miles east of Ramsey. If there was any doubt of it before this time, Hash Hunt had fully established himself as a respectable northern farmer.

Time passed smoothly for the young couple, in the beginning at least, as they settled into a life of farming and child-rearing. Their first, Robert, was born in 1873, a year after their marriage. Next came Florence, Rose, James, Sherman, Henrietta, and Leonard, all born in fairly regular order between 1874 and 1886. The eighth child born to Hash and Ella Rose was another boy, whom they decided to call Haroldson Lafayette Hunt, after his father. After more than twenty years up north, and after enriching his adopted new world with seven children, Hash decided it was time for a namesake. Ella Rose, for her part, was happy to see the long line finally completed. She was as tired as could be and growing older. Lord! Lord! She had had enough of child-bearing. Junior, who entered the world on February 17, 1889, would be her last.

By the time Junior was born, whose name was later shortened to June, life had grown a little harsher in the farmlands in southern Illinois. Many farmers as nearby as

Kansas had gone broke from the drought, and a major depression gripped the country in the 1880s. Hogs and other livestock were slaughtered and eaten by the farmers themselves since no one could afford to buy meat, and in the winter they were forced to burn their own rotting corn to keep warm, having been unable to sell it in the market.

Conditions in Carson Township were only slightly better, and Hash just managed to scrub out a meager living from the soil and feed his eight growing children. To supplement his income and further enhance his standing as a loyal Yankee farmer, Hash decided to enter politics. In 1894 he was elected sheriff of Fayette County, as a Republican no less; his abandonment of his southern tradition and his acceptance as a pillar of northern society were now complete. Hash was the first Republican ever elected to this office, and it was with a certain smugness that he assumed his office in the old Greek Revival courthouse in Vandalia, the county seat, twelve miles south of his farm.

The great old building had been the state capitol back in 1839 when Abraham Lincoln was beginning his career as a legislator in Vandalia. And now Hash Hunt was taking office in the homeland of his former enemy, the Emancipator of the slaves and scourge of the South. With his full beard and sturdy girth, Hash bore a somewhat stagy resemblance to Ulysses S. Grant as he presided over his sheriff's office in the land of Lincoln. His routine kept him away from his family for days at a time as he performed his new duties and slept nights in his quarters a block down the street from the great old courthouse. Twelve miles north on the family farm, James acted as surrogate father and tended the farm after the oldest son, Robert, got married and bought a place of his own a few miles west, closer to Ramsey.

Returning to the old farmhouse on his land after spending a week in Vandalia, Hash Hunt would storm through the house, sipping a bit of his own homemade corn whiskey from a jar, and thundering to anyone within earshot his views on the world, on the hard times that had spread throughout the nation like a pestilence, on the politicians who had brought these conditions about, and on the bare living he was able to scratch out from his farm and his sheriff's salary. Hash had managed to survive the depression of the 1880s while others, farmers and shopkeepers alike, went broke and hungry around him.

Like many men who feel that true success has somehow eluded them and their time to make it has irrevocably passed them by, Hash Hunt took out his resentment on those closest to him, driving a wedge of alienation between his family and himself. Age had grayed his hair and beard a bit, and thickened his body, and he was a formidable figure as he raged through the house, sipping his homemade corn brew and terrorizing his wife and children with his tirades. Ella Rose drew more and more into herself, quietly accepting his verbal assaults and doing her duty as a proper Christian wife, turning her attentions to her youngest, Junie, in her loneliness and fear. Junie was her pet, her baby, and he looked to her for refuge against this strange, violent man who filled him with terror every time he entered the house.

Hash, paradoxically enough, came to resent this special relationship between his youngest son, his namesake, and his quietly suffering wife. Young June should have been his special son, the one who bore his name, and yet the boy had come along at a difficult time, a time when money was in short supply, when Hash was growing more and more distant from his wife with each passing day, and when he was least inclined to take the boy under his wing and raise him in his own image.

Returning unexpectedly one day from Vandalia, Hash Hunt stormed into the kitchen of his farmhouse and saw his wife, now a graying full-blown woman of fifty-two, bent over the long rough-oak kitchen table kneading bread dough. Standing on a milk box in front of her as she worked the dough, the seven-year-old Junie had his face upturned as he suckled her naked breast. Now Hash had heard stories from James, the oldest boy still at home who was working the family farm, that Ella Rose was nursing Junie longer than was natural. Hash dismissed these stories at the time, having preferred abolishing the thought to facing something that seemed shameful and repugnant to him.

"Good God, woman! What's going on right here in my own house?"

The farmhouse was quiet as death. Ella Rose pulled back in fear, covering her naked breast as she stared into the enraged face of her husband. Junie kept to his mother's side, backing away from the erupting violence that had come upon them suddenly.

"Have you no shame? Nursing the boy like he was still an infant!"

Ella Rose struggled to reclaim her composure. Junie stood back, regarding his father with a mixture of fear and hatred. At the moment fear predominated, though hatred won out when the man was absent.

"Don't make it out to be more than it is, Hash," Ella Rose said, making a cautious attempt at defending herself and her son.

"More than it is? Don't I have eyes to see for myself? I'm not blind and stupid, woman. Dear God! It's a shameful thing I see going on between the two of you."

"Not in front of Junie, Hash. Please. You'll regret your words later on."

"I'll regret nothing except not listening to my own instincts. I've been blind for years. Too busy to put my foot down when it mattered most. Let this be the end of it, you hear! I'll listen to no pale excuses. This has to end at once or

I'll know the reason why not. Dear Lord! I've been a fool all these years in my own house."

Hash's word was final. Ella Rose never exposed her bosom to her youngest son again: whether out of fear of her husband or out of her own shame was never explained to young June. The boy came to hate and resent his father all the more for taking from him what was the most important thing he had known so far—his intimacy with his mother. Hash tried to assume a more active role in family affairs from that day on, but the effort was a hollow one; his heart simply was not in it.

"Why," he would rail on one occasion after another, "didn't I stay down south? There's a place along the Mississippi Delta, on the Arkansas side of the river, where the soil is rich and alluvial. A man could really make things grow down there. Dear God, we could be living like kings if I had gone to Ditch Bayou near Lake Village instead of coming up here."

Junie listened to his father's lament in silence. He said nothing to this strange and violent man who dominated the life of the family when he was home, but he would never forget his words. In his daydreams young Junie made up fantasies about how life would be down there, in that rich alluvial soil along the Mississippi Delta, and he longed to be there with his mother, just the two of them together. Later on he would do something about those fantasies. But not quite yet. His time was yet to come.

Life at home when his father and brother James were not around was agreeable enough for the growing boy. He hated James, the surrogate master of the house who was more like Hash than any of the other sons, but he enjoyed an especially warm relationship with his sisters and his brother Leonard. The girls, in particular, had teased him often enough about being Ella Rose's favorite and about the inordinate amount of time he had spent at his mother's breast. But the teasing was good-natured and playful, unlike James's sneering and resentful taunting. The girls regarded Junie as their own special pet, as well as Ella Rose's. Sherman and Leonard were nicer than James; particularly Leonard, who had always been his favorite.

They all looked upon young Junie as the family prodigy. They thought he was smarter than all the rest of them put together, and he used to dazzle them with his unusual memory and his ability to read by the time he was scarcely out of diapers. Ella Rose educated the boy herself, reading to him from the Bible in Greek, Latin, French, and German, and then translating all the foreign words into English for him. She also gave him the *St. Louis Globe Democrat* to read for himself when he was three years old. June gained a reputation throughout the region as a child genius, despite the fact that he never attended the local school. His entire education was received from his mother and from his sisters' readers, which he devoured when they came home from school.

Junie's memory also served him well in games of chance, particularly card games, which he played with his older brothers and sisters. He was able to beat them all at Authors, a game played with special cards divided into sets, each one relating to a different author; and he also beat them regularly at Flinch, another popular card game at the time. Life would have been just wonderful for June if he could have spent it exclusively with Ella Rose, his sisters, and his brother Leonard.

Hash Hunt was not nearly so impressed with his namesake's mental agility as the others were. And right from the beginning June had problems with James.

"You think you're better than the rest of us, don't you?" James badgered him incessantly when they were alone. "You think you're smarter than we are."

"I don't. It's not true."

"You act like you're Lord God Almighty and the rest of us have to work like slaves. You're mama's pet, that's all you'll ever be."

Junie glared at his older brother through eyes filling with tears. He was hurt, frustrated, and angry. James was just plain unfair, but it did no good to argue with him.

"Don't mind James," his sisters consoled, when they were alone. "He's just jealous, that's all. He don't mean what he says."

June was determined to show his father that he could do more than read and beat everyone else at card games; he was not a mama's boy. As he grew he developed his body as well as his mind. He learned to ride bareback and enjoyed putting the various farm horses through their paces on wild romps through the fields. He fished and swam in the big stream that cut across the middle of their farm. And when he grew a little older, he worked with James in the family business, weighing fruit and vegetables on the big scales, totting up orders and receipts, and keeping the books in order. He was growing into a handsome young lad, the best-looking of all his brothers, and it was clear he was going to be tall and strong like his father.

But the more he tried to please the old man by helping out in the family business and turning himself into a boy's boy, the more bitterly Hash criticized him and complained that he was his mother's pet. And the bigger he grew and better he became at dealing with their business associates, the more James resented him. There was nothing in the world he could do to please his father and older brother, and after a while he just stopped trying, deciding it wasn't worth the effort. They were making life miserable for him and nothing he did seemed to please them. When Congress declared war on Spain in 1898 and James enlisted, young Junie's enthusiasm for his brother's heroic act had little if anything to do with patriotism. The sinking of the *Maine* in Havana Harbor, resulting in the loss of two hundred sixty American lives, crystallized popular support around the war effort. James was shipped off to the Philippines and, for the moment at least, June was able to breathe more easily.

# 2.

Hash Hunt's term as sheriff enhanced his reputation in the county. The depression ended and boom times returned to America. Hash's business began to prosper, and through his political activities, he was able to make some valuable business contacts. He acquired more farmland near the churches that stood at the crossroads north of Vandalia, and started his own bank in the small farm town of Ramsey, west of his property.

Ramsey, at the turn of the century, was a quiet village with about six hundred inhabitants. They were farmers who worked the land in the countryside around the town. Most of the farms were fairly small, smaller than Hash's, and the People's State Bank, which Hash formed with some business associates, provided most of the working capital for the harvest season. Junie had a wonderful opportunity to observe up close the workings of the American free-enterprise system when his oldest brother, Robert, started his own bank in Ramsey to compete directly with his father's. Hash little appreciated this unique form of incestuous capitalism, but it was a great source of merriment among the neighbors.

Pretty soon the family ranks began to thin out. Robert was long gone, married and now in competition with his old man. James was a grizzled veteran of the Spanish-American War. And now Sherman decided he had had enough of life down on the farm and took off to the wilds of Montana to try his hand at

[13]

ranch work. The loss of Sherman from the family homestead was an event June could cope with. He got along well enough with this brother, but they were not especially close. But when Leonard decided to follow in Sherman's footsteps shortly afterward, Junie was devastated. Of all his brothers he liked Leonard the best.

It wasn't long before he tried to find out for himself what running away from home was really like. It all sounded so adventurous, camping out in the fields alongside streams and rivers, working with cattle and livestock on ranches, and maybe working in logging camps way out there in the Northwest. Wanderlust seemed to run through the entire family; June's father certainly had it years ago, and recently his older brothers. And now, at twelve, Junie tried it for the first time. He ran off a few miles upstate, sleeping under trees on the side of the road a night or two at a time. Ella Rose was frantic and pleaded with Hash to do something about it, but the old man did little. What with all his ranting and raving, he had never exercised much control over his sons.

By the time June was fourteen years old, his absences had taken him farther from home, once as far as fifty miles to the northeast, where he found work on a farm harvesting corn. He had discovered that many other young vagabonds were on the road, boys and girls alike, whose families were too poor to feed them properly at home. On occasion, he had hooked up with a gang of them, and slept in teenage hobo jungles around open campfires.

All this, however, was preliminary to the big move that would set the pattern of his life for the next thirty years. Now in his sixteenth year, June Hunt was nearly full-grown. He had shot up to his full adult height of six feet. His shoulders were broad and muscular, his body full and solid. In two years he would be a natural two-hundred-pounder. With his favorite brother gone from the house and life at home becoming more disagreeable each day, June Hunt decided that his time had finally come. There was simply no good reason to continue living at home any longer.

After stuffing the barest essentials into a rucksack—a change of underwear, some socks, an extra shirt or two, and two decks of cards—and bidding a tearful farewell to his mother and sisters, June Hunt left the farm and headed south on foot on a warm spring day in 1905. He was just a few months past his sixteenth birthday.

In Vandalia the boy walked past the old Greek Revival courthouse where his father used to ply his trade as sheriff. To this, to the town, and to the man who had ruled his life with his terrifying rages, he bade goodbye. June Hunt headed to the railroad yard south of town; here the freight trains stopped on their way west, into the heartland of America. With nothing but his bedroll and the clothes on his back, the sixteen-year-old hopped aboard a train. He was now another bindlestiff thumbing a ride across the country. The train took off and headed west. His time had finally begun.

# 3.

WORK WAS FAIRLY EASY to find for America's itinerants in the early days of the twentieth century. There was great demand for manual labor on the farms and ranches, and in the logging camps in the Northwest. June Hunt was young and strong. He was used to hard work and anxious to try his hand at new and challenging jobs.

June had been to St. Louis before with his family, but this was his first time in the great, bustling city on his own. The railroad needed able-bodied men to work as section hands. June signed on and was assigned to a crew that was shipped off to the western part of Kansas to repair tracks. He was for some time a member of the section gang, but eventually he tired of the job and felt the need for a new challenge. When he saved up a bit of money, he packed his kit and hit the road again. He worked his way from Kansas to Colorado, washing dishes here, laboring in the sugar-beet fields there. From Colorado he worked his way further westward into Utah, where he herded sheep and eventually got a job tending a carload of sheep on a train to California. In Santa Ana the young man found work with a road-building contractor, for whom he drove a dump wagon that spread sand and gravel. Each new job gave him a valuable new experience, and experience was to him the best education of all.

It seems that most adventurous young Americans headed west in those days, away from the confinements of civilization back east toward the wild western land, where, they imagined, a semblance of the old frontier spirit still remained. Most westbound adventurers eventually landed in California, enticed by the vast and alluring green Pacific. June was no exception. And he found California much to his liking, especially the lush blonde beauties, who appeared as plentiful as the succulent fruit that grew in this golden sun-soaked land. With his good height and his hard solid body, his deep-set blue eyes and rugged looks, he had little trouble in attracting more than his share of young females. His sexuality was strong and developing, and he exuded an aura of raw animal magnetism.

When he had had his fill of road work, as well as the girls who grouped around the roadside camps near Santa Ana, the same way they do around military camps and other places where men live and work together, young June headed north. Farming in California was much different from what it had been back home in Illinois. The farms were bigger and the machinery more complicated. He learned to drive a mule team at the Irvine Ranch, planted trees, and hauled olives on horseback, something he had never done before.

And then came San Francisco, as sooner or later it always does for young American wanderers eager for adventure. June Hunt had saved some money from his various jobs, and he headed for San Francisco's Barbary Coast, a stretch of honkytonks, flea-bag hotels and roominghouses, noisy gambling halls, and dark streets filled with sailors, drunks, and prostitutes. Junie was now in his element. Here were adventure and excitement of a kind different from what he had been accustomed to.

The boy found a room in a rundown roominghouse filled with sailors on leave, merchant seamen, and riffraff from the distant corners of the globe. Ofttimes in the early morning, as he lay awake on a thin lumpy mattress unable to sleep with a bellyful of gin after a night of roaming the seedy bars and gambling joints along the waterfront, he could hear the noises in the hallway outside his bedroom door. Occasionally a hand would grip the doorknob, turning it in an attempt to get inside. June, awake, would clench his fists, ready to spring into action to defend himself.

When June was not cruising the nightspots looking for a place he had never been to before, he would take a turn at poker in one of the many gambling halls that dotted the waterfront. His memory for numbers was photographic. He could remember what cards had been played, and this gave him a good idea of just how good an opponent's hand was likely to be. He was a countdown artist with an incredible ability to calculate probabilities based on cards that had already been played, and this natural talent grew sharper with each game. As a result, he was a winner more times than not, and he found that poker could provide him with a lucrative source of income.

One night June approached a streetwalker after an especially successful night at the card table, and she brought him back to her own hotel, which was just down the street from his. They undressed and hopped into her bed. June took his pleasure and was generous with the wad of dollars in his pocket. The woman saw that he was a handsome and an exciting youth with a bankroll, and that he was considerate in his lovemaking, unlike the drunken sailors and sadistic creeps she was used to dragging in off the streets, riffraff that might beat her up and steal her hard-earned money.

"Where you stayin', honey?" she asked him as they were lying back smoking a cigarette after they had finished.

"Oh, just down the street. That rattrap down on the corner."

The girl sat up quickly and dashed out her cigarette in the ashtray she balanced on her knees.

"Oh, honey. Look, you gotta leave there right away. That place is no good. It's just plain trouble."

June looked at her more amused than concerned. After two nights in the joint, he didn't need her to tell him what a nightmare it was.

"I can take care of myself pretty good. It ain't the best place in the world, but I been in worse."

"No, honey, no. You don't understand. It's more than what you think. The saloon downstairs, they hire, well, they hire girls like me to slip a powder into the guys' drinks and then they shanghai them off someplace. The guys wake up a day later out on a ship somewhere."

June was intrigued and horrified. He had heard stories about whores slipping Mickeys into sailors' drinks and setting them up so they could be shanghaied, but he thought all that belonged to the old days when the Barbary Coast was really something. In the old days, sure, but in this day and age?

"Tomorrow morning," the girl continued, "they're roundin' sailors up for a whalin' cruise. I swear to God. You gotta leave there right now."

June didn't need any more convincing.

He left the girl and went to his room. In five minutes his possessions, such as they were, were packed. And he was off into the night, a young American hobo leaving scarcely a trace of his existence behind. June carried his belongings to a different part of the city and took a room on the third floor of a good hotel, one of the only two high-rise buildings in town. A few days later he wandered back to the waterfront and looked up the pretty young whore who had warned him to leave. He found her in one of his haunts, not far from the spot where he first picked her up

"They're all gone," she told him. "They rounded them up at six that mornin', two hours after you left. They took them away on a whalin' ship headin' north, up to Alaska, I think. You got away just in time."

June worked around the San Francisco area for a while, mostly on farms north and east of the city. Then one day, after he had been in the city a few months, a friend of his told him about tryouts for a semipro baseball team in Reno, Nevada.

"I'm heading over there tomorrow," the boy said to him. "I've had enough of busting my back out here like a slave. Once you make the team you get free room and board and a few dollars a month pay, depending on how well the team does."

"I don't know," June was hesitant. "I played some baseball back home, but not that much. You probably got to be pretty good to get on a team like that."

"You got nothing to lose. You're big and strong. You can probably hit the ball pretty far when you connect. That's what these teams look for, the long-ball hitter. More important than anything else."

His friend was right. He had nothing to lose and the idea of trying out for a baseball team, farfetched as it sounded, held a certain appeal for him. It would be one more experience to add to a growing list of adventures. So what if he didn't make the team? It would be fun trying and he might learn something new as well.

The next day he and his friend hopped a train and made the trip northeast through Sacramento into Reno. They arrived at the training camp along with an army of other hopefuls, mostly itinerants like themselves, who were starry-eyed over the notion of being paid for playing a sport they had played for nothing all their lives. They were assigned beds in a large bunkhouse near the ballfield, and in the morning they were called out to take a turn at bat facing one of the regular pitchers on the team. June's friend may have been right in saying that he could probably wallop the ball a mile if he connected, but June never had a chance to prove it. The ball went streaming past his bat as though it were streaked lightning. He might as well have been swinging a club made out of Swiss cheese for all the connecting he did. It was immediately apparent that, whatever else he might do in life, he was not destined to become a professional or even a semiprofessional baseball player. June chalked up the episode as another great learning experience, and began to plan his next move.

No sooner had June packed his rucksack and said goodbye to his friend than he learned that his trip to Reno was fortunate after all. On the morning of April 18, 1906, the San Andreas fault shifted violently, and the city of San Francisco was ravaged by one of the most devastating earthquakes in its history. The golden city on the bay was rent by one cataclysmic jolt after another. Streets split open and buildings were shaken from their foundations and toppled like so many toy blocks, including the high-rise hotel where June had been living a few days before. The lovely sun-drenched city, which had lured so many of the nation's restless and adventurous, was leveled.

This was June's second close call in the space of a few short months. Much as he loved the city and the surrounding area, June respected numbers more than anything else in life. Everything else was fickle and fleeting, but numbers were constant and eternal. Two warnings were all he needed. The boy threw his bundle over his shoulder and headed southeast.

# 4.

THERE IS A VALLEY running through the forests and timberlands surrounding Flagstaff, Arizona, and nestled in this valley were logging camps where men turned trees into logs and shipped them off to mills farther down the valley. June turned up at a logging camp in the Pecos Valley; the camp was located alongside a branch line of the big railroad that connected Flagstaff and Phoenix. The gang with which June signed on was composed mostly of white men. Down the valley beside another branch line, closer to Prescott, was a logging camp filled with Mexican workers.

June had never worked in a logging camp before, and he found the rough, hard outdoor work agreeable to his nature. The spring sun was hot this close to the Mexican border. The countryside was wild, as wild as any he had seen on his footloose odyssey; it was marked by wide gaping canyons, blistering desert, and a broad expanse of high forests and low-slung valleys running through them. The men who worked in the logging camps were a tough breed—big, brawny, and quick to fight. At night, after a long, physically punishing day of work, they liked to sit around the campfire drinking whiskey, smoking, and playing poker.

Now and then June and a few friends would go down to the Mexican camp after work. They would stand around the camp drinking beer and whiskey with the Mexicans, and watching them play a card game June had never heard of before. The Mexicans called their game cooncan and they liked to gamble heavily on it. If anything, the Mexicans were even heavier drinkers and gamblers than the white loggers, and June was fascinated by them.

Cooncan was played with a Spanish card deck consisting of forty cards. The deck had the same cards that were in an American deck except for the eights, nines, and tens. After watching the Mexicans play the game a few nights, June had it figured out. It was a game of skill, strategy, and cunning. June never did believe in luck. Only suckers, he believed, trusted in luck where gambling was concerned. The numbers said it all, and the player with the ability to count down numbers and commit them to memory had the odds on his side. With fewer numbers to worry about in this game, June could more easily project probabilities than he could in poker. He observed that most of the Mexicans played the game recklessly, drinking and gambling heavily, trusting their game mostly to luck.

Most of the white loggers avoided gambling with the Mexicans, figuring it was just not their game. They preferred to stand around drinking and kidding with them instead. One night June asked if he might sit in for a hand or two. His friends laughed and clapped him on the back, wishing him good luck. The Mexicans laughed as well, making a spot for him around the crate beside the open campfire. They were always happy to see a gringo put his money on their game since most gringos weren't any good at it.

June dealt the cards around the crate, the firelight dancing on the slick coated paper. He won a hand and when the deal passed from him and moved around the circle, he continued to win fairly big. The crowd of men closed around the players as the mood changed considerably. The drinking, laughing, and earlier camaraderie dissipated quickly. One by one, the Mexicans were going bust and the atmosphere turned sour.

The white men rocked nervously from foot to foot, glancing at each other, and growing uncomfortable as the mood turned against them in this alien camp. June, however, was oblivious to it all; he was raking in pot after pot. When the Mexican participants went bust, their places around the crate were taken by others, who came from the bunkhouse with new money for the game. Their pride was at stake now; this gringo was beating them badly at their own game.

One of the white men leaned forward and whispered in June's ear. "Let's go, old buddy. These Mexes are startin' to look ugly." June waved him off and continued to win sensationally. Old faces left, new ones appeared to take their places, and the result was the same. One by one the white men drifted off after several more attempts to get June to fold and leave. But the boy seemed possessed as he took them hand after hand. He came to his senses only when he realized that the game was slowing down and the money drying up. Then it dawned on him what had happened. The stack of money in front of him amounted to almost $4,000. He looked up into a sea of dark somber faces. Their money was gone. He had wiped out the entire camp. Only pride had kept them in the game to the bitter end. Macho pride.

June got up and smiled graciously. "Adios, amigos. Muchas gracias." No one smiled back. He was the only white man left in camp. June waved and started to move off. He kept to the tracks and walked as fast as he could without appearing to be running. When he was beyond the camp and could no longer see the campfire licking the night with its orange and yellow tongues, he stuffed his winnings into his tobacco pouches and ran north along the tracks. After running a good distance toward his own camp, June cut left, away from the tracks and into the woods. He was afraid the Mexicans might try to overtake him on a handcar if he stayed along the tracks. Running through the thick woods, with only the moon and stars lighting the way in front of him, he angled toward his camp. The going was slow and tricky.

After what seemed like an eternity of bulling his way six or seven miles through the woods, June reached the outskirts of his own camp. The men had retired now and the camp was still. A sense of foreboding seized him and he hesitated before stepping into the clearing and crossing the open field to the bunkhouse. The tobacco pouches weighed heavily against his skin, buttoned up inside his shirt. He had $4,000 in there, the most money he had ever had at any one time in his life. These white men were strangers to him; he had worked and drunk with them, played cards with them, but he didn't really know them much better than he did the Mexicans whom he had just taken at their own game. How could he trust these brawny strangers who knew he had made a killing that night, saw him do it in fact? What was to stop two or three of them from jumping him in his bunk, leaving him with a knife between his ribs, and slipping off with his winnings?

Again the numbers spoke to him: $4,000. A stake. These lumberjacks would never see that much money one time in their whole lives. He was different from the rest of them now. He had money and they would resent him for it, try to take it away from him. He was in fact a stranger between two camps, unable to turn to either in safety. The numbers said it all and June slipped quietly back into the woods. He found a soft spread of grass beside a tree, away from the beaten track between the camps. He decided to bunk there for the night, what was left of it at least.

After the men had their breakfast and strolled off to work, June left the woods and entered the camp. The place was empty now, still as death itself. June chuckled to himself as he stuffed his handful of belongings into his rucksack and tossed it across his shoulder.

"Probably think the Mexes got me. Probably think I never got out of there alive."

The boy had been carefree ever since leaving home, but now, with a stake of money in his pockets, he was freer than he had ever been before. He headed north along the tracks, trying to decide what his next move should be. With $4,000 cash to his name, he could go virtually wherever he wanted.

Now seventeen years of age, June had been a loner all his life. His brother Leonard was by far the best friend he had ever had, but after Leonard took off with Sherman a couple of years back June felt abandoned and lonely. He had come to accept this as his natural condition in life. A lone wolf. His own man. He trusted no one and depended on no one.

On his way north June fell in with a young man a couple of years older than himself who reminded him strongly of his brother Leonard. For that reason more than any other June opened up to him a bit, and almost immediately began to think of him as a buddy, the first one he had ever had except for Leonard. June didn't know it at the time, but Steve would be the first and last true pal he would have throughout his entire life.

Steve took a fatherly interest in June. He admired the younger boy, this towering giant of a boy-man who had done so much and had so many experiences of his own, and June looked upon Steve as an older brother, a father-figure, and a friend, all in one. Steve told him about the wheat harvest that was now getting under way up north, so the two of them hopped a train that took them through Colorado and Nebraska and ended up in the northwest corner of South Dakota, just above Rapid City. Along the way June told his friend more about himself than he had ever revealed to anyone else. He told him about life back home where the churches stood at the crossroads in Carson Township, about his problems with his father and his brother James, and about his more pleasant relationships with his mother, his sisters, and his brother Leonard. He told Steve about his adventures in the West, about his near misses in California, and about the wild night of card playing with the Mexicans down in Arizona. He also told the older boy what he had learned from it all, and they discussed with each other their philosophies of life. They found that they agreed on most things. They were true buddies, with a good chemistry between them. June would never be this close to anyone else the rest of his life.

From South Dakota they followed the wheat harvest to North Dakota. The summer was coming to an end and the early-September air was beginning to take on a bit of a chill, the first warning sign of encroaching autumn. After work one evening, June and Steve were alone in the bunkhouse. The other men had gone off to the nearby village for a night of drinking. The season was ending and pretty soon all of them would have to move on in search of new work. June took out a deck of cards and the two of them played a few hands of solitaire idly while they chatted. They soon became bored playing just for fun, so they decided to put a little money on the game to make it more interesting.

In turnabout solitaire, each player pays the other $52, a dollar a card, for the deck. One player then goes first and tries to run the deck as far as he can until he has no more moves left. For each card he runs he gets back $5 from the other player. When the run of that player is over, the other player takes a turn, and he gets back $5 for every card he runs. The money usually balances out fairly evenly in the end since solitaire, unlike most other card games, is a game of chance rather than skill.

June picked the higher card on the draw and got to go first. The cards were falling well for him and he started a good run.

The cards just kept on falling in place, as though he had stacked the deck himself. His luck ran high, and within minutes, he had run out the entire deck. According to the rules, the game was over and Steve had to pay him $5 a card for a total of $260.

"I never seen anything like it," Steve said incredulously. "The whole deck! I never seen anybody run out a whole deck before."

"I can't believe it myself. Pure luck, that's all it was. Keep your money. That was just for fun."

"No, no. You beat me fair. I owe you $260."

"Hold onto it. It was just a friendly game that got out of control. I don't want your money."

"Fair is fair, June. I always pay my debts." Steve counted out $260, most of the money he had saved up from working the harvest, and tossed it on the blanket in front of June.

"Look. I don't feel right about this. You're my friend. This wasn't supposed to be a serious game. I don't need the money."

"Well, I don't need it either. I lost it fair and that's all that matters."

"Take back $100 then. You can't go away from here broke."

"I'll be okay. It's your money. I don't need it."

"Well I don't need it either. Here. Take back $50 then."

"No. I don't want it. You beat me fair and square and that's all there is to it."

But I still got most of that other money I won from the Mexicans. What am I supposed to do with it all?"

"Why, hell. You don't wanta keep bumming around the country all your life like a regular hobo. You're young and smart. Why don't you go to college?"

June stared at his friend and started to laugh. "Me go to college? You must be crazy. I never even set foot inside a grade school."

"So what. You got a better education at home with your mother. You said so yourself. You can read and write, and you know how to count better than anybody I ever saw."

June laughed and kept staring at his friend. College! Why not? This job was coming to an end and he had all that money in his pocket. He had already done about every kind of job he could think of, from washing dishes to logging and farming and ranching and road work. What was left for him? College was one experience he had never even thought of before. Why not? It would be exciting and fun.

Years ago, when he was a little boy on the farm in Carson Township, he had heard some neighbors talk about a college in Indiana. Valparaiso College it was called, the "poor man's Harvard" since it was about the only reputable college within reach of the farm boys with whom he had grown up. It was already September and the school term would just be starting. Steve would soon be moving off in his own direction, without any money as it turned out, and June would have to plan his next move.

He and Steve shook hands and said their goodbyes. They promised to stay in touch and keep each other informed of their whereabouts. They would meet again soon and go off on another great adventure together. That's what they promised. They never saw each other again.

# 5.

JUNE ARRIVED A FEW weeks late for the start of the fall term in 1906. Despite his lack of formal education, he talked the dean into letting him enroll for the fall semester. His money was good and his sister-in-law, Robert's wife, had graduated from the college a number of years back, when it was known by a different name. Besides, students were not then banging down the doors to enter the place, and government handouts were few and far between.

The seventeen-year-old boy signed up for Latin, algebra, rhetoric, zoology, and history. He had learned some Latin at his mother's knee as a growing boy, and the logical symbols and formulas of algebra appealed to his quick and calculating mind. After the life of action and adventure he had led, the sedentary life of a college campus was welcome relief for him. He applied himself diligently to his studies, as he had with every new learning experience, and his teachers were impressed by the hard-working six-foot two-hundred-pounder in their class. June had a voracious appetite for knowledge and experience of all kinds, and in all his subjects he scored high up in his class.

June's new bunkmates were younger and more innocent than those he had grown accustomed to, and he quickly turned this to his advantage. It didn't take him long to break out a deck of cards from his bindle and get a poker game going. The fair-cheeked college kids were easy marks for him, and June added considerably to his earlier winnings from the Mexican loggers. He managed to cover his college costs and then some. "It's like shooting fish in a barrel," he chuckled to a friend between classes one day. If Valparaiso was known as the "poor man's Harvard" before June's arrival, its student body was a hell of a lot poorer for his having been there.

He signed up for a second term, but just as the spring session was getting started, he developed a bad case of tonsillitis and came down with a fever. The illness refused to break and he found himself growing homesick for his mother and sisters after nearly two years of wandering. He was beginning to get a little bored with classwork and easy poker winnings in the dorm. So, shortly after his eighteenth birthday, in 1907, June decided it was time to go home. He was tired and sick and weary, and quite lonely as well, although he would never have admitted this to anyone, and could hardly admit it even to himself.

Ella Rose was an old woman. That's the first thing that entered June's mind when he stepped across the threshold of the old farmhouse in Carson Township. Ella Rose was getting old, had been old before he left although he didn't notice it so much at the time. Seeing someone every day blinds one to the subtle changes taking place in slow motion before one's eyes. She was over sixty now and showing it. The boy held her tightly and she sobbed quietly against his chest.

His sisters were married and gone, and Sherman was wandering somewhere in the Northwest the last time anyone heard from him. James too was married, but he lived nearby and still ran the family farm business. Hash, grown gray and stout, shook hands stiffly with his youngest son. The two of them, father and son, stared into each other's eyes, sizing up each other as they had always done in the past. They never did have much to say to each other, and the occasion of June's return to the family homestead was no exception. Hash occupied himself primarily with banking business these days, as did Robert, who remained his father's main competition.

The biggest surprise of all for June was the presence of Leonard, who, as chance would have it, was also home recuperating, he from a recurring attack of tuberculosis. Leonard had broken off his travels with Sherman when he fell ill a few weeks earlier, and had been home nursing his health and helping James when he could in the family business. He and June welcomed each other warmly; indeed, theirs was the warmest reunion except for June's long moment with Ella Rose.

Leonard was twenty-one now, three years older than June. He was slightly taller than his younger brother but not nearly so powerfully built and full-bodied. He was a good-looking young man but, again, June had the more rugged features of the two. The two boys enjoyed each other's company all the more for their lengthy separation, and they resolved to set off together the next time, just as soon as the warm weather arrived and their health was restored.

They pitched in together, helping James on the farm and their father in his bank a few miles west in the farming village of Ramsey. Bank work had little appeal to them, particularly to June, who much preferred being outdoors in the sun using his body as well as his mind. This was the happiest time of all for June, being with Leonard and Ella Rose once more after his lonely wanderings of the past two years. The brothers had many stories to exchange about the things they had done and seen and the places they had been to, and Ella Rose warmed to the presence of her two hulking sons in the house again.

When the air grows warm and fragrant with the lush bouquet of blooming things, young men in pursuit of adventure grow restless again. Their blood begins to flow like the streams rushing along their beds toward lakes and rivers. They must leave home again; must leave mothers and family behind and go out into the big world. So it was with June and Leonard. In the warm spring of 1907 they packed their bundles and started off together.

# 6.

THE TWO BROTHERS, now young men, headed south toward the logging camps in Arizona where June had made his big killing in the card game with the Mexicans. June had told this story several times to Leonard and the two of them laughed heartily each time. Leonard longed to see the canyons and desert and timberlands of the Southwest since most of his wanderings with Sherman had been through the far Northwest.

They found work in a logging camp in the national forest just outside of Flagstaff, not too far from the place June had worked on his earlier visit. Their work consisted of cutting down high-soaring pine trees with two-man saws, and the brothers grew closer than ever as they shared the joy of common labor.

One day June found himself on one end of a two-man saw opposite a big middle-aged man named Lou. Everyone called him Lou the Limberer because that's the only name he would answer to. An air of mystery surrounded Lou the Limberer. One story making the rounds was that he had been a northern banker who was forced to take to the road for reasons best not mentioned. Nobody asked too many questions in the logging camps and bunkhouses of America since most of these itinerant workers did not take too kindly to strangers prying into their past.

Lou the Limberer took a liking to June. He was in awe of

June's prowess in poker and respected his physique. The young man had broad shoulders, a barrel chest, a slim waist, and narrow hips. Somewhere along the line Lou had gotten the impression that June was from Arizona, perhaps because the young man talked about the area so much.

"Look at that boy's muscles. Arizona Slim can cut down a tree faster than anybody I ever saw. Yessir. Arizona Slim can do just about anything he wants to."

The name stuck. From that day on the men called June Arizona Slim, or Slim for short. Even Leonard called him Slim, clapping him on the back and laughing when he did so, and June decided right away that he liked his new name. The name had about it a sense of adventure and mystery, which appealed to the young man's vagabond nature.

When their work in Arizona was finished, Slim and Leonard traveled west across the border into Southern California. Their sister Florence was living in San Bernardino with her husband, Jack Wright. Slim had not for several years seen Florence, the second-oldest of his brothers and sisters and fourteen years older than he. Florence was happy to see her younger brothers again, and the young men stayed with her and Jack for a couple of weeks, loafing in the hot California sun and replenishing their strength after the tough physical labor of the logging camp.

After the domesticity and idleness of their brief hiatus, the brothers grew restless once more. One day they came down to breakfast with their rucksacks packed, exuding an air of departure. Florence knew this moment was coming. She had sensed it building the previous few days and had resigned herself to the certainty that the paths of their lives would be separating once again. Before they could leave she pulled her younger brother aside and took his hand.

"Promise me before you go, Junie, that you'll write to me and let me know where you are and how you're doing."

The young man shifted uneasily. Outward displays of affection embarrassed him. "Slim, remember? My name is Arizona Slim now," he said, making a weak attempt at humor.

"You'll always be Junie to me, my little brother. I don't care how big you get. You've got to promise you'll stay in touch. It's important, Junie."

"I promise. I'll write you and let you know where I am."

"Mom and pop are getting old and the rest of us are spread all over the place. We can't just let the family fall apart. We've got to care about each other and keep from growing into strangers."

"I understand. I won't break my promise."

"And take care of Leonard, you hear? Keep an eye out for him."

"Leonard!" Slim was taken by surprise. "He's older than I am. He ought to watch out for me."

"You're stronger than he is, June. You're stronger and smarter than all the rest of us. You're different and you'll go far. Leonard looks up to you even though he is your older brother. He wants to be just like you, but he's not a natural survivor like you are. You've got to keep an eye out for him."

"I will, Florence. Don't worry. Everything will be just fine."

Slim was a bit troubled when he took his leave of Florence. She had made him look at Leonard through different eyes all of a sudden. All his life he had looked up to Leonard and depended on him as a buffer against the hostilities of his father and his brother James. Florence had made him see Leonard's vulnerabilities. She was right; their roles had changed. Leonard was following him around now as he had taken the lead. Florence had forced a sense of responsibility on him and, at first, he resented her for it. He was a loner, answerable only to himself, and he did not want to feel responsible for anyone else. But he knew she was right. This wandering existence was good for him. Leonard loved the life too. But Leonard, at the same time, seemed a bit baffled by it all.

Despite his slight misgivings, Slim brought Leonard along with him on a lumber boat up the coast of California to Oregon. In all his travels Slim had never been to the great logging camps of the far Northwest before. He had heard much about them from Leonard, who had spent a good deal of time there with Sherman, and he decided it was time to see this part of the country for himself. He hoped to see Sherman again, whom he had not seen since he left home when Slim was still in his early teens. But Sherman had moved on to new stomping grounds without letting anyone know of his whereabouts. Slim pondered on this for a while. Sherman, apparently, was the brother he was most like after all.

The brothers traveled and worked together in Oregon until their work was finished. Then they wandered slowly toward the Midwest. Slim was true to his word; he wrote Florence a letter from every place they visited, telling her about their activities and what they were doing. This was a point of honor with Slim: whatever deficiencies he had as a human being, he regarded his word as a sacred trust. Once he had made a promise, he would not think of breaking it. His curious philosophy and code of ethics and honor were continuing to take shape.

By the time they had wandered into the Dakotas, to work the wheat harvest there as Slim had done a few years before when he was on his own, it was clear that Leonard was getting tired of their itinerant existence. He had become increasingly homesick and the restless lifestyle was wearing down his health. The harvest season was coming to an end and Slim was mapping out their next move, when Leonard asked him one evening after work, "Do you ever get tired of all this wandering around? Do you ever feel like going back home for a while and maybe settling down?"

Slim looked up from his map and stared at his older brother.

"Can't say I do, Leonard. Why? You thinking of heading back to Illinois soon?"

"What's going to come of all this roaming around from one place to another? I mean, what are you hoping to get from it? What are you looking for in life?"

Slim sat back on his bunk and grew more reflective. "I really don't know what it is I'm after. I just kind of enjoy it, I guess. Traveling from place to place, working different jobs, it's what I like doing best. I never thought much about doing anything else."

"Well, I just thought sooner or later it would come to an end. We'd get it out of our system and go back home to settle down. I been thinking lately more and more about packing it in and teaching school or something. A change of pace is what I need."

Leonard's voice had taken on an apologetic tone and Slim moved quickly to reassure him.

"Well, hell, Leonard, if that's what you want to do, I think you should go right ahead and do it. You been looking a little rundown lately anyway. Wouldn't hurt for you to go home and rest up a bit, get your health back in shape."

"You think so? Maybe that's what's best for me after all. Go home and settle down for a while until I get restless again."

"You bet. That's exactly what you need. Get your strength back again and decide the next step for yourself."

In the fall of 1909, about two and a half years after they had started on their long journey together, the brothers decided to go their separate ways. Leonard had a racking cough which had been plaguing him more and more recently, and his health had been deteriorating in general during recent months. Slim had mixed feelings about seeing his older brother take off without him. Leonard was still the one person he was closest to in the world, and his feelings for him came as close to love as any feelings Slim had allowed himself to entertain for anyone except his mother.

As for Slim's next move? He had studied the map carefully and made up his mind. He had never been out of the country before, not even to Mexico, although he had twice been in Arizona and not too far from the border. This time he would head north to cross into Canada. It was time to see another country, time to visit our northern neighbor to see what life was like up there.

Slim, still mindful of his word, kept Florence informed of where he was at all times. He told her of his travels with Leonard and about Leonard's weakening health and his decision to return home to get a job teaching school.

Arizona Slim fell in love with Canada at first sight. This wild, raw, gaping country stirred his soul and filled him with wonder. So much land, so much wide-open space to see and explore. And so few people living there. To Slim, it was virtually a new frontier, much wilder and less developed than the sprawling, unpopulated stretches of his own country. Lakes, mountains, rivers, and vast uncharted wilderness— Canada had them all.

He roamed mostly through Saskatchewan, in places called Regina, Moose Jaw, and Swift Current. He traveled farther north to Central Butte, Lucky Lake, and Riverhurst. Finally he came to Elbow, on the Saskatchewan River, just at the junction where it veers westward toward Alberta. Arizona Slim worked around Elbow for a while, then moved a few miles farther north to a logging camp along the river in Outlook. He wrote Florence a letter telling her about the vast, incredible beauty of this land, about the logging camp in Outlook nestled in the midst of a soaring forest of pine trees that sloped down the side of the mountain all the way to the edge of the Saskatchewan River.

Early in 1910, as he awoke to the clean, fresh, biting cold of the northern winter morning, Slim received a telegram at the camp. Tearing the ominous yellow envelope open with his thick, work-scarred fingers, he read:

JUNE
RETURN HOME IMMEDIATELY STOP LEONARD DEAD
STOP SO SORRY.
FLORENCE

Slim stared at the words, so simple yet so final, on the yellow page. Leonard dead. Just like that. Is that all there is to it? Leonard, whom he idolized as a child and, well, yes, whom he loved—say the word, damn it—as a boy and young man. Dead. Just like that.

The young man wrestled with the turbulence inside him during the trainride south. This was a terrible new experience for him, much more disconcerting than anything else that had touched him on his long odyssey. He had seen and done it all, had packed five lifetimes of adventure into his teenage years, and was hardly a man yet. But nothing had prepared him for this moment of unexpected and overwhelming grief. This was the toughest experience of all.

By the time he reached Vandalia and headed north to the farm near the churches at the crossroads in Carson Township, the young man had himself nearly under control. He knew he would soon be seeing Leonard, his remains. But somehow he would have to endure. There had never been anything like this grief when he held his mother to him, then his sisters. Nor did it abate when he clasped the hands of his father and brothers. Then came the dread moment. He stared down into the unnatural, frozen face of Leonard lying so quietly in his box. Was this waxen figure the one with whom he had worked and laughed a few short months ago? The brother he had known and cared for all his life? Alas! It was. Was Leonard still inside that shell? Or was he off in space, wandering where he had never been before?

Slim couldn't wait to leave home as soon as Leonard's remains were lowered into the ground. But as he was preparing to do so, another unexpected event occurred, preventing his departure. Hash got sick. He complained of pains in his stomach one morning. He said he was feeling weak and rundown. Indeed, he did not look well and started losing weight as well. The family took him to St. Louis, to a hospital in the city closest to home. While Hash was being treated for the cancer slowly spreading through his system, Slim helped James run the farm. Robert tried to make a banker out of him, figuring that his youngest brother would be a natural with his quick head for figures, but Slim could not stand the confines of indoor work.

Sherman also returned to the family homestead at this time, and Slim made a point of getting to know him better now that they were both a bit older and able to regard each other as equals. Slim's suspicions were confirmed. He now knew that of all his brothers and sisters, he and Sherman were closest in temperament and disposition.

Hash lingered for months, but it was clear from the beginning that the cancer was getting the best of him. The year ended and a new one began. Finally, a little more than a year after the family buried Leonard, Hash died. He was buried on March 24, 1911, in Fayette County in a plot next to Leonard's. Slim watched silently as the last clumps of earth were thrown over his father's coffin. The emotion he had felt at Leonard's funeral was a thing of the past. He and Hash had never been close. As a boy he alternately feared and hated his father, a fact he could now acknowledge to himself without feeling guilty. Guilt was another emotion the young man had steeled himself against. He had become even harder since Leonard's death.

With his father and closest brother dead, Slim agreed to do some traveling for the family business. Traveling was what he liked doing best, and James needed someone to travel as far south as Arkansas to buy livestock and trade in the southern markets. Arkansas had fascinated him since the days when Hash, liquored up, would rant on and on about the rich, alluvial soil along the Mississippi Delta. The young man had never forgotten those words, and longed to see the place that, with the alcohol, had stirred his father's imagination to fever pitch.

So to Arkansas Slim went in the early fall of 1911 to buy some hogs. As he was returning north with three carloads of them, the train stopped for a brief layover in Little Rock, a city new to Slim. He got off to do some browsing and decided to buy a new suit. The weather was hot and he was wearing a thin shirt with the sleeves rolled up, revealing his thick, heavily muscled forearms. The shirt clung to his chest and shoulders because of perspiration, outlining the contours of his powerful physique. Slim entered the store and started picking through the racks. He found a suit he liked for $10 and decided to try it on.

A group of men standing across the street in front of their hotel observed the young man as he walked into the store. They nodded to one another, crossed the street, and followed him inside. One of the men, the apparent spokesman for the group, approached him as he was tugging the suit jacket across his broad shoulders.

"Excuse me, young fellow. You mind if we have a word with you?"

Slim looked down at the plump middle-aged man in surprise. He and his companions were strangers to him. The last thing he expected was to be accosted while trying on a suit. The men looked prosperous and had an air of confidence and power about them. Slim was cautious.

"I suppose so. What's on your mind?"

"Me and my friends here are in the fight game. Promoters. We're always on the lookout for fresh new talent and we couldn't help noticing what a fine strapping lad you are."

"Oh?"

"You ever think of doing any fighting? In the ring I mean."

"Me?" Slim was relieved. With all the card playing he had done, his first thought was that this encounter might somehow be related to that. "Why, hell no. It just ain't my game."

"Well look at the size of you. You're built like a bull. You could be the next white hope to take on Jack Johnson, the nigger champ."

Slim laughed. "I hardly ever been in a fight in my life."

"We could teach you, son. That's our job. With that build of yours, you could be a natural."

"Well, thanks for the kind words, but no thanks, it just doesn't interest me. Sorry."

The men left reluctantly, leaving Slim to select his suit and head back to the train and his carloads of hogs. The young man thought about the incident during the trainride home. He found it amusing and flattering as well. The next white hope. Why couldn't they have asked him if he wanted to play baseball instead. Baseball had been his one notable failure in life. That was something that would really have interested him.


Hash Hunt's estate was settled in the fall of the year. By the time of his death, Hash had managed to accumulate substantial real estate holdings throughout Fayette County and as far away as St. Louis. His five-hundred-acre farm had prospered under James's husbandry, and his bank business in Ramsey was also doing well.

The estate was divided equally among all of Hash's survivors. The old man knew his offspring well. He knew his youngest son had no interest in his bank or farm, so he left him about $5,000 in cash while most of the others received a combination of cash and shares in the businesses.

The year 1911 was drawing to a close. The frigid blast of winter from Canada would soon assault the land. Arizona Slim had to leave. Nothing of interest remained for him in Carson Township. No ties bound him save those to Ella Rose. But this time was different. When he had left home in the past, he always knew he would return to his family in the not too distant future. He was merely running off to explore the world and get himself an education. His home was still the farm in Carson Township, near the churches at the crossroads. That was where he belonged, to that land and to those people, while he was wandering far away.

Ella Rose held him tightly, as though she would never let go. She too knew that this time was different. Her youngest boy, Junie, her favorite, was now not merely running away from home. This time he was leaving for good.

# Book II

# The Gambler

# 7.

*THERE'S A PLACE ALONG the Mississippi Delta, on the Arkansas side of the river, where the soil is rich and alluvial. A man could really make things grow down there.*

Hash's words had been emblazoned on the young man's mind probably the first time he heard them. As a small boy he had countless times watched his father storm drunkenly through the house, drink in his hand, filling the air with ringing incantations about the rich soil of the delta country. Hash's dream was about to become his son's reality.

Slim got off the train in Lake Village, across the river from Greenville, Mississippi, not too far from Ditch Bayou, the place his father used to talk about. He knew he had begun a new phase of his life. In all his previous wanderings Slim had been an itinerant, observing life and people and places as he passed by. Never had he felt that he belonged to any one place. This time, however, he felt he would sink roots. He would make this land his own. He would belong to it.

If Slim was fulfilling an early fantasy of his father's, he was also digging up his roots in yet another way. Hash had been a Confederate soldier who wandered north and made himself into a northerner. His youngest son was now a blue-bellied Yankee who had decided to come back home to the South.

Cutting off his own roots, he was reestablishing those of his father and grandfather before him.

Lake Village was a sleepy farm community and the seat of Chicot County. It lay near the western bank of Lake Chicot, which snakes gracefully along the Arkansas side of the Mississippi River. The thousand or so residents of Lake Village were mostly cotton farmers who traded with merchants in Louisiana and over to the west. They sold their cotton through the local brokers, and also made an active market trading land, horses, and other livestock. Greenville, the nearest city, was directly east across the muddy, winding Mississippi River, and the local farmers would ferry across once a month or so to load up on supplies and have themselves a time.

Slim arrived in town in the closing days of 1911, and found the winter not nearly so harsh as it was in Illinois. He had his father's inheritance in his pocket, plus a few thousand dollars he had saved from poker winnings and laboring wages. He was not yet twenty-three years old, was reasonably well off financially, and seized by a towering ambition to make something of himself now that he had decided to settle down.

The land and the people in Lake Village were unlike anything he had grown accustomed to up north. This was wet black cotton land, a species of earth entirely different from the lush brown northern wheat and corn land. Before the Civil War, when the vast, stately plantations reigned supreme in the land around Lake Village and Ditch Bayou, these cotton lands had sold for over $100 an acre. After the fall of the South, however, particularly after the Battle of Ditch Bayou, in which Hash had fought and which was peripheral to the Siege of Vicksburg, a massive depression destroyed the once booming economy of the delta country. The area had not yet recovered by the time of Slim's arrival; black cotton land sold for $15 an acre.

The people too were different from those the young man had known back home and in his travels. He had known Mexicans; indeed, had beaten them badly in their own card game. But most of the men he had rubbed shoulders with and bunked with in the logging camps and farms and ranches of the West and Northwest were fair-skinned white men like himself. They were white Christian men, Protestants mostly, of English, Scottish, Dutch, German, and Scandinavian extraction. White Protestants predominated in Lake Village too, but they lived side by side and in apparent harmony with their former slaves and with a large colony of Italians who had moved north from Louisiana. In addition to a large percentage of blacks and Italians, Lake Village had a fair sampling of swarthy Cajuns, French settlers, mulattos, and other mixed breeds that had migrated from the Gulf Coast. Arizona Slim was quick to notice how "different" these people were from those he had previously encountered, but what disturbed him most was the fact that all these people were established in the life of the community while he, a northern stranger, was regarded as the "foreigner" in their midst.

Perhaps the most different of all the people in Lake Village was the only Jew in town, Sam Epstein, who had emigrated from Russia and settled awhile in New York City before wandering south. Sam could have chosen to live in the established Jewish community across the river in Greenville, Mississippi, but he preferred to live apart from them in a town full of white, black, and swarthy Gentiles.

Epstein came to Lake Village around the turn of the century. He opened up a general store in town and a few years later bought land, planted cotton, and reaped his crop with the first cotton gin the people in the area had seen. By 1911, the year Slim arrived, Sam Epstein was rich and prosperous—and reluctantly accepted by the Christian folk.

Slim had never tried his hand at cotton farming. He was ambitious, full of optimism, and anxious to get started. He immediately looked around for a suitable spread of land and within weeks found what he thought he was looking for. A local farmer had just put his land up for sale and Slim went out to take a look at it. The forty-acre farm was located outside town on the old road that leads directly west to Montrose. On it was a little farmhouse in need of much repair, but the young man was eager and figured it would be a good place to get started. He asked some townsfolk what they thought of the place and they were quick to reassure him.

"Best cotton land you'll find in these parts," one oldtimer said. "Nosiree. You got to go pretty far to find a better piece o' land for growin' cotton."

"What about flooding?" Slim asked. "It's pretty high up on the levee out there."

"That's as high as it gets," the old man said, spitting out a squirt of tobacco juice. "Why, hell, there ain't been a flood out there in thirty-five years."

Slim was convinced. He had found the place he was looking for. As he went back to the farm to make an offer, the locals gathered around the old man and treated themselves to a good laugh.

"That's one dumb Yankee sumbitch," a farmer said to the old man. "What he don't know about cotton farmin' can fill a book."

"Says his father was a Confederate soldier. Fought at Ditch Bayou," said another.

"He's still a blue-bellied Yankee sumbitch," the old man replied. "Don't matter what his daddy and granddaddy was. He's a Yankee."

The farmers laughed and nodded in agreement. The oldtimer summed up the feelings of all the townspeople perfectly.

Slim took possession of the farm on January 30, 1912, for the sum of $1,050, which he laid out in cash. He moved out to the old farmhouse and threw himself immediately into his assumed new role of southern cotton farmer. This was a brand-new adventure for him and he was full of energy and enthusiasm. He planted his cotton and sat back to await the results.

Two weeks later the rains came and the water began to rise on the levee. Slim was concerned at first, but found reassurance in the fact that the land hadn't been flooded in thirty-five years. The law of probability was on his side. The water continued to rise at an alarming rate and spilled over the levee, inundating his land. His crop was destroyed. When he walked through town the men chuckled quietly to themselves, shaking their heads in mock commiseration.

"First time in thirty-five years," the oldtimer said with a smile on his face. Slim felt their hostility wash over him. Probability had been on his side, but it had failed him in this instance.

"Probabilities are not always dependable," Slim said out loud to no one in particular. Without realizing it at the time, he had formulated another component of his developing philosophy. Probability worked in the long run, but it was not always dependable. You needed better odds.

The land lay under water for three solid months. Slim noticed, however, that the adjoining property, also up for sale, had remained relatively dry during the flooding. He had lost money in the failure of his crop but was not wiped out. He decided to plunge in deeper and made an offer for the adjoining land. Using what was left of his savings, he put down a deposit and took out a mortgage in the local bank. By borrowing heavily, he was able to add nine hundred sixty acres to his original forty. He now had a plantation-size spread, a fact that was another source of resentment among the locals. In no time flat, this blue-bellied Yankee had swooped into town and acquired one of the largest farms in the area.

Gambler that he was, Slim decided to make back his loss by counterattacking at once. Only by taking an even bigger plunge than the first one could he hope to recoup his loss and come up with a profit. He borrowed money from Sam Epstein, the Jew, the most different of all the different people in Lake Village, and decided to go for broke with a last-minute corn crop. The water level was subsiding and the rains apparently had stopped. Slim planted his corn and the weather broke just right for him. It appeared, at first, that he was going to come in with a successful corn crop right on the heels of his cotton fiasco. But luck was not riding with Arizona Slim this year. The gambler, game as he was, was running a losing streak. Just as it seemed he was going to harvest a successful corn crop, an epidemic of cutworms hit the area. They descended on his corn and made a feast of it. The young would-be southern farmer was devastated. His luck was running out. First the floods, now the cutworms. His first attempt to conquer the South and make it his own had ended in failure. The year 1912 was a disaster. Arizona Slim was wiped out. He owed the bank for all his land, and he owed money to Sam Epstein. He was a foreigner in his own land, an unacceptable northerner among all these different people. Worst of all, they had seen him fail, sat back and watched it happen, and had themselves a good laugh.

Arizona Slim was wiped out. He was twenty-three and broke. He had blown his father's inheritance and all his poker winnings. These southerners had beaten him. He was dead broke and owed a lot of money.

# 8.

THE FERRY SAT IN ITS slip east of Lake Village, on the far side of Lake Chicot along the west bank of the Mississippi River. The night air was cool and a soft breeze blew west across the river from Greenville on the other side. The river was wide here and ran swift and brown to the south on its way through Louisiana toward the Gulf. The ferry was crowded tonight with farmers and their wives traveling over to Greenville to have themselves a time. Arizona Slim stood against the railing, looking down into the dark churning water beneath him. Across the way the lights of Greenville shone brightly against the backdrop of the night sky, welcoming the next boatload of visitors from the sister state to the west.

The hottest spot in Greenville, the place where all the rich planters, businessmen, and politicians went to play high-stakes poker, was the Planters Club in the center of the city. The best poker players in the area would gather there around the green felt-lined tables on Saturday nights for the big games. The men were mostly middle-aged and successful; numbered among these veteran poker players were some of the most prominent people in town. Slim had become friendly with a young man his own age named Dixon Gaines, whose father was a politician in Chicot County. Dixon told Slim about the big games in the Planters Club, and Slim saw them as an opportunity to make back some of his crop losses. He decided immediately to turn to the thing he knew best, poker playing, to get back on his feet.

"Hell, you can't go over there to play with them," Dixon said to him one day.

"Why not?"

"Those men will eat you up alive. They are veteran poker players over there. Professionals. You can't hold your own with them."

Slim smiled broadly and patted his friend on the shoulder. "Well, Dixon, maybe I'll just sit in one night for the hell of it and see what happens. Just for the hell of it."

When the twenty-three-year-old young man showed up at the Planters Club with a grin on his face and a black cheroot stuck confidently between his teeth, the men around the table looked at one another in surprise. This boy, big and tall and strong as he was, was no older than their own sons.

"You want to play poker with us? Why sure, boy. Pull up a chair and get acquainted."

Slim sat in and drew a hand. Dixon was right. These men were tough veteran players, the best and smartest he had played against. Poker games in the logging camps and bunkhouses had been a Sunday-school picnic compared to this. But Slim was a veteran too, despite his young years. Hadn't he been playing cards with his brothers and sisters from the time he was hardly out of diapers? And hadn't he been gambling with and beating grown men when he was a fair-cheeked teenager? He had packed several lifetimes of experience into his twenty-three years. He was a tough grizzled professional himself, even though these gamblers were old enough to be his father.

The young man held his own right from the start, and then some. He couldn't take these men to the cleaners as he had most of the itinerant workers he had played with. They were too smart and cagey for that. But he was able to win a little, enough to pay off some of the money he owed and keep himself properly fed. That a mere twenty-three-year-old could hold his own against the best poker players in the area, even come out a winner, was enough to give him a reputation. It wasn't long before the folks in Greenville as well as Lake Village began to talk about that Yankee boy who played cards so well. Arizona Slim had come to Arkansas to be a farmer, and he had earned a reputation as a gambler instead. When he wasn't taking the ferry across the Mississippi for the Saturday night poker marathons in the Planters Club, he was playing poker and checkers in Lake Village with the local farmers. He even played poker and checkers with Dixon Gaines' father, and beat him. The farmers who laughed at his first disastrous attempts at farming slowly began to respect his prowess as a gambler. The blue-bellied Yankee boy had found his niche. He had won grudging acceptance in this strange southern land, although not at all in the manner he originally intended.

His success at the gaming tables did not preclude his continuing effort to succeed as a cotton planter. Slim could not accept failure, particularly his own. He was determined to succeed at everything he attempted. The new year came in and he reached his twenty-fourth birthday. Planting season was about to begin and Slim planted his cotton. The Mississippi had overflowed the previous year, so there was a good probability it would not happen again this year, the second year in a row.

Once again the rains came and the Mississippi started to rise. The water on the levee out at Slim's farm west of Lake Village inched higher and higher toward the top. The water level kept mounting. The rains kept falling and the river rose dangerously, threatening to overspill its banks. The water crested over the levee and flowed across the young man's entire plantation. His crop was inundated the second year running. Probability had failed him once more.

"Probabilities are not always dependable," the young man muttered to himself. It was grim consolation as he gazed across his flooded farmland. Failure again. Ruin. His cotton was destroyed. His money gone. Wiped out. Thank God there was poker. Thank God for that at least. He had to return to the poker tables to get back some money.

Around this time, shortly after the failure of his second cotton crop, Slim met an attractive young girl in town named Mattie Bunker. Mattie's father, Nelson Bunker, had migrated to Lake Village from Ohio right after the Civil War. In doing so, he must have passed pretty close to Hash Hunt, who was heading north at the same time. This ironic development, Mattie's father and his own father migrating in opposite directions simultaneously to seek their fortunes, appealed to Slim's adventurous nature. He was not a romantic, did not believe that all things were ordained in heaven despite his mother's religious background, but did feel a certain star-crossed affinity with the Bunker family because of this similar twist in their families' histories. He pursued young Mattie as diligently as he pursued everything he wanted in life. The young girl liked him well enough, and was taken by his rough good looks and strong physique. Nelson Bunker also liked Slim, but he was a practical man and told his daughter to maintain a wait-and-see attitude toward her suitor.

"He's seems like a nice enough young man," he said to Mattie. "All the men down at the club find him fair and honest. But what kind of prospects does he have? He calls himself a farmer, but so far as I can see he's a professional gambler more than anything else. Don't rush into anything,

Mattie. Wait and see how things work out on that farm of his out there."

The months rolled by and Mattie continued to hold him off at arm's distance. Equally frustrating for Slim was the fact that he liked Nelson Bunker a lot, truly admired this man who had turned himself into a southern cotton farmer and established himself as a local civic leader. Hadn't his own father done virtually the same thing with his own life up north— prospered as a farmer and got himself elected sheriff of the county? The parallels were uncanny. Nelson Bunker was the flip side of Hash Hunt. He was Slim's spiritual father, a substitute for the real father to whom he had never been close. He had to win Nelson Bunker's approval, had to become an accepted member of his family.

When Mattie continued her coy game, playing hard to get and making life generally difficult for him, the young man turned his attentions to her older sister, Lyda, who was the village schoolteacher. Not quite so pretty as her sister Mattie, Lyda was getting dangerously close to becoming an old maid at a time when most available young girls were married off before they were barely out of their teens. Lyda was two weeks older than Slim, exactly the same age difference that existed between Ella Rose and Hash. This was another curious irony that flabbergasted the young man when he first discovered it. The better he got to know the prim, shy, self-effacing schoolteacher, the more she reminded Slim of his own mother. Lyda was flattered by Slim's interest in her, and she welcomed the opportunity to put one over on her pretty young sister, who had been more popular than she all their lives. In her quiet way she was also headstrong, determined to have her way once she made up her mind to do something. She was less her father's daughter than Mattie was, and therefore less susceptible to his control. He had cautioned Mattie about the young gambler and she had listened. Now Lyda had an opportunity and she was going to make the most of it. She was as determined as the young man who wanted her, who wanted to share his life with her, and become a part of her family.

The year 1914 brought the prospect of a happier and more prosperous new season. Slim had managed to sustain himself by his winnings at the poker tables as he courted Nelson Bunker's older daughter. But now it was time to see if he could make some money from cotton.

Once again the young man planted his cotton. Once again he turned his gaze skyward toward the heavy rains that threatened to destroy his dreams with their relentless deluge. The Mississippi, brown and murky, began to swell. The water inched higher and higher on the levee, threatening to flood the land. And then the rains stopped. The water crested and then started to subside. Lower and lower the level dropped on the levee. This year would be different. This year the young blue-bellied Yankee cotton farmer would be spared the devastating floods. This year his crop would come in. This year was his. "Probabilities are sometimes dependable," he chuckled to himself.

When World War I broke out in Europe that summer, Slim received another ominous telegram from Carson Township. This one announced that his mother was seriously ill and unable to leave her bed. The year had started off beautifully, but this news cast a dark cloud over his first success as a cotton grower.

Slim took the train north to Carson Township to be at his mother's side. Ella Rose was old now, a gray woman wasted with sickness as she lay on her deathbed. But Ella Rose could not leave this world without seeing her youngest boy once more. The family, what was left of it, was together again, as aging families always are in the presence of death. Slim held his mother's hand and looked down into the face of this woman with whom he had once shared so much, this woman who had been the center of his universe not so long ago. She had become a stranger to him during the past ten years, ever since he left her side and started his wandering. He had put time and distance between himself and all his family, but it was Ella Rose who felt his absence the most, who felt as though a vital part of her own flesh had been taken away from her forever.

Ella Rose had seen her Junie one more time, and now she was ready to meet her Maker. They buried Ella Rose in September 1914, just before her seventy-first birthday. As earth was thrown over her coffin, it was clear to all the brothers and sisters that an era in their lives had come to an end. What had bound them as a family was now gone. James and Robert had decided to make their home in Carson Township, but the others had no reason to return. Their last root was plucked up.

Slim's break was now complete. On the train back to his adopted home, Lake Village, Arkansas, the young man mused. He knew that an era in his life had ended. He thought about the girl who waited for him back there, who reminded him so much of Ella Rose, who was two weeks older than he was, the same age difference between Ella Rose and Hash. He decided then that she would become his wife. He married Lyda Bunker two months later, in November.

# 9.

S LIM LEFT THE OLD rundown farmhouse on his land
and moved with Lyda into a small frame house in the
center of town. The young couple was off to a good start.
Neither was particularly warm or passionate. Both had cool,
practical, calculating natures, and both had what they wanted.
Lyda had won the former suitor of her younger, prettier sister,
and Slim had become a member of Nelson Bunker's family.
He had a wife who reminded him of his mother, and a father-
in-law whose life was the mirror image of his own father's.

As war raged in Europe in 1914 and into the next year, the
economy of the United States started to boom. The demand
for cotton for military uniforms increased dramatically and
prices skyrocketed. Land values, particularly farmland, also
took off. Slim brought in another successful crop in 1915, and
with his profit acquired additional farmland. As the manu-
factured prosperity of the war years increased, one could turn
a quick buck more easily by speculating in farmland than by
plowing the land and growing cotton. The gambling aspect of
land trading appealed to Slim at this stage of his life more than
did the tough manual labor of walking behind a mule and
planting seed. Leveraging his money, he would put down less
than twenty-five percent in cash and borrow the rest from the
bank or from the seller of the property in an installment sale.
This land he would immediately sell, and then roll over the
proceeds into a new piece of property. All the established
cotton farmers in the area and across the Mississippi were also

caught up in the speculative frenzy. They abandoned their lifelong professions to become wartime land traders. As long as land values kept rising, a trader could sell his property for a profit, buy a new piece of land, and never have to worry about paying off the notes. It worked just fine; everybody grew rich as long as the bull market continued.

Notwithstanding all his trading, Slim retained his original thousand-acre farm since he was encouraged by his two successful crops. His land was producing a bale an acre and the price of cotton had soared from $30 to $600 a bale as the war continued. In addition to trading land and growing cotton, Slim discovered a new game, which suited his nature perfectly. He learned of a market for speculating in the future prices of commodities, including cotton. This was another way a risk-taker like himself could make a lot of money with a relatively small investment. Since he was convinced that the price of cotton would keep rising as long as the war was on, he started buying futures contracts on margin. By borrowing as much as ninety percent of the price of the contract, a speculator could multiply his investment five, ten, twenty times over if cotton kept rising. Slim leveraged himself to the fullest, borrowing heavily to buy land and futures contracts, and he parlayed his winnings into a sizable profit.

Slim's luck had clearly turned for the better. He was making money with other people's money, another key element in his constantly developing philosophy of life. And his farm was producing for him and bringing in a healthy income. He had it both ways now. And successful as a gambler and farmer, he threw himself headlong into the mad whirlwind of the wartime economy.

Slim was active on another front as well. He became a family man with the birth of his first child, a daughter named Margaret, a year after his marriage. Lyda was happy with her baby and with her marriage. Her husband's success as a businessman as well as a gambler vindicated her decision to marry him against her father's reservations. Nelson Bunker came to respect her husband's business abilities, and the two men got along well together.

But Lyda had assumed that Hassie, as she started to call Slim shortly after she met him, would give up his gambling as soon as he started to prosper as a farmer. She knew about his legendary prowess in the poker marathons over in Greenville and in Lake Village. Indeed, she had been reminded of it enough by her own father. But she thought he had gambled only to recoup his losses from his crop failures, and that he would give up card playing once he had established himself in the cotton business. Now that he had, however, she couldn't say that she noticed any letup in his penchant for poker games. If anything, his gambling fever had risen with his prosperity.

"I just don't understand it, Hassie," she lamented on more than one occasion.

Slim growled, showing his displeasure with her choice of nicknames for him.

"But it just doesn't seem right to call you Slim. It sounds so . . . so mysterious. Besides," she added mischievously, eyeing his developing paunch, "it's just not appropriate any more."

Slim grudgingly acknowledged the kernel of truth in her words. Now that he could afford to hire field hands to do his labor for him, and his activities were confined mostly to the gambling tables and the trading halls, his body had begun to thicken. The good life was fleshing out the hard lean body of his logging days.

"Everything in life is a gamble, Lyda. Poker's only part of it. You think farming and real estate aren't gambling? Everything we've got comes from gambling. And the only way to get more is to keep on gambling."

"But you've made so much already. We're well off now. I hoped that maybe it was time to give some thought to preserving what we've got instead of risking it all the time."

The idea of preserving what he had was repugnant to Arizona Slim. It flew in the face of his philosophy of life. A gambler who knows what he is doing learns to minimize his risk and maximize his reward. Risk and reward. Profits and growth. Preservation and retrenchment sounded too much like stagnation and death. Taking risk was what living was all about. It was the substance of life. Lyda would never be able to understand this. It was not her nature. She thought he gambled merely to get back onto his feet. Because of her failure to understand that risk was an essential in her husband's makeup, she misjudged him completely.

And so the poker games continued amid the cotton boom, the land trading, and his speculation on futures contracts. They took place in the Planters Club in Greenville and in Lake Village, where Slim learned to beat the mayor.

Luke Howell, the mayor, had a reputation for being the tightest player in town. He and Dixon Gaines, Sr., the father of Slim's friend, were reputed to be among the sharpest there were. But it was Luke, in particular, who gave Slim the most trouble. The young man observed his style of play, betting against him cautiously and holding his own until he finally figured out Luke's flaw. He played his hand tightly, close to the vest, but he didn't know how to bluff. He just couldn't do it. Slim believed that someone who couldn't bluff would never be a first-rate player. Good, yes, but not great. He bided his time with Luke, waiting for the right opportunity. It finally came.

Slim's cards were running poorly one night. He just couldn't draw a big hand. To compensate, he started bluffing outrageously. The first time it worked. Luke dropped out and Slim threw his cards face down, making it obvious he had nothing. The next time he bluffed, Luke folded again, and Slim acted as though he had just pulled off the smartest bluff in the world. Now Luke was mad. Slim had him where he wanted him; he had set him up perfectly. Luke would not drop out so easily the next time Slim acted as though he were bluffing. Slim knew that Luke would try to outbluff him just to get even.

The young man waited until he had a big hand and then made his bet, pushing his chips brazenly toward the center of the pot. Sure enough, Luke refused to fold, even though Slim, countdown artist that he was, knew the mayor couldn't possibly have more than a pair. Luke pushed out a huge stack of chips, seeing Slim and raising him considerably. The other players, knowing the mayor was not one for bluffing, dropped out.

"Oh, oh, he's got it," said Dixon Gaines, Sr., as he folded.

"I've got a notion to call you, just for practice," the young man said.

But Slim stayed in and met the mayor's bet. The young man had doped the situation perfectly. Luke had nothing. He had tried to bluff Slim back in anger. Slim laid down three of a kind on top of the mayor's pair and raked in his winnings. Luke was furious but the others stood up laughing, appreciating the perfect setup.

"Goddamn, that was the prettiest thing I ever saw," said Dixon Gaines.

The other players, who had been fortunate enough to drop out, whooped in agreement.

"How'd you know I was bluffing?" Luke scowled.

Slim smiled but said nothing.

"That boy's got a photographic memory, that's all there is to it," Dixon answered for Slim. "That's the whole secret of his game."

"Also," Slim added, "most people have a lazy shuffle. They

tend to let cards clump together. If you can remember the way cards went into the deck before the shuffle, you got a pretty good chance of figuring out how most of them will be dealt out.''

Lyda gave birth to their second child, a boy, on November 23, 1917, almost two years to the day after Margaret was born. Slim had wanted a son right from the start. He was determined to rectify what, in his own mind, had been one of his father's biggest mistakes. His namesake would be the first among his sons, not the last. He would not wait to create a son in his own image. This boy would also be named Haroldson Lafayette Hunt, or young Hassie for short, as Lyda insisted on calling him.

In 1917 the United States entered the war, but Slim, a twenty-eight-year-old farmer, land trader, and father of two small children, was exempt from the military draft. While his countrymen went off to save Europe from despotism and the world for democracy, he stayed home and prospered from the wartime economy. The price of cotton kept soaring, and land trading reached epidemic dimensions. Speculators could hardly wait for the ink to dry on their deeds before they scouted around for a new buyer. Property changed hands at such dizzying speeds that clerks were working overtime just to keep the records straight. Cotton and land. There seemed to be no end to the incredible upward spiral. Anyone with enough cash in his pocket for a small downpayment and a taste for a little action could get rich overnight. It was easy. Borrow, buy, and sell. As simple as that. Everything was going up, so everyone could make a profit. Just like that. It was the American way.

Arizona Slim kept winning at poker, and he was involved in various business deals with his Jewish friend, Sam Epstein, his

French pal, R. D. Chotard, an Irishman named Milligan, and his Italian crony, Frank Grego, who was the manager of the Planters Club in Greenville. The impression made by the ethnic varieties available in Lake Village never left Arizona Slim. So struck was he by their differences from the people he had grown up with and those he met during his travels that he could hardly mention these companions without referring to their nationality.

"That Italian over in Greenville is really quite a good person," he would say to Lyda on more than one occasion.

Lyda didn't say much about it at the time since she realized there wasn't much she could do, but she knew that her husband also regarded Frank's sister, a singer at the club, as "quite a good person" too. Hassie was frequently away from home, looking around for new parcels of land to trade, and his reputation as a man with an eye for the ladies as well as a fast buck was starting to make the rounds in Lake Village.

Together with some of his friends and business associates, Slim acquired a huge tract of land in Louisiana, some twenty-five hundred acres, for less than $30 an acre. Land values in Louisiana had lagged behind those farther north, and the men felt that the boom would soon spread toward the Gulf area, causing their parcel of land to skyrocket. They put down a little cash and mortgaged the rest, sharing the expense of paying off the note. They bought up additional land, together and individually, throughout eastern Arkansas and western Mississippi, again taking out big loans to finance the purchases. The risk was minimal what with the war raging in Europe, the demand for cotton and other goods increasing every year, and land prices soaring out of sight.

Poker, cotton, land, and war. How could you go wrong? Borrow, buy, and sell. Get rich overnight. Pyramid your profits into a fortune. It was the American way. This boom, it seemed, would never end.

# 10.

NEW ORLEANS WAS AN EXCITING, thriving city during and immediately after the war. It was a seaport city, and most of the cotton heading for Europe was shipped from its ports. The city was alive with planters making deals for their cotton; with speculators trading commodities in the futures market; with gamblers shooting craps and playing poker in the gaming halls; with sailors from dozens of countries, wearing colorful uniforms, speaking many languages, and cruising the cobblestone streets; with prostitutes, white, black, and every shade in between, soliciting openly in the saloons and on the streetcorners.

Arizona Slim took to New Orleans immediately. It reminded him of San Francisco and the Barbary Coast. Old memories revived. His circumstances were different now, however. No longer was he the lean, hard, strapping teenage youth of the ranches and logging camps in search of new experiences. Now he was a prosperous twenty-eight-year-old gambler, farmer, and trader visiting the city on business. His body had taken on weight and his hair had already begun to thin a bit on the crown of his head. He was dressed somewhat sloppily, indifferently, in a rumpled and baggy suit, even though he could certainly afford better. A cigar was clamped eternally between his teeth; lit or unlit seemed not to matter— he just liked to know it was there. With a layer of fat fleshing out his cheeks, giving him a plumpish and burly look, there was not much chance of anyone now mistaking him for a great white hope. He looked more like a promoter these days, more like the men who had approached him in the clothing store in Little Rock than like the powerful young man he had been then.

But he was an imposing figure of a man, still—tall, prosperous, good-looking. Slim had a good deal of business to attend to in New Orleans, visiting his cotton factors and buying futures contracts on the commodity exchanges, and he usually took care of it alone, leaving Lyda and his two young children home in Lake Village. Lyda didn't like this arrangement but had grown used to it by now, accepting it as her lot in life, as Ella Rose had accepted Hash's frequent absences when he was sheriff of Fayette County. On this particular occasion, however, he had his family along because his daughter, Margaret, had to have her tonsils removed. He took a room in the Grunewald Hotel, where he had stayed on previous visits to the city, and sent Lyda off with the children to see the doctor.

The Grunewald, in addition to being the focal point for most of the important business dealings in the city, was famous for its marathon poker games, which attracted some of the best-known card players from all over the country. Most men of means gravitated, at one point or another, to New Orleans, it being a vortex of commerce and high life. Professional gamblers made the rounds of all the major cities for the big games and eventually found their way to New Orleans.

Slim wandered down to the Planters Club in the hotel to check out the afternoon action. The sun was high and hot outside, but the club was dim and noisy and the air was thick with billowing clouds of tobacco smoke. The games in the afternoon tended to be on the light side, limit games, warmups for the high-stakes games that got started after dinner. Slim bought himself $100 worth of chips and sat down at one of the tables. The big talent had not arrived yet. The high rollers were saving themselves for the no-limit game that night. Slim coasted easily through the afternoon, and by the time he left to go out for dinner he had run his stake up to $700.

He had heard that the best talent in the country would be there that evening for the no-limit game. Slim had played against the best poker players in his area at the Planters Club in Greenville, but never against the legendary players from Chicago and New York, whose names were famous in gambling circles everywhere. Lyda was frantic as he prepared to go down to the big game after dinner, and he tried to reassure her.

"Don't worry. I have the advantage on them. I know who they are but they don't know me. As far as they're concerned, I'm just another planter from the delta, easy money for them."

Slim was not disappointed when he arrived at the table. Sitting around the table for the no-limit game were Jinks Miller, a man he had been hearing about for years, White Top, Nick the Greek, Indian Jack, John Crow, and other luminaries of the poker table. He may have beaten the best at home, but in this game he had graduated to the major leagues.

The game the men would play was five-card stud, the favorite of most professional poker players since it required a minimum of luck and a maximum of skill. Dogs would be allowed in the game. A little dog was the deuce to the seven in different suits with one card missing, and a big dog was nine to the ace. Both dogs ranked higher than three of a kind but lower than a straight. Slim had played this version of poker before, and he knew it complicated the game considerably since it forced the player to consider different combinations when he was counting down and locating cards in his memory. It was not a game for those with less than total concentration.

The game went well for Slim right from the start. He was winning steadily, beating the best there were, men who made a living from their winnings. These were players with big-money backers who would send them stake money for a game in return for a piece of the action. People like Nick the Greek, for example, never had to risk their own money since wealthy shippers and restaurateurs financed their games. Yet here was Slim, the cotton planter from Arkansas who should have been an easy mark, adding to his winnings from one pot to the next. The gamblers looked around at one another, wondering who he was. They had never heard of him before. Arizona Slim he called himself. They thought he must have invented some form of cheating unknown to them.

As the game drew down to the wire, it became more of a head-on competition between Arizona Slim and Jinks Miller, the wily old veteran. The time was approaching midnight and Slim intended to make this his last hand, win or lose, since he found that his powers of memory and concentration deserted him after that hour. Slim was playing with a small pair, one in the hole and one showing alongside his ace. Miller also had an ace showing, and the rules called for the first ace to make the bet. Slim pushed forward a stack of chips and Miller met his bet, staring him straight in the eyes. They drew their next card. Miller caught a king, Slim a lower card, but none of the face cards revealed a pair. Miller made a huge bet, brazenly indicating that he had paired his face-up king with one in the hole. Each knew the other could not have a pair of aces from counting down the earlier cards. Slim hesitated a moment, trying to figure if Jinks, in fact, was sitting with a pair of kings. In a second he determined that he wasn't. If he had a king in the hole, chances are he would have raised on the second card. He met his bet.

Then they drew their last card. Slim watched his opponent carefully and saw him give a kind of jerk, an imperceptible flinch of his eyes and head that spoke volumes to Slim. Precisely then Slim knew he had Miller beaten, and he also knew that Jinks had just figured out how Slim had beaten him. Slim threw down his triumphant pair and scooped in his winnings, a total of $10,200 for the night. The men around the table looked at Slim in admiration. He was clearly one of the best they had ever seen, a thorough professional. If he had discovered a new form of cheating, it certainly escaped them. They knew everything there was to know about cards and cheating. Arizona Slim was one of the best.

Slim left the table with the feeling that he was probably the best poker player around. He had yet to meet anyone he couldn't beat. He had over ten grand in his pocket and a new lease on life. He had not mentioned anything to Lyda yet, but he had gotten himself into a bit of a hole. Land values were still moving up, but not soaring as rapidly as they had been in recent years. Consequently, it was more difficult to turn land over as quickly as it had been. That meant speculators were being forced to hold onto their heavily mortgaged property longer and longer. And that meant coming up with the cash to pay off the notes.

Yes, Arizona Slim could use that money he won tonight. His bills were beginning to pile up a bit higher than he had bargained for.

# 11.

IN 1920, TWO YEARS AFTER the war ended, land values reached a peak and actually started to fall. Speculators who had borrowed heavily to buy farmland suddenly found themselves with huge tracts of acreage, mortgaged to the hilt, which they could no longer sell. Slim kept on acquiring land as it fell in price, figuring that it was only a temporary dip in the market and the boom was not yet over. In doing so he was putting himself deeper and deeper into debt. He was buying land nobody else wanted at what he thought were bargain prices only to find that there were no other buyers around as the market kept on sinking.

He was now in debt to the banks for what amounted to a fortune. He was forced to make a move. Sizing up the economic situation, he concluded that, with the war over, demand for cotton should be falling off. The price of cotton was bound to follow that of land. He went to New Orleans and told his factors to sell his entire cotton inventory. He was determined not to be caught holding tons of a product nobody would be needing any longer. Then he visited his broker and took an enormous short position in the cotton futures market. By reversing his position and selling contracts instead of buying them, he stood to make a large profit if the price of cotton started to drop.

His timing was off, however. Incredibly enough to him, the value of his land kept plummeting with no buyers in sight while cotton prices continued to climb. Logically, land and cotton should have been moving together. Slim was getting whipsawed in the worst possible way: the commodity he had just sold, cotton, was going higher and the land he owned, and could not get rid of, was falling lower, forcing him to pay off all those notes. In addition to his already substantial financial bind, he was now getting margin calls from his broker as his equity dropped with rising cotton prices. He was on the wrong side of both markets. He had backed himself into a corner and gotten sandbagged like an amateur. Arizona Slim, the veteran gambler and poker player who had beaten Jinks Miller, Nick the Greek, and other famous professionals from all over the country, had allowed himself to get a little too cocky. Just as he was starting to believe that he was the smartest gambler in the world, that everything he put his hand to would turn to gold, his entire world began collapsing around his head. He was learning humility in the worst possible way, but the only way that really counts.

Slim refused to admit he made a mistake about the direction of cotton, and he used up all his cash to meet his margin calls rather than liquidate his positions and accept a loss. He reasoned that, if only he could hang on long enough to his short position, cotton would eventually start to fall in price and he would make back his fortune. But the market refused to cooperate. Cotton prices continued to rise and he was suddenly out of cash. Unable to come up with money for additional margin calls, he was forced to sell out his position against his wishes. He was bust, bankrupt, without a penny to his name. His plantation lands were mortgaged to the banks for over $200,000, and there were no buyers in sight for any of it.

As it turned out, Slim was right about an eventual collapse in the cotton market. In 1921 prices hit their peak, and then they immediately began to plummet. Cotton dropped from over $600 a bale all the way back down to $50. Delta planters who were sitting on all that farmland, who had gotten rich during the great boom of the war years, went broke overnight. Yes, Slim's reasoning had been right. Cotton was destined to nosedive after the war. But his timing had been off by a year. He had failed to take into consideration the lag factor. He assumed that cotton and land would move in the same direction simultaneously. Logically, they should have; but markets are not always logical. They have a way of fooling us. Slim had gotten so cocky from all his gambling successes that he didn't think it was necessary to hedge himself just in case there might be an outside chance he could be wrong.

The postwar depression hit Lake Village hard. Lyda was more furious than ever with Hassie because of his gambling. Even though his financial disaster had occurred in the cotton and land markets, she was inclined to blame it all on poker. This added another ironic twist to Slim's life. Poker had been the one area where he had been able to sustain himself and make back losses from other ventures, but it was his poker playing that Lyda picked on.

In any event, it was time once again for Arizona Slim to reassess his position. He had just turned thirty-two. He was a married man with two small children. He owned some fifteen thousand acres of land spread out across three different states and mortgaged to the tune of $200,000. And he was completely out of cash. In addition, cotton prices had hit rock bottom, which meant it would be a long while before he would be able to make much money farming again. What were his options?

Should he remain in Lake Village? Try to raise some more money to buy up additional land at unbelievably low prices? He had just heard about another tract of farmland in Louisiana which a farmer was virtually giving away for the price of the back taxes owed on it. Eventually all this cotton land would move back up in value and he would be rich, if only he could ride out the depression and pay his bills in the meantime.

But this depression was mean. It was cutting deep and hard, down to the marrow. Everyone in the area had been devastated by it. All those rich planters and land traders who had so much such a short time ago now had nothing. What should he do? Should he stay in Lake Village and try to gut it out? He mentioned the possibility of leaving the area to Lyda.

"Are we going to bury ourselves here for the rest of our lives? If our land ever regains its value, we'll be rich. Meanwhile we're sitting on over fifteen thousand acres. We could rent it out and help pay off the notes."

"But where would we go? Everything I've ever had is right here."

"I was thinking maybe of El Dorado. There's a big oil boom just getting started over there. Some people are striking it big."

"Oil? But you don't know anything about oil."

"There's not much to know as far as I can see. Either you strike it or you don't. Why not give it a try? We can rent our land out and go over to El Dorado."

Lyda was not buying. She had her house and children and her family in Lake Village. That much she was sure of. She had no idea what kind of crazy schemes awaited her in El Dorado. Oil, poker, gambling. That's all Hassie was interested in. He gave no thought in the world to security for his family. At least she knew she was safe in Lake Village. She could survive there among friends and family. Better that than going off to starve to death amid strangers in some oil town.

They decided that he would go over to El Dorado on his own to look around and see what was going on. If there was anything there for them, if he could find a way to make a living in this oil business, he would send for Lyda and the children. Otherwise, he would return to Lake Village and try to revive his cotton business. His biggest problem now was that he was so broke he didn't have even enough cash on hand for the journey.

"I got to borrow some money to expense me a few days in the oil-boom town," he mentioned to a friend.

One of the banks he did business with agreed to lend him $50 more, on top of all the money he already owed it, but only if he could get three cosigners for the loan. He talked to his friends—Sam Epstein, R. D. Chotard, and Milligan. They agreed to cosign the loan. He told Frank Grego about the big oil money that was being made over in El Dorado, and Frank said he would like to go along with him. Because of the depression, action at the Planters Club had virtually ceased; no money was available for keeping alive let alone for gambling. Frank needed a change of scenery as much as Slim did.

Cranking up the engine of his battered Dodge touring car, Arizona Slim and Frank Grego headed west out of Lake Village, on the road that would take them through Montrose, Hamburg, and Crossett on their way to El Dorado, ninety miles away. The old dirt road was pitted and muddy in spots, but they would make El Dorado by early afternoon if they didn't get a flat.

Lyda felt desolate and abandoned as she watched her husband drive off. Slim was leaving her behind as he had left Ella Rose sixteen years before. She would be alone with Margaret and young Hassie until big Hassie had a notion to send for them. Or until he came home whipped by the oil business, ready to settle down and try his hand at cotton farming again.

She had one small consolation at least. It was Frank Grego he was taking with him. Frank's sister, like herself, was being left behind.

# Book III

# The Family Man

# 12.

IN SOUTHERN ARKANSAS, about twelve miles north of
the Louisiana border, the town of El Dorado sits amid
hilly pine forests. Dirt roads run out of town north and west
into rolling farmland and fruit orchards. The countryside
around El Dorado is lush and gentle; undulating hills and
valleys flow peacefully toward the horizon. The earth is
generous, yielding an abundance of corn, cotton, potatoes,
rye, and millet. On Saturdays the farmers come with their
families to El Dorado, driving wagons laden with produce
from their fields. They gather in front of the red-brick
courthouse in the middle of town and trade eggs, butter,
vegetables, and melons for dry goods and staples. When the
trading is over, they head for the hotels and restaurants with
their families and have themselves a night on the town.
Saturday afternoon marks the end of the workweek for them.
Saturday night and Sunday they rest and enjoy themselves
before beginning another week of hard labor on the farms.

But change seldom respects idyllic life. As El Dorado
suddenly discovered in early 1919. The town was transformed
almost overnight. Wagonloads of men, strangers, from all
over the country invaded. These aliens were not farmers like
the locals. They came garbed in heavy leggings, thick-soled
boots and shoes, flannel shirts, and corduroy jackets. They
filled the local hotels at night, and during the day trekked the

creeks and valleys, the beech and pine forests, the fields and farmlands. They had come to El Dorado looking for oil.

The farmers had heard stories about the big oil strikes in Oklahoma and Texas, but no one believed it could happen in Arkansas. Others had drilled and failed in different parts of the state as early as 1910. Unlike Texas and Oklahoma, Arkansas was just not oil country.

But still the strangers came. They practically took over El Dorado. True, after they had stayed awhile and done their surveying, they left, but only to return a short time later with long wagons filled with derrick timbers, boilers, piping, and heavy drilling equipment. All of which they transported to the pinehills and the fields north of town, where they erected their derricks and rigs across the rolling countryside. The quiet was soon broken by the rumble of heavy wagons, by the thunder of steel striking the tool dresser's anvil, by the giant serpent hiss of forced hot steam, by the banging of hammers and the grating rasp of men sawing wood. The farmers observed all this; resentment mingled with awe. They took none too kindly to these strangers invading the privacy of their world, yet they were fascinated with the possibility that their soil could yield up anything but the products they had been growing all their lives.

And then one day it happened. A man from Tulsa, Oklahoma, named Bruce Hunt—no relation to Slim but equally adventurous—borrowed $250 from a friend of his and leased over twelve thousand acres of land a few miles west of El Dorado. He formed a partnership with a geologist, J.J. Victor, and the two of them contracted with the Constantin Refining Company to drill the land. They started a well on a spot they called No. 1 Hill, and on April 22, 1920, at a depth of twenty-two hundred feet, the earth suddenly erupted as an explosion of gas, estimated at forty million cubic feet, roared from the casing head. The strike also produced a trickle of oil, about eight barrels.

Although not tremendous in itself, the discovery was the first concrete evidence that oil was to be found beneath these arable lands. The news spread instantaneously. A new army of prospectors descended upon the once peaceful farming town, and a forest of derricks sprang up across the hills and fields, crowding out the pine trees as the towering rigs lunged toward the sky.

The initial oil strike, meager as it was, merely whet the prospectors' appetites for the big payoff which they all felt would come in a matter of time. Their patience and labor were rewarded on January 10, 1921, less than a year after the first find. Another partnership, Busey-Mitchell, had only recently completed its first well, Armstrong No. 1, in the hills southwest of El Dorado, when the land erupted with a new explosion of gas and a great black gusher of oil. The strike was enormous. The local farmers hopped aboard their wagons and rode over to the well to stare at the roaring geyser. Immediately the word went out that the first big oil strike had just occurred in El Dorado, Arkansas.

Within weeks, thousands of strangers came pouring into town from all over the country. The Vicksburg, Shreveport & Pacific Railroad put on special trains to carry people to El Dorado from Shreveport, Louisiana. The Rock Island Line and the Missouri Pacific added a total of five runs daily from Little Rock to El Dorado. Additional special trains were set up in Tulsa, St. Louis, Chicago, and New York. By the end of the month twenty-two trains were daily unloading fortune-seekers from across the entire nation in El Dorado, now dubbed the Oil Capital of Arkansas. In addition to the trains, every road leading into town was clogged with hundreds of wagons, riders on horseback, and automobiles of every description, including Model-T Fords, Starrs, Overlands, Dodges, Saxons, Marmons, and Pierce Arrows. Two ingenious men flew into town from Oklahoma City, some three hundred ten air miles away, in a three-seat Laird Swallow. The trip took three hours and twenty-eight minutes, something of a record for time and distance. Six days later, a commercial air service started regular flights from Shreveport to El Dorado.

By the beginning of February, El Dorado had grown from 4,000 to 15,000, and it was growing every day. The big hotel in town, the Garrett, put cots into its hallways to accommodate the strangers, and started renting space in the chairs in the lobby. The same scenes were repeated in the Star, Central, and Arcade hotels down the street. The lobbies and the streets in front of the hotels and roominghouses were packed with a rolling sea of humanity from early morning to the middle of the night. The hotels themselves became instant goldmines, and were bought and sold for huge profits within days. Dr. Busey, whose well started the big oil rush on El Dorado, bought and sold the Arcade within days, and the man to whom he sold it resold the place the following day. Rufus Garrett, the owner of the Garrett Hotel, leased his establishment to a gentleman named Paul Marks, who sold the lease to two men from Shreveport a few days later for a huge profit.

The initial flow from Armstrong No. 1 was as high as ten thousand barrels of oil a day. The land around the well skyrocketed in value overnight. A tract of sixty-five acres a half mile away shot up to $10,000. Days later speculators from Shreveport bid the price of a nearby one-hundred-acre tract up to $21,000. Enormous fortunes were made in a matter of days and weeks. The officials of El Dorado, together with the county government and the chamber of commerce, tried to join hands in an effort to suppress excess profiteering and to

[82]

keep out undesirable elements. But things were happening too quickly for anyone to control. The strangers kept coming and money kept changing hands. Dr. Busey had made one fortune and was busy looking for another. And Captain Eugene Constantin, whose company had drilled the No. 1 Hill well, was planning to retire to a castle he had bought on a seven-hundred-eighty-acre estate just forty-five minutes from the elegant heart of Paris.

By early February 1921 the fever was too far out of control for any legislature or chamber of commerce to do much about it. Oil. Land. Instant money. The party was on. Professional oilmen, amateur speculators, hustlers, gamblers, prostitutes, sightseers—they were all in El Dorado searching for adventure, excitement, and fortune. Barely a few short weeks had passed since the first blockbuster well came in, and the action was just getting started.

# 13.

WHEN ARIZONA SLIM and Frank Grego hit town early that first afternoon in March, 1921, El Dorado looked like a Mardi Gras celebration gone berserk. The main drag through town, South Washington Street, had been renamed Hamburger Row by the invading oil prospectors. Enterprising entrepreneurs were erecting rickety shacks and stalls on the wooden sidewalks, which ran the length of Hamburger Row on both sides of the street. To the passing strangers vendors hawked their wares, including food, durable boots, leggings, and other items of clothing suitable for the oil fields, cots and bedrolls for those without the price of a room, and games of chance, such as shell games, cards, and craps. Prostitutes, whiskey, and oil leases were also for sale. The dirt street was ribbed from the weight of heavy wagons loaded with men and machinery, and the mud was so deep in spots one could sink to his thighs.

Slim and his buddy took a cot at one of the stalls on Hamburger Row and then went down the street to check out the action at the Garrett Hotel. The lobby was swarming with people, some of whom were sleeping in chairs and bedrolls, while others were shouting at one another, making deals, buying and selling oil leases, swapping the latest rumors about oil shows in one place or another. Arizona Slim's adrenalin started to pump amid this excitement. He found the new manager of the Garrett, the one who now held the lease from

Rufus Garrett, the owner, and talked him into setting up a poker game in one of the rooms in the hotel. Slim would run the game and cut the hotel in for a piece of the action.

Once again Arizona Slim was back in business doing the one thing he knew best, the one thing he had to do to make himself some stake money and get back onto his feet again. The same night he opened up his first game to any and all comers. The hotel had cut a slot in the table with an iron box underneath into which Slim shoved the house's share of his winnings. The game was an immediate success, with prospectors and local merchants flocking to his room in search of the latest action in town. A local restaurant owner, R.E. Robinson, newly rich as a result of the oil boom, sat in on one of the first games. Slim played him along beautifully, letting him build up his opening bet of fifty cents to a win of $50 for the night. Robinson went away from the game, rubbing his hands in glee and bragging about the game to all his friends.

"This is the game I been looking for all my life," he told the other merchants in town.

Three nights later he returned with a group of well-heeled friends, and they all sat in for a high-stakes game. By the end of the night Slim had cleaned them out and walked away with a new lease on life. He managed to put a small bankroll together after only a few days in El Dorado. He could now afford to walk away from the Garrett and set up his own games. He no longer needed to cut the house in for a percentage now that he could afford a place of his own.

He and Frank Grego moved into an old frame building on Hamburger Row, farther down the main drag from the Garrett. The first floor of the building housed a pool hall, and in the dirt street out front stood a couple of gas pumps, which served as a filling station. Slim's reputation as the gambler who had cleaned out Robinson and his friends after only a few days in town followed him to his new establishment. He advertised his game as the most honest in El Dorado, in which every man had a fair chance to beat the house. He set up some poker tables down in the pool hall and opened the doors to the trade.

Slim and his partner, Frank Grego, prospered from the start. He lived up to his word and quickly established a reputation as an honest gambler whose games were completely aboveboard. He also expanded his games to include blackjack and craps, and he offered the public the best odds in town. An oil driller named Charles Casey, who was the same age as Arizona Slim, was a regular customer and he spread the word to his friends in the oil fields.

"The man's got the best tables in town. He's tough to beat but he's honest. Gives all comers a fair shake. That's more'n you can say about most of those operators."

Slim opened up accounts at several of the local banks, as soon as he made some money, to establish a line of credit for himself. He was careful not to stick the bank with any bad checks from his games. If a check bounced, he made it good with cash from his own pocket. He realized that, in a town full of hustlers, con artists, and outright thieves, a solid reputation was the best stock in trade a man could have. He was careful from the start to keep his slate clean, careful not to give anyone just cause to say anything that would mar his reputation for fairness and honesty.

With all his success in the gambling business, Arizona Slim kept his foremost goal in mind—to get into the oil business. The problem now, however, was that the price of oil leases was being bid up to astronomical new heights every day with all the frantic trading that was going on. The standard lease called for a prospective oilman to pay a farmer or landowner so many dollars per acre, plus an annual rental fee, for the right to drill for oil on the owner's property. If the prospector was fortunate enough to hit oil, he would then cut the owner in for royalty payments, usually 12 1/2 percent, as long as the wells kept producing. There were many variations to these leases, some requiring the prospector to commence drilling within a set period of time or forfeit all his payments, but the basics were about the same. A prospector would go out and lease some land, and then talk up the oil potential in the land to other investors, showing geological surveys and pointing out nearby producing wells, in order to raise money to start drilling. Local farmers had caught on to the hustle early on in the game, and had started charging outrageous sums for the right to drill on their land. Leases might change hands two and three times a day, with one speculator paying a farmer $25 an acre for the lease and then going into town and selling it an hour later for a profit of $2 an acre, and so on in an endless cycle of hustling and trading. For every honest oil prospector in town, there were probably fifty con artists who were interested more in quick profits than in punching holes in the ground.

After about three months in El Dorado, Arizona Slim had his first big opportunity to get his hands on a decent lease without paying through the nose for it. His opportunity came the same way most of his opportunities had come in the past: by way of a marathon poker game. By June, with over a hundred wells producing in the fields around El Dorado, farmers were charging the staggering sum of $1,000 an acre for leases on their land. One promoter had leased a forty-acre tract, subdivided it into one-acre plots, and resold them to eager prospectors. One such prospector was sitting in on a poker game at Slim's establishment when he had a run of bad luck and ran out of cash.

"This here's all I got left to my name," he said to Slim, tossing his lease into the pot.

Slim seized the tailor-made opportunity immediately. He knew the man had finally drawn a good hand and was going for broke. Slim was holding a pair of queens, not enough to take the pot. One card remained to be played and there was one queen left in the deck that had not been dealt yet. If he pulled it, he would win the hand. It was a long shot but the only one he had, and he decided to go for it. Each man pulled a final card and Slim almost leaped from his chair; he had his third queen. The prospector threw down his hand, confident he had won the huge pot with his two pairs, but his hopes collapsed when Slim laid down his queens and scooped in his winnings. Arizona Slim was now in the oil business.

It was June 1921. Arizona Slim had been in El Dorado for a little more than three months. He had an oil lease in his pocket and he was now in the oil business. Or almost. First he had to go home and promote some money to drill a well. That meant coming up with $10,000 or so to punch a hole in the ground. He would go home to see Lyda and the kids. And do a hell of a lot of fast talking among the local merchants while there.

# 14.

WHEN LYDA SET EYES on Hassie again, she hoped he was returning to Lake Village to settle down for good this time. Instead, he came home bubbling over with enthusiasm about all the money that was to be made in oil in El Dorado, about all the wells that were bringing oil up out of the ground, and about the potential for future discoveries. He tried to talk her into moving there with him and joining him in all this excitement, but Lyda was still not convinced. Everything was still up in the air. Anything could go wrong and then where would they all be? It was better to wait until he had something more substantial to offer them there.

Slim looked up his old associates and pitched them on the prospects in the El Dorado oil field. He had his lease and now he needed some cash money to drill his well. Wells all around his land were gushing up enormous black fountains of oil. They couldn't miss. They would all get rich in oil money the way they got rich on cotton and land trading during the war. His enthusiasm was catching, and El Dorado oil fever spread throughout the town. Slim's father-in-law, Sam Epstein, the mayor of Lake Village, Dixon Gaines, all his old poker partners and business associates came down with the fever. They knew Slim was a hustler, but they also knew he was honest. He could be trusted to be fair with all of them if he hit it big. Arizona Slim raised his cash and then some. When he left town, heading west again in his beatup old Dodge, he had enough money in the bank to drill his first well. He was officially in the oil business, or at least he would be in a very short time.

Slim's acre was on a huge stretch of sloping land owned by a farmer named Pickering, and he decided to christen his first well Hunt-Pickering No. 1. The farm rolled on endlessly down into the valley and up the far hills toward the horizon. The well was on a proven part of the field, and the wells surrounding Slim's were disgorging huge black gushers of oil. It was an eerie sight, all this lush idyllic farmland forested with towering derricks and crawling with men and heavy drilling equipment. The farmers themselves had become interested more in the thick dark liquid that lay deep in the earth than in the crops that grew from the topsoil. Rivers of oil coursed through the earth, and Slim was more convinced than ever that he would tap into them as his drill bit broke the ground for the first time.

His determination paid off on his first try. Hunt-Pickering No. 1 threw up a black geyser after only a few weeks of drilling. His excitement was short-lived, however, when the gusher subsided, then started spurting sporadically before it stopped completely. Arizona Slim was acquiring an on-the-job crash course in the oil business. He discovered in short order that it wasn't enough merely to strike a vein and bring up some oil, not with other wells pulling oil out of the ground all around. It wasn't a question of whose patch the oil was under; the most important thing was who could get it out of the ground the fastest. Slim's equipment was old and rudimentary. He was surrounded by more powerful rigs, rigs which could sustain the gas pressure to deplete the lode faster than his could. He needed better pumping equipment, and that meant raising additional cash money, at least $3,500 or so.

He shopped around El Dorado and found a small outfit that would use its own equipment to pump the oil faster than he could on his own. This refining company would bring up the oil and share the profits with him. All went smoothly at first. The oil started flowing again, and the company channeled it into its pipeline to the refining plant. Slim was back in the running and he began to count all the money he was going to make. Rich again! A successful oilman on his first try. And then his luck went sour once more. The drilling outfit went bankrupt while the well was being drilled and had to cease operations. Slim had yet to collect a nickel from the company; his dreams of an instant oil fortune receded. He was forced to abandon his first well for lack of cash to continue pumping the oil he knew was there. His first attempt ended in failure, but it did teach him an important lesson: it was not enough to find oil; he had to be prepared to get it out of the ground faster than the other guy. It was an expensive lesson, but at least he had learned it early in the game.

Arizona Slim returned to his gambling tables in the old frame building on Hamburger Row and started at the beginning again. Throughout the summer of 1921 he built up his winnings at the poker tables. He traded oil leases with the other hustlers in the shacks along the wooden sidewalks, and he visited Lyda and his two small children on odd weekends in his old jalopy. By the early fall he had raised enough money to start another well.

"That man's been doing everybody he can ever since he hit town," Charles Casey remarked to Harry Reeves over a drink one night at the Garrett Hotel. Reeves, an El Dorado merchant, had been observing Slim in action since he hit town.

"He's got one of the keenest business minds I ever encountered," Reeves said. "I seen him outtrade people who are supposed to be pretty smart."

"He runs an honest poker game, though. He even pays off the niggers when they get lucky and win a hand of black-jack."

"Tricky but honest. That sums him up pretty good, I'd say."

By November, Slim had accumulated enough money to lease a twenty-acre patch on a farm owned by Tom Rowland. He signed a note agreeing to pay Rowland a bonus of $10,600, and then he subdivided half of the twenty acres into smaller leases and sold these off to investors in El Dorado. By holding ten acres for himself and selling the remaining land, he was able to come up with enough cash to pay the note he owed Rowland and put aside the money he would need for drilling. In doing this, he was utilizing a system he would follow all his life: put up a little cash of his own; pyramid the investment into a larger stake by selling shares to others; and take the big plunge with other people's money.

Slim put his rigging in place and his drill bit hit the ground for the second time that year. The cold damp Arkansas winter was just taking hold. The fields and woodlands surrounding the town were gray and bleak as oilmen bundled up against the biting winds. The dirt streets in El Dorado crusted over with frost and ice; the rutted mud froze into a swirling pool of murky ice along the length of Hamburger Row. The merchants shuttered their rickety shacks on the wooden sidewalks against the damp winter cold, and heated them as best they could with wood-burning stoves. Ordinarily, life in the town and on the farms surrounding it would have come to a halt during the bleak months. But this was not an ordinary time. El Dorado was an oil-boom town, the Oil Capital of Arkansas. Wagonloads of men and equipment daily jammed the old dirt roads leading from town to the farms and woodlands, to the growing forest of derricks that stretched toward the cold gray winter sky. The cold months little discouraged the men from their frantic quest to dig holes into the earth, to tap the flowing rivers of thick black oil that lay there, and to pull out that oil faster than everybody else.

This time Slim was prepared. His pumps were new and powerful, his equipment the best he could find. He was determined to hit oil and make a pile of money for himself and his investors. He had done his homework and picked his site well. As the old year ended and the new one began, his rig was plunging deeper and deeper into the earth. After several weeks of drilling he hit paydirt. The wellhead erupted in the middle of January 1922, about a month before his thirty-third birthday. This one was a gusher, a powerful black geyser that looked as though it would produce forever.

On the strength of his first big strike, Slim had no trouble finding a new lineup of investors for a second well on his ten-acre site. He put the new rigging in place within weeks of his first discovery, and on March 12 his second well came in, this one even bigger than the first. Again he raised additional cash for a third try.

The first two wells were throwing up a total of ten thousand barrels a day and he knew he had to act immediately to capitalize on his recent successes. This was another technique he had learned in his years of wandering, trading, and gambling. Nobody wants anything to do with a failure; people are afraid that failure may be contagious. Everybody wants a piece of a successful man for the same reason. Thus a winning streak has to be exploited immediately. There is no guarantee it will last forever. Fail to exploit a success while still fresh in people's minds and the opportunity may vanish.

Arizona Slim parlayed his own successes on Tom Rowland's farm into a stunning winning combination. He talked up his wells to everyone with whom he came into contact. He wrote letters to old associates and acquaintances in Arkansas, Mississippi, and Louisiana. He wrote to his brothers in Ramsey, Illinois. James was particularly enthusiastic and sent Slim some money, buying shares in the oil royalties that flowed from the wells.

Slim's third well came in big in June. In the space of six months he had birthed three big producing wells. With this newfound wealth he paid off his old debts and scouted around for new leases in different parts of the field. He was on his way toward accumulating a new fortune. He had done more than merely regain his feet; he was flying high on oil money. The potential for success was enormous, a success much larger than what he had achieved growing cotton and trading land during the war years in Lake Village.

Slim rented a house in El Dorado, in a good part of town away from the main drag, and sent for Lyda and the kids. He again had a home, money, and prosperity to offer his family. Lyda no longer had to worry about what would come of them all in that strange boom town ninety miles from home. She could join her husband and live in style. Hassie had come through after all. Maybe now that he was well on his way to becoming a rich, successful oilman, he could see his way clear to giving up those dreadful gambling games of his.

# 15.

ARIZONA SLIM CUT A memorable figure as he strode through El Dorado in his white planter's suit, his thinning auburn hair combed neatly back from his forehead, and a long black cigar clenched between his teeth. He was a familiar sight to everyone, the drillers and the oilmen, the local merchants and the entrepreneurs, and the farmers whose land had suddenly made them worth their weight in gold. In the beginning he had been known as the gambling man and hustler who could outtrade the sharpest heads in town. But more recently he had proven himself as an oilman as well, and that added the element of dignity to his bearing. Slim was known as a man of action rather than a man of words, and Harry Reeves, the El Dorado merchant who had gotten to know him pretty well, asked him as they were chatting one day why he seemed to have so little to say.

"What I learned, Harry, was by listening," Slim replied, and walked away.

Lyda also was becoming a familiar sight. Not seldom was she seen strolling along Hamburger Row with her two children on her way to the Quaker church. Always she was properly dressed in fashionable clothes, despite the pioneer atmosphere of El Dorado, and always did she have a friendly smile and a pleasant word for everyone she passed.

"Good evenin', Lyda," Harry Reeves said, tipping his hat to her as he met her late one Sunday.

"Hello, Harry. How are you tonight?"

"Just fine. On your way to church I see," said Harry, smiling down at the children.

Six-year-old Margaret and four-year-old Hassie, freshly scrubbed and dressed for the occasion, stared up at the big friendly man.

"Yes," Lyda replied. "I take the children with me every week."

"And how's Mr. Hunt tonight?"

"He's just fine, Harry. He's off playing poker again, as usual."

Harry detected a tinge of resentment in her voice which she tried unsuccessfully to hide. He looked down at her midriff, observed the swelling beneath her light cloak, and smiled at her.

"I guess it's showing now," she said, smiling. "I'm expecting around the first of the year."

"Congratulations, Lyda. And give my best to your husband too," said Harry, tipping his hat and strolling off toward the Garrett Hotel.


During the summer of 1922 oil was pumped from the ground at a furious pace in the hills and fields about El Dorado. The Gilliland Oil Company had built a pipeline connecting El Dorado with Haynesville, Louisiana, and the Shreveport–El Dorado Pipe Line Company laid branch lines into Homer, thirteen miles farther south on the road from Haynesville to Shreveport. The Southern Oil Corporation put down a four-inch pipeline to transport oil to its new loading station on the Rock Island Line just south of Shreveport.

The fields immediately surrounding El Dorado were now fully exploited; rigs pumped oil on every available square foot of land. So prospectors began searching for leases in the hills and farmlands farther to the north and west. New strikes were made in Irma, East El Dorado, Woodley, Stephens, and Smackover, which was a short distance north and slightly to the west of El Dorado.

Smackover was, by far, the most productive field of them all. Before 1922 it had been a hamlet of sixty poor farmers, lying alongside the Missouri Pacific Railroad line. Following the first big discovery of oil by J. T. Murphy on April 14, 1922, however, the population of Smackover multiplied fortyfold, to some twenty-five hundred eager prospectors. The Murphy well hit a huge pocket of gas, in addition to the oil, at a depth of about two thousand feet and produced a flow of thirty million cubic feet of gas a day. The VKF Oil Company's No. 1 Richardson well shortly afterward came in with a major oil strike, occasioning an influx of men and equipment into Smackover every bit as overwhelming as that into El Dorado. Within a year over a thousand wells were pumping twenty-five million barrels of oil, exceeding the production of the original field in El Dorado.

All this oil wealth, aside from making the Arkansas oilmen some of the richest men in America, helped transform El Dorado from a dusty oil-boom town into a shining urban center. The money was put to work pulling down the shacks along Hamburger Row and replacing them with proper shops and stores. The wooden sidewalks were ripped up and new cement walks laid. The rutted dirt main street resumed its name, South Washington Street, but not its condition; the mud was covered over with a smooth coat of tar down the entire length. The old mud roads and fields off South Washington Street were also paved, and the area was zoned for building lots. El Dorado now exuded an air of affluence and southern cosmopolitan glamour it had never known before.

In a matter of weeks and months the town began to spread

outward from the main drag, the focal point of which was the brick courthouse in the center of town. The oilmen bought plots of land and built houses where nothing but open spaces had existed. Residential sprawl had come to El Dorado, as it eventually came to Smackover and other oil communities in the rolling hills north, east, and west of El Dorado. The oil flowed from the ground as though it would never stop, creating instant fortunes for a growing army of oilmen and their families. It was boom time in southwest Arkansas and northern Louisiana.

Lyda gave birth to a third child, a girl they christened Caroline, on January 8, 1923. Slim was content with his growing family but was also beginning to get a bit restless. His self-contradictory nature was pulling him in different directions. Despite his farm boy roots, he was obsessed by a need to take great risk, master new fields, and acquire vast amounts of money. But the wealth itself seemed to mean little to him. Once he made a fortune, he took no steps to preserve it and enjoy the luxuries it could provide. His pleasure was in the struggle itself. Taking new risk with the money he had worked so hard to accumulate was more important to him than anything else. It was as though he had to keep proving himself, had to keep on finding new challenges for his restless nature, even if it meant losing everything he had.

Likewise, the establishment of a growing family was another obsession of his. Lyda was valuable to him more as a conduit for his genes than as a wife, companion, and lover. Reproduction was his goal, the creation of offspring who would carry his name and serve as images of himself. He saw his family as an extension of himself rather than as a collection of human beings of which he was part. It was another aspect of his paradoxical nature that he was determined to enlarge his family even though he was anything but a homebody. He was content to know that Lyda and the kids existed, but he shared little if any of his life or himself with them.

Consequently, it was no surprise that he began to expand his field of operation farther from his homestead shortly after the birth of Caroline. He acquired new leases and drilled some wells in Smackover, north of El Dorado, and then roamed south of town to Junction City on the Arkansas-Louisiana border, and then to Homer, twenty-seven miles southwest of Junction City on the road toward Shreveport. Both Junction City and Homer were in the middle of oil fields, and Arizona Slim developed successful wells in both areas.

At this stage of his life, with Lyda and the three children comfortably ensconced in El Dorado and money from the oil wells rolling in faster than he could spend it, Slim began to get a craving for some faster action. He had proved himself as a cotton farmer and a land speculator back in Lake Village before finally going bust in the aftermath of the war. He had conquered a new field and established himself as a successful oilman. Life was again becoming too easy for him. He needed faster action and new challenges. Thus he invested some money in a gambling casino in Junction City with some underworld figures from Shreveport, and it wasn't long before he was spending more time around the craps tables than in the oil fields.

His establishment was one of the most popular spots in Junction City, and he enjoyed strolling among the customers in his white suit, chewing on a cigar, talking about the oil business and gambling techniques with the men, and getting chummy with the ladies who hung around the bar and gambling tables hustling for an easy buck. The casino had poker, blackjack, and dice tables, three games Slim enjoyed the most because they required memory and countdown skills rather than blind luck.

Slim got to know an oil-refinery worker who had migrated to Junction City from eastern Europe after spending some time working in Mexico. Slim, amused by the man's thick accent and convoluted speech patterns, took a liking to him. He decided to take him under his wing in much the same manner one takes in a stray dog and makes a favored pet of it. Slim observed the European in action at the craps table, making foolish bets and losing his hard-earned wages. He strolled over to him, draped an arm across his shoulders, and pulled him aside.

"Listen here, my foreign friend. I'm gonna give you some free advice because I like you."

The man, who was about Slim's age, was insulted by Slim's method of addressing him and by his patronizing tone, but he also welcomed whatever help he could get.

"You're betting the field and that's a sucker bet. If you want to play dice like an American, bet the thrower to shoot a natural or crap out on his first roll. If he gets a streak going, bet him to make his point with half your winnings two or three times in a row, then quit. No guarantee you'll win that way. But you reduce the odds to almost fifty-fifty if you bet like that."

The man was grateful for the advice, which he never forgot, but he could never get Slim to call him by his name, no matter how many times he told it to him. After a while he dropped the subject, realizing that his benefactor enjoyed his little game and nothing was going to change him.

Slim opened another gambling house, this one in Homer, and also in conjunction with some mysterious figures from Shreveport. He wandered north to Little Rock, the city where he had been touted as the next white hope by the fight promoters thirteen years earlier, and over to Hot Springs, the mob-run town known as Sin City, fifty miles west of Little Rock. His craving for excitement and new adventures brought him into contact with the racketeers who controlled the gambling action in both cities, and he invested his own money in their clubs.

His relationship with Lyda had never been close, and now he was growing more and more distant from her, geographically as well as emotionally. He was a stranger to his children as well, who saw him but briefly when he visited home now and then. He stayed seldom more than a few days. The wanderlust was becoming more chronic every day. Nothing Lyda would do or say could tie him closer to the family nest, could get him to abandon his mania for gambling and wandering off on his own. Although Hassie was not one to flaunt it, Lyda more than just suspected that there were other women in his life, women he met in his various clubs, women who worked as secretaries and clerks for him in his oil business.

"That Hunt's a man's man," she had overheard the men in town remark on more than one occasion. "He's a real man in more ways than one, if you know what I mean," they said, winking and laughing the way men do when they thought she couldn't hear them.

# 16.

IN 1925 EVERYTHING CAME to a head. Oil production in El Dorado, Smackover, and the fields around these major centers, had reached a peak and was starting to decline. The output at Smackover rose to seventy-two million barrels before the field seemed to shoot its load. For the past year Slim had been given considerable thought to selling out part of his oil operations. He sensed that production was nearing a peak, and he didn't want to be caught holding the bag when the market dropped the way the cotton market fell a few years earlier. Moreover, he was getting a bit bored with it all, bored with the easy money that flowed from the ground, and bored with the suckers who frequented his gambling establishments. He felt the urge to venture even farther from home, perhaps to a new state to try his hand at something altogether different.

The year started off badly for him and Lyda on a personal level. Lyda gave birth to a fourth child, a girl they called Lyda Bunker Hunt, in February, around the time of Slim's thirty-sixth birthday. The girl was sickly at birth and died within a month. Slim didn't blame his wife openly for her death, but it served to aggravate the strain that already existed between them. Slim was bitter about the loss of his newest offspring, the latest extension of his ego, and he seized the death as an opportunity to arrive at a decision he had been leading up to for months.

Sensing that the oil boom in southwest Arkansas was running out of steam, he decided to unload the greater portion of his producing wells in Smackover. He made a deal with the Louisiana Oil and Refining Company whereby he would carry a note for $600,000 in return for most of his Smackover wells. Whereupon he approached one of his banks in El Dorado and discounted the note, that is, he sold it to the bank for about $400,000 in cash; the monthly payments on the note would go to the bank, instead of to Slim, over a period of time, amounting to a total of $600,000. Besides his remaining Smackover wells, he held on to his wells in El Dorado, Junction City, and Homer, but production was already declining steadily. By acting when he did, he was able to sell off most of his bigger wells for a huge chunk of cash.

Without informing Lyda of the next step in his plans, he moved quickly to soften the blow he would soon deliver. He used some of his money to buy a full square block of land in El Dorado, away from the main drag and in the middle of the finest residential area in town. He contracted to build an enormous, rambling three-story house on that land and move his family from the house they had been renting. Lyda was ecstatic. She had been morbidly depressed over the death of her infant girl, but Hassie's actions helped take her mind off it a bit. Perhaps he was finally changing after all. Perhaps he meant to settle in with her and the children and give up his incessant gambling and carousing. Perhaps he was tiring of his restless life as he approached middle age, and would soon turn himself into a husband and a real father to his children.

He suggested that they take a trip together while the house was being built, drop the children off in Lake Village with her family, and go off on a second honeymoon to New York City, a place he had never been to but always wanted to visit. Lyda couldn't believe this was finally happening. She had longed for this kind of closeness with Hassie ever since they met, but had all but resigned herself to the fact that it would never be. And now, out of a clear blue sky, he seemed to be changing overnight before her eyes. In the spring of 1925 they set off on their journey, heading north on the train that would take them to the great magical city that was the real capital of the country.

The honeymooners stayed at a hotel in midtown Manhattan, and spent most of their time taking in all the breathtaking sights, eating in the finest restaurants, and going to all the Broadway shows in the theater district of Times Square. Arizona Slim was spellbound by it all. He had been to big cities before. Hadn't he been almost shanghaied in San Franciso, and barely escaped with his life a day or so before the great earthquake struck? Hadn't he spent a good portion of his youth in St. Louis with Hash and Ella Rose? And later on, had he not visited Chicago to play poker with some big-city gamblers? But New York was in a class by itself. There was nothing to compare with its towering buildings and vibrant streets jammed with endless streams of people on the move, searching for excitement. He was overwhelmed.

It was the Broadway musical, however, more than any other experience in New York, that struck a chord within him. Notwithstanding all his wide-ranging adventures, from farming to trading to land speculation to gambling to oil, Arizona Slim was still an unsophisticated man. He was at heart a farm boy who had been extremely successful in several walks of life, but who still did not know what he wanted to be when he grew up. The musicals he saw on Broadway appealed to this childish aspect of his nature in a way nothing else could have. The snappy tunes, the dancing, the costumes, and the set designs made an intensely vivid impression on him. The songs ran irresistibly through his head long after he left the theater. Incessantly he hummed the tunes and sang the words in his mind. By the time he and Lyda boarded the train for

Arkansas, Slim knew that the Broadway musical must play a big role in his life from now on.

They moved into their large three-story house toward the end of the summer, and Lyda had never been so happy in her entire life as she was now. She had even managed to blur the memory of little Lyda's death during the whirlwind events of recent weeks. Hassie had finally come home, to be her husband and a father to their three children. She and Hassie were going to be together after all.

But Slim had other ideas. The fine new house, the second honeymoon to New York City—these, he thought, made up for the years of neglect. He had paid her off: treated her to a grand time and settled her comfortably with the children in the finest house money could build. His conscience was clear. Now, early fall 1925, was the time to deliver his bombshell. One night after the children had been put to bed, he told her of his plans.

"I'm going to be leaving for a little while, Lyda."

Lyda stared at her husband in something resembling a state of shock. He might as well have struck her on the forehead with his fist.

"What? What's that you're saying, Hassie?"

"I got to go off to Florida on some business. There's a wild real estate boom going on down there everybody's been talking about. I want to go down and see for myself what it's all about."

"By yourself, Hassie? Aren't . . . aren't we coming along with you?"

"It'll only be for a little while. If there's anything to it, I'll send for you and the kids. I'll know better after I get there."

A week later, Arizona Slim got behind the wheel of his car and headed southeast toward Florida. He left a wife who was three months pregnant with a fifth child.

# Book IV

# The Bigamist

# 17.

REAL ESTATE FEVER WAS already out of control in Florida in the summer of 1925. The postwar depression had struck Europe harder than the United States, and by the time Calvin Coolidge was sworn into office as president in August 1923, right after the death of Warren Harding, the American economy had already gotten off to a roaring good start.

Much of this newfound prosperity could be traced to the mass production of the automobile. Under the Coolidge administration, the businessman was considered a king. The American industrialist had become the final authority on the conduct of society, replacing the statesman and the priest as the dictators of our destinies. The automobile was the most ubiquitous symbol of American ingenuity and business know-how. Americans who had spent their lives within ten miles of their homes suddenly had the ability to meander farther from the family nest. Many families took to the roads and headed to places where the weather was warm year round, places where they could enjoy the sight of palm trees swaying in tropical breezes during the winter, places where warm ocean water rolled onto white sand, places where fantasies turned into reality. Southern California was one of those magical places whither people went in their new automobiles. Shortly afterward, Florida was another.

For the first time ever, working-class Americans could

journey to these tropical paradises where only the rich had gone before. Industrious entrepreneurs were quick to recognize this new trend and find a way to capitalize on it. One such gentleman was George Edgar Merrick, the son of a Congregational minister. Merrick had bought some inexpensive land outside Miami and built a gabled house out of coral rock. He called it Coral Gables. George bought additional land in the same area and started building Mediterranean-style homes on his development, which he advertised as America's Most Beautiful Suburb. Coral Gables was incorporated as a town and George Merrick's utopian community grew into a city of two thousand homes, a business district, schools, banks, hotels, and clubhouses. He built long graceful streets lined with palm trees, and built his own lagoons with marinas where people could keep their boats. Merrick created nothing less than an American paradise in a place where only swamps had existed. To promote his paradise, he hired William Jennings Bryan, the eccentric American who in 1896, at thirty-six, had run for president on his Cross of Gold platform.

William Jennings Bryan was now an old man who was known more for his fundamentalist religious crusades than for his political clout. His beliefs had made him a subject of ridicule in intellectual circles, but he still had a hard-core following of small-town American fundamentalists. George Merrick put Bryan on a raft covered with a sun umbrella and set him afloat in the middle of his lagoon, where the old crusader lectured the visitors who flocked to the shores on the benefits of life in Coral Gables. When Bryan finished his talk, dancing girls came out and put on a show that was regarded as just out of this world. Since most of Merrick's land was below sea level, creating something of a drainage problem during the wet season, the crafty entrepreneur dug trenches which he called canals and imported gondolas with real-live Italian gondoliers from Venice. By this masterstroke of promotional genius, he was able to sell his swampland as an aquarian paradise on earth.

The success of Coral Gables led to the development of similar communities around Miami. Carl G. Fisher cut down the trees on Miami Beach, buried the stumps under five feet of sand to fill in the swamps, and built islands with villas and lagoons on them. He then subdivided his development into building lots and sold them off to the tune of $40 million. Joseph W. Young did the same thing for Hollywood-by-the-Sea, and Miami was developed and advertised as the Wonder City. Farther to the north, Fort Lauderdale became the Tropical Wonderland, Orlando was billed as the City Beautiful, and Sanford as the City Substantial. Even places no one had heard of before were promoted up north as tropical paradises by unscrupulous hucksters. One group started selling to northerners building plots, sight unseen, on Manhattan Acres, which supposedly was only three-fourths of a mile from the prosperous and fast-growing city of Nettie. Nettie, it turned out, was an abandoned turpentine camp in the middle of a swamp. Likewise, the beautiful tropical paradise of Melbourne Gardens turned out to be a clump of palmettos stuck in the middle of an impenetrable mudflat.

Despite the element of fraud and outright thievery, the development of Florida continued at a hectic pace. Real estate values soared to incredible new heights. In the early stages of the boom a lot in the business center of Miami Beach was bought for $800. A few years later it was resold for $150,000. A strip of land in Palm Beach, worth $240,000 before the madness set in, was subdivided into building lots and sold for $1.5 million in 1924. Fortunes were made by people whose tiny patches of previously worthless Florida land were suddenly sold for hundreds of thousands of dollars a few years later.

In 1920 Miami was a city with no delusions of grandeur. A

sleepy semitropical community of thirty thousand, it was set in the middle of a mangrove swamp. By 1925 Miami had evolved into a vast real estate exchange with a population of a hundred fifty thousand. More than two thousand real estate offices in the city employed over twenty-five thousand agents. Properties were sold in the streets sight unseen, sometimes changing hands two or three times the same day. The city government passed a law prohibiting the sale of land on the sidewalks to eliminate traffic congestion. Busloads and carloads of people from New York, Ohio, Illinois, and other northern states were descending on Miami by the hour. Hotels were jammed to capacity and the visitors camped in the parks, in the bus terminals, in their automobiles, and on the sidewalks in front of the real estate offices.

The fever spread sixty miles up the Atlantic coast where an American Riviera sprang up overnight. It spread its contagion farther north to Jacksonville, near the Georgia border, and then swept west across the middle of the state, over to the Gulf Coast, where it infected the residents of Tampa, St. Petersburg, and Sarasota. There was no stopping the contagion. Real estate fever was running amok. Every American wanted his own place in the land of eternal youth, sunshine, and leisure. Paradise on earth. All here in Florida.


Arizona Slim entered the magic land in the early fall of 1925, driving south along the west coast toward Tampa. The boom had already peaked in Miami. Although real estate values had started to soar along the west coast as well, a few bargains could be found here and there.

He rented an apartment for himself in the center of Tampa and made the rounds of the local real estate offices. On one of his first visits, an attractive young woman got up from her desk and walked over to greet him.

"Franklin," she smiled. "Why, Franklin Hunt, what are you doing down here?"

Slim looked at the lovely young woman closely. She looked familiar; he was sure he should have recognized her, but he couldn't quite pin her down.

"Don't you recognize me? I was a waitress in El Dorado when I met you. Frania Tye. I used to be Fran Tiburski in those days."

Now it came to him. Of course. Fran the waitress. No wonder he didn't recognize her right away. She had caught his eye the first time he set eyes on her in El Dorado and a serious flirtation began. He used the name Franklin, as he always did when he was on the prowl, and she got to know him as Franklin Hunt, the well-to-do oilman. Fran Tiburski was a knockout when she was a waitress in the oil-boom town. Here in Florida, in the land of eternal sunshine, swaying palm trees, and short clinging dresses designed to show off a maximum of golden-tan skin, she was absolutely stunning. What an incredible coincidence, what a godsend that she should turn up again in his life when he was beginning to drift restlessly in search of new challenges, as he had done in his youth.

Arizona Slim and Frania Tye hit it off immediately. He started seeing her every day, and she helped him locate a one-hundred-acre spread of land directly north of Tampa for which he put down $10,000 as a binder. He searched the area for other deals, and in spare moments when not with Frania or tending to business, he started composing musicals in his room. The tunes he had heard in New York City while attending the Broadway shows had become an obsession with him. He was convinced he could write romantic musicals himself, perhaps even better than the professionals did it. All day the lyrics and melodies ran in and out of his head, and he committed his own songs to paper: "Wherever Dreams Come

True, I'll Be with You"; "Happy the Days, and Sublime, When We Were Sweethearts."

He was infatuated by the romance, by the corny escapist atmosphere the musicals provided, and in his own mind he tried to turn them into reality. In his need to run away from an unhappy marriage, to find some deeper calling for himself now that the easy oil money had started to bore him, the musical fantasies were blown up out of proportion. He was determined to create his own paradise, to make his dreams and fantasies come true while pretending that the realities of his life, namely Lyda and his family in El Dorado, no longer existed.

In this romanticized, make-believe world, the land of unrealistic real estate values, blazing sunshine, blue-green water, and clean streets lined with palm trees, all of which looked as though they were part of a movie set, the border line between fantasy and reality was all but obliterated. Arizona Slim fell madly in love with Frania Tye; he was thoroughly convinced that, at long last, he had finally met the great love of his life. He had to have her, possess her, and make her life a part of his own, not merely for a weekend or even a month-long affair, but forever.

In the musical that his life had become, he had cast Frania Tye as the heroine, the shining golden girl with whom all boys fall in love in their dreams.

He was drifting now, emotionally as well as geographically. He was still trying to find out what he truly wanted to be when he grew up. He found his paradise in the Broadway musical. And he found his dream girl in a real estate office in Florida. He proposed to Frania Tye and she accepted. They were married in a quiet ceremony in Tampa on Armistice Day, November 11, 1925.

# 18.

FRANKLIN AND FRANIA SPENT the next six weeks
honeymooning up and down the coast of Florida.
This was the second honeymoon of the year for Arizona Slim,
but this time it was with the woman he loved.

Arizona Slim felt young again, so blissfully young, as he
drove around the sun-drenched state with his Frania, check-
ing out a spread of land here and there, and singing tunes of
his own composition, she laughing at his side. While they
were totally absorbed with each other, the rest of the country
was washing its Thanksgiving Day dishes and beginning to
prepare for the Christmas season. But even as the honeymooning couple traveled, sheltered from reality in their own
little bubble of excitement, the real world slowly was encroaching on their euphoria.

In every town they visited, newspapers carried headline
stories about the beginning of a real estate crunch. Arizona
Slim had arrived on the scene apparently at the top of the
cycle. Land values had already peaked in the Miami area and
farther north along the Atlantic coast. Having started later on
the west coast than on the east, the boom was still gaining
momentum when Slim first arrived in Tampa, but the
handwriting was now on the wall. If Miami was experiencing
an incipient real estate collapse, it was only a matter of time
before the good times ended in Tampa as well.

The last people to put down binders on land in developments to the east found themselves holding the bag. The buyers seemed to have disappeared overnight. Investors who had used up all their money in downpayments were defaulting on their notes when they could no longer resell their property. Developments that had been started remained half finished because of a lack of customers and cash. The city fathers of the new communities, the mayors, planners and developers, the chambers of commerce all staged parades and rallies in a vain attempt to revive the sudden slump. John W. Martin, governor of the state, held a press conference and declared in florid words, "Marvelous as is the wonder story of Florida's recent achievements, these are but the heralds of the dawn." He was joined by Davies Warfield, president of the Seaboard Air Line Railway, which had made a ton of money carting visitors to the Sunshine State. Warfield predicted that the population of Miami would continue to grow to a million happy residents within the next few years.

If the peaking of the real estate boom was not bad enough in itself, nature intervened in a way that brought everything to a state of total collapse. Paradise suddenly experienced a twist of fate that served to remind everyone that utopia is an illusion. With reckless fury a hurricane came roaring up the Atlantic coast from the Caribbean. It smashed into Biscayne Bay and drove its waters over Coral Gables, destroying the Mediterranean-style homes and turning the city into one gargantuan Venetian canal. The storm deposited a five-masted schooner into the middle of Coral Gables; tossed huge steamers and yachts onto the streets of downtown Miami; lifted trees out of the ground, roots and all, and sent them flying through the air until they crashed-landed atop the new Spanish villas with their red-tiled roofs; hoisted automobiles as though they were so many baseballs and launched them into storefronts and houses; and ended four hundred lives, seriously injured sixty-three hundred, and left some fifty thousand people homeless in a paradise that had quickly become a hell on earth.

Arizona Slim was one of the lucky ones. Sensing that the decline in real estate values in and around Miami would spread west across the state even faster than the boom did, understanding that bad news travels faster than good, he turned his car north toward Tampa. He was able to make a deal on his one-hundred-acre spread, taking a small loss on the $10,000 he had put down as a binder, before disaster struck. Professional gambler that he was, he knew that it was better to bite the bullet and take a small loss than to hang in too long, hoping against hope that the market would soon turn back in his favor again. Slim got out almost whole at a time when thousands were being wiped out in a rapidly falling market.

He and Frania ended their six-week honeymoon in Tampa on New Year's Day 1926. The curtain had been brought down on Act One of their musical for a brief intermission. Frania didn't want to see her Franklin leave her side, not even for a minute. They were so happy together, enjoying themselves in the sunshine and planning their future. But Franklin had business to attend to in El Dorado, he said. She would close the apartment and await his call to come and join him. He would send for her just as soon as he got things organized. He couldn't wait to have her with him again.

So Arizona Slim got back into his automobile and headed up the west coast of Florida. He had to go home and tend to his oil business. And besides, Lyda was due soon, and he wanted to be there for the happy occasion.

# 19.

WHEN HASSIE RETURNED to his three-story house in El Dorado, Lyda was entering her ninth month of pregnancy. His oldest child, Margaret, was ten now. A prim, unsmiling little girl with a seriousness that seemed to go beyond her tender years, she was very much her mother's daughter. Eight-year-old Hassie, little Hassie as he was called at home, was cut in the image of his father. He had his father's reddish-brown hair, his naturally powerful physique, and an unusual way of using his mind that prompted strangers to deem him a bit different. He was, in fact, different from most other boys his age. He kept to himself a lot. His intelligence was immediately evident to everyone who met him, but it was strange and disturbing, a preternatural intelligence that appeared at times to border on the psychic. A haunted look in little Hassie's eyes hinted at either genius or dark spiritual turmoil. It was still too early in his life to say which way he would go. Caroline, the baby, was just turning three and was of course the most uncomplicated. She was a pretty blondish girl, quick to smile for family and strangers alike.

Little Caroline was still too young to have noticed that her daddy wasn't home a lot. Margaret, however, had developed a brittle bitterness regarding her father. He was a virtual stranger to her and her mother, and she treated him with a proper coldness during his rare visits home.

But it was little Hassie who was most troubled by his

father's neglect. Margaret had discovered long ago that she could get along very well, thank you, without him if that's the way it had to be. She was a good friend to her mother, who needed her and loved her, and that was enough. But it was not enough for little Hassie, who felt personally rejected by this strange man who entered his life only now and then, without warning, and then disappeared with barely a word for him. This man had named him after himself, had given him his looks and quick intelligence, and then apparently decided that his son was not quite up to snuff. That's how little Hassie viewed his situation anyway. His own father had created him in his own image and then rejected the finished product. He was so much like his old man, but evidently not similar enough to make him happy. Why else would his father breeze in and out of his life with barely a word of recognition?

Lyda had perhaps changed the most. She had been crushed by Hassie's bombshell announcement in the early fall that he was going off on his own again. Just when she had begun to feel that he was changing, just after they had enjoyed such a good time together in New York City, just as she had gotten her hopes up that their marriage would be based on a more solid and intimate foundation, that's when Hassie had let her down the hardest. Unprepared for his announcement, she had been hurt as never before. Never, she vowed immediately, would Hassie do that to her again. If there was ever any chance that their relationship could change for the better, that chance was forever lost. Never again would she bare her feelings to him as she did; never again would she allow herself to become vulnerable. She erected a steel wall of defense between herself and her husband.

For his part, Arizona Slim had never been an introspective man. If he had doubts about the consequences of his actions, he was quick to shunt them aside. He had learned ages ago how to cope with remorse, how to deal with guilt and self-

[119]

doubt. Like all ruthless, driven men, he had developed a gift for rationalizing his actions that went beyond any semblance of logic and reason. Arizona Slim had a cold, hard, calculating intelligence. On a psychological level he was an immensely complicated man, but the moral side of his nature was simple. He did not love Lyda, perhaps was incapable of truly loving anyone, but he provided her with the good life, paid her off with material goods, and therefore owed her nothing. If he spent little or no time with his children, well, he was a busy man with much on his mind, and they were well taken care of in other ways. It was Lyda's job to bring them up properly; his job was to ensure proper shelter and care for them, and that he had done successfully by anyone's standards.

What of his relationship with Frania? What of his bigamous marriage, which was illegal if nothing else? Why, laws were made by a bunch of fools, and the country would probably be better off with hardly any government at all. It was the businessman who made this country what it was, without any help from the politicians, if you please. Calvin Coolidge was the greatest president this country ever had. Silent Cal kept his mouth shut and let the businessman do what had to be done to make the country great. If all politicians were like him, there wouldn't be any problems with a bunch of silly laws. So much for legalities.

But what of the more serious social and emotional consequences of his double life? What would happen if Lyda and Frania found out about each other? And how would it affect his children? That was his business and nobody else's. He was taking good care of Lyda and the kids, providing them with a new home and making sure they were all dressed and fed properly. If he needed Frania for other reasons, and could afford to take care of her as well, that was nobody's concern but his. Frania, true, was not the smartest girl in the world. Conversation with her tended to get a trifle common, if not downright boring, after five hours or so in a car. But she had a rare beauty and a romantic side to her nature which he wanted and needed. Lyda was a good mother and homemaker, and Frania was an exciting companion and stimulating lover. He needed Frania's flesh, and he also needed Lyda for her domestic qualities. If he was man enough to take care of both of them, why should anyone complain? It was his business alone.

No, Arizona Slim entertained not a twinge of guilt or doubt when he returned to El Dorado in January 1926. His main problem was logistical. Where would he set Frania up, and how would he arrange his time, to manage both sides of his life efficiently? It was a fairly complicated problem, but one he was sure he could resolve. He would have to divide his life into compartments. That might be too much for a lesser man to handle, but he was sure he was big enough to find a way.


Lyda gave birth to another son, Nelson Bunker Hunt, whom they nicknamed Bunkie, on Washington's birthday, February 22, 1926, five days after Slim's thirty-seventh birthday. Slim spent a few weeks at home with Lyda and the family, then sent for Frania and rented a house under the name Mr. and Mrs. Franklin Hunt in Shreveport, Louisiana, sixty miles southwest of El Dorado.

With his logistical problem taken care of, for the moment at least, Arizona Slim went about the business of putting some structure into his oil interests. He formed H.L. Hunt, Inc., and the Tenable Oil Company, which included some of his early financial backers among its shareholders. He fleshed out his corporations with a staff of secretaries, managers, and administrators, but all major decisions he reserved for himself. Wisely, he surrounded himself with some of the best talent in the oil business, men with a solid track record of sniffing out oil and the ability to pump it from the ground at the lowest cost.

One such individual was a man named Jick Justiss, a former muleskinner whom Slim had met at a poker table in El Dorado. Jick had a quick, cunning mind, and was a pretty good poker player to boot, a quality Arizona Slim held in high esteem. Justiss developed a reputation as a good fisherman, that is, he had a talent for salvaging old drilling equipment that had broken in the wells and been abandoned, and Slim put him in charge of drilling and field operations. Jick was devoted to Arizona Slim, the man who virtually picked him off the streets and provided him with a career, and he thought nothing of working on Thanksgiving, Christmas, and other holidays for him without asking for extra pay.

Roy Lee was an individual Arizona Slim had picked up during his earlier drilling days. Lee had a quick mind for figures and some experience working in the oil fields to the west in East Texas. Lee insisted on wearing a jacket and tie no matter how hot and humid the weather.

"That man just don't sweat," Justiss was fond of telling other employees when Roy was not around. "I think he's just too cheap to give away a free drop of honest sweat."

His stinginess and loyalty were put to good use by Arizona Slim, who made him general office manager, head accountant, and bookkeeper, all rolled into one. Lee endeared himself forever to his boss when he replied, upon being offered a raise in pay before Slim had struck it big, "Not now, sir. You really can't afford it now, Mr. Hunt."

With Jick Justiss in charge of field operations and Roy Lee riding herd over the office staff, Arizona Slim was able to go off on his frequent trips and tend to his gambling establishments with the knowledge that his oil interests were being managed properly in his absence.

"I never seen anything like it," one secretary remarked to

another when they were alone. "Those two look after this business like it was their own. You'd think it was their own money they were protecting."

"Mr. Lee thinks nothing of making me work Sundays and holidays. He fired one girl last week who refused to stay late one night," replied the other.

"Mr. Hunt pays very well, though. That's how he gets away with it. He rewards people well for their loyalty."

"I still think Mr. Lee could be a lot bigger on his own if he wasn't so devoted to Mr. Hunt."

"Yes, but he enjoys working for the great man. He thinks Mr. Hunt is God Almighty Himself. He'll do anything Mr. Hunt wants him to just for the privilege of being near him."

"Well, he pays us regular and that's all I care about. He never missed a payday yet. And that's more than I can say about some of these other outfits around here."

With Frania set up in a house in Shreveport, Arizona Slim decided to expand his drilling operations farther south into Webster Parish, in the oil fields east of Shreveport. This provided him with a legitimate excuse to spend a little more time away from Lyda and the kids in El Dorado, and a little more time with Frania in Shreveport. Slim had already set up housekeeping, after a fashion, as early as the end of January, a full month before Bunkie was born. As Lyda was beginning her final month of pregnancy, Slim was slipping away to Shreveport helping Frania get the house set up down there. His infatuation with Frania was still in full bloom. He was enchanted by her fair tanned skin, blue eyes, and lush blonde hair that draped in flowing waves over her shoulders. She was fun to be with; not bright and intelligent like Lyda, but fun-loving and quick to laugh. She loved it when he read his music to her, and she even joined him in singing the tunes. He had tried that once with Lyda but she only laughed at him and told him he was being a fool.

Franklin decided right from the start that Frania would have to bear his babies. With her blonde hair and light eyes, she definitely came from good stock. She had the good pure beauty and he would supply the brains. What children they could make together! Pure and healthy Americans. They wouldn't be dark and mixed like some of those foreigners he had met in his travels. Sure, he liked some of them well enough. Frank Grego, his old Italian buddy who had finally gone back to Greenville, was as good a man as a lot of real Americans Slim knew. Even the Jew from Lake Village, Sam Epstein, was a fine honest businessman. But you could never tell, even with them, what kind of genes they had mixed up inside them. Frank's sister was a rare dark beauty and he surely had enjoyed some good times with her. But he would think long and hard before he let her have his babies. God knows what kind of a mixed breed she might deliver.

Frania's family had evidently come from somewhere over there in Europe too. Where else would she have gotten the name Tiburski from? But she obviously had a pure strain in her with her coloring. No mixed blood in her family. Franklin Hunt and Frania decided from the start to have a family. She conceived a child in late January, about a month before Lyda gave birth to little Bunkie. And on October 25, 1926, she delivered their first child, a pink baby boy, whom they named Howard.

# 20.

WITH PROHIBITION IN FULL swing by the early 1920s, Johnny Torrio, the notorious Boss of Bosses in Chicago, hired a twenty-three-year-old hoodlum from the Five Points gang in New York City to run his liquor business in the Windy City. Al Capone had already established a reputation as a ruthless executioner despite his tender age, and he moved to Chicago to manage the speakeasies and liquor distribution business under Torrio.

Capone performed his duties well. He eliminated his boss's competition and helped Torrio expand his string of speakeasies throughout Chicago and Cicero, a nearby suburb. Capone established his headquarters in Torrio's main gambling emporium, the Four Deuces, located in an office building on South Wabash Avenue. Capone created a furniture dealership as a front for the club, and printed a set of business cards which read:

ALPHONSE CAPONE

Second Hand Furniture Dealer
2220 South Wabash Avenue

Capone was so good at his job that when Torrio retired, he succeeded his boss, running the entire operation on his own. He diversified his business from liquor to gambling and prostitution, and was grossing an estimated $100 million a year by 1926. He built a private army of seven hundred dedicated hit men, most of whom were well trained in the use of the sawed-off shotgun and the Thompson submachine gun. He ran over a hundred sixty speakeasies with an iron fist, and started making inroads into the political arena as well.

Al Capone used his money to get his own men elected to office, including the mayor of Cicero. He donated lavishly to charities and was praised highly in public by politicians and businessmen alike. Meanwhile, he went about the business of slaughtering his competition in imaginative new ways. Dion O'Banion, leader of a rival gang who owned a florist shop specializing in orchids, was greeted in his shop by three of Capone's top lieutenants one day. While the man in the middle, whom O'Banion knew and trusted, shook his hand, his two buddies pumped him full of bullets and left him lying among his orchids. O'Banion's gangster-style funeral featured a $10,000 coffin and twenty-six truckloads of flowers, including a basket with a card on it "From Al."

Other rivals, such as the Genna and the Aiello gangs, were riddled with machine-gun bullets as they left their homes in broad daylight, taken for friendly rides from which they never returned, mowed down by submachine guns as they rode in their automobiles, and tossed out hotel windows. Alphonse Capone was only twenty-seven years old in 1926, but he had already established himself as the single most powerful individual in Chicago and near-lying Cicero. His reign of terror was invincible, for the moment at least. He was Chicago's Boss of Bosses and his gambling emporium, the Four Deuces, played host to some of the heaviest rollers in the country.

Arizona Slim had gambled in Chicago before, way back when he was a youth drifting across the country on his own, then later on when he had established himself as a successful cotton farmer and oilman in Arkansas. After he had hit it big in the oil business, however, he started traveling north to the Windy City more and more frequently. Because of the amounts of money he played for, as well as his acknowledged skills at the poker table, he was treated as a man of respect whenever he visited the Four Deuces.

Shortly after the birth of Howard, his first boy by Frania, Arizona Slim organized a party of some of the highest rollers in El Dorado and took them on a gambling jaunt to Chicago. Among his party was Pete Lake, El Dorado's own bon vivant, who owned and operated the Star Clothing Store, which he won in a poker game a few years back. Pete dressed in loud flashy suits, mostly checks and plaids, with a lavender, pink, or red handkerchief tucked flamboyantly into the breast pocket. He was a skillful gambler and a free spender with a reputation as a lady killer as well. Slim also brought along some of his business associates from the oil fields, men who were gamblers and risk-takers in their business and personal lives.

Pete Lake had a weakness for the bottle as well as the poker table, and after a long night of hard gambling and drinking he turned his attention to an attractive redhead on the stool at the end of the bar. Pete sidled up to her, put his arm around her waist and offered to buy her a drink. When the girl indicated she wasn't interested in his advances, Pete grew abusive and started insulting her loudly. Arizona Slim, who had been talking to someone else at the other end of the bar, looked over to see what the commotion was all about. He almost gagged when he saw his friend in action. Rushing as fast as he could along the bar, he arrived at the scene just as two towering goons were approaching from the other side.

"You idiot!" he hissed at Lake. "You just insulted the boss's girlfriend."

The two men stopped, looked first at Lake and then at Arizona Slim.

"This guy a friend of yours, Mr. Hunt?" one of them asked.

"He had a little too much to drink. He didn't know who he was talking to."

"Well, I dunno. The boss told us to take him outside and teach him a lesson."

"Where's Al? Let me talk to him a minute and see if I can get him off the hook."

A few minutes later, Slim was ushered through a door at the rear of the club as Pete Lake and the rest of the party waited uncertainly at the bar. Five minutes later he reappeared and grabbed his friend by the arm.

"I had to apologize to the little dago for you. He don't like you one bit. Come on. Let's get out of here now before he changes his mind and decides to turn you into a sausage."

Pete Lake's knees were banging together like castanets when they got out onto the sidewalk. Drunk as he had been before the incident, he had sobered up instantaneously as he sat there on the stool awaiting the verdict. Each second that passed was a separate eternity in itself. Perhaps five minutes elapsed in all, but it seemed to Pete like a lifetime in hell. Capone was dictator of all Chicago. He decided things according to his own whim. There was no authority beyond him, no one else to appeal to. His word was the final law. Arizona Slim had come through for him, but it was the last favor he would ever do for Lake. Pete had violated his friendship. He had jeopardized Slim's reputation, even his physical well-being. He had committed a grievous sin in Slim's eyes.

Later on, Pete would realize that Arizona Slim was in the back room pleading as much for his own name and reputation as for Pete's health. The code Slim lived by was not that different from the one that governed the actions of Chicago's boss. Honor. Trust. Respect. Arizona Slim and Al Capone came from different backgrounds, different worlds light years apart. But they followed the same rules. They were more similar than either man would care to admit. Slim had no recourse but to cut Pete down to size in no uncertain terms. The words he spoke to Pete on the journey back to El Dorado were the sharpest he had ever directed at anyone.

# 21.

FRANIA GAVE BIRTH TO Haroldina on October 26, 1928, two years and one day after the birth of Howard, their first child. A little more than four months later, on March 6, 1929, Lyda delivered her sixth baby, the fifth to live, William Herbert, in El Dorado.

After his return from Chicago, Arizona Slim developed a fairly rigid routine in both his personal and professional lives. He spent the holidays with Lyda and the children in El Dorado, figuring he owed them that much after spending Thanksgiving and Christmas in Florida with Frania in 1925. Right after New Year's Day he traveled south to Shreveport, living for a while with Frania and his new family while he looked after his oil interests in Webster Parish east of the city. Then he would take off, sometimes over to Texas and Oklahoma, other times as far west as California, where he checked out new oil sites. Always on his travels he found time to fit in a gambling expedition to Chicago or New York, where he played poker with the top professionals of the country.

In 1927 Slim sensed that the fields in southwest Arkansas and northern Louisiana had seen their best days, even though his wells continued to produce and provide him with a handsome living. He was a wealthy man by anyone's standards, but the restlessness that drove him to Florida in the first place never fully left him after he returned to El Dorado. He felt that he had gone about as far as he could and made as much money as he could in the El Dorado–Shreveport oil-boom area. He had more than enough money to carry him through a lifetime. If he sold all his oil interests, he would net out a couple of million dollars at least.

But then what? He was not yet out of his thirties. The money itself was not the object with him. He craved new action, new excitement, new challenges. He thought Frania would bring him more satisfaction in life, perhaps provide him with a reason to stay closer to home and give up all his restless wandering. He discovered, however, that after a few weeks of playing house with her, he was as bored as ever he had been with Lyda, and itchy to be on the move.

If anything, Lyda was easier to take than Frania. Lyda made no demands on him and had long ago ceased to object to his absences. She let him come and go without complaint, accepting her fate in silence. But Frania was not exactly the long-suffering type. She was high-spirited when he met her; indeed, that's what attracted him to her initially. Her beauty. Her love of fun and excitement. Her delight in his musical endeavors. Married life and child-rearing failed to dampen this native enthusiasm. So, when he first announced after spending a few weeks in January with her that he had to take off on his own to check out some business interests, she was not shy about venting her feelings.

"And just what am I supposed to do while you're gone? There's nothing to do around here but go out and stare at the oil wells."

"It'll just be for a little while, Frania. I won't be gone more than a few weeks."

"It might as well be a few years as far as I'm concerned. We had such a good time in Florida, Franklin. We used to sing and laugh all the time. Why can't it be like that again? You're so . . . so serious all the time now."

[131]

"Life can't be like that all the time, Frania. Life can't be one big honeymoon that never ends."

"Oh, phoo. Go on then. Go off and tend to your business if you want to. See if I care. Maybe one day when you get back I won't be here anymore."

But Frania stayed because she had to; she had no money of her own, and no means of supporting herself and her babies. Franklin was upset by Frania's outbursts. She was still his dream girl. She was still his lovely blonde beauty, the golden girl whom he loved more than anyone else in the whole world despite her common mind. She was the perfect girl to have his children, to bring healthy new babies into the world for him. But this nagging was intolerable. Didn't she understand that he loved her and needed her and wanted to take care of her, but that he also needed his freedom? Freedom of movement, freedom to come and go as he pleased, was an essential element in his life.

Just because he went off on his own from time to time didn't mean he loved her any less. Why couldn't she get that through her head? Why couldn't she understand that the way Lyda did? If her disposition was only a little more like Lyda's, life could be so pleasant for him. Why did she have to make things difficult, not to say downright unpleasant, by nagging him all the time?

So Franklin went his own way because he had to. Much as he adored his golden girl, his freedom meant more than anything else in life to him. And Frania continued to complain because she could not bear being left alone. All the reassurances in the world could not take the place of having a happy-go-lucky, fun-loving husband at her side.

But Franklin Hunt could not stay at her side for more than a few weeks at a time. Just long enough to love her up a bit and get her pregnant with another October baby. And Hassie Hunt could not stay at Lyda's side for longer than a few weeks or so. Just long enough to look in and make sure everything was running smoothly. And long enough to make her pregnant and bring a new piece of himself into the world again. And then Arizona Slim had to leave his women for a spell; he had to go off by himself into the great wide world again. Franklin. Hassie. Arizona Slim. His many-faceted nature pulled him here, pulled him there, then pushed him by himself in search of new adventures.

Searching. Drifting. Wandering. Gambling. Franklin. Hassie. Slim. Off on his own looking for something new. Returning. Fathering. Tending to business. Then drifting and wandering. Perhaps one day he would find what he needed to make him truly happy, to make him content and at peace with himself and the world around him. Perhaps. One day. But not now. Not quite yet. That time had not yet come.

# Book V

# The Oilman

# 22.

To THE WEST OF EL DORADO lies Rusk County in East Texas. Located between Henderson and Overton, the county is marked by rolling farms and pasture lands that are thickly covered with towering oak, pine, and gum trees. The farmers in the southern part of Rusk County, about fifty miles west of Louisiana, had scratched out a meager living growing cotton, sweet potatoes, and corn since before the Civil War. The year 1929 was bad for the local farmers. The weather was dismal and the crops failed, bringing a depression to the area earlier than it descended on the rest of the country. The farmers tried to supplement their income by raising poultry and producing truck crops, but times were rough and many were hard pressed to pay their debts.

The promise of oil beneath their land had raised their hopes in 1927. That year the Pure Oil Company discovered a favorable oil structure in Van Zandt County, farther west, and two years later, on October 14, 1929, the company developed its first successful well there. Rumors started flying that Rusk County was also sitting on a sea of untapped oil, and it was only a question of time before some diligent prospector drilled into it.

Of the people looking for oil in and around the county, none other was more persistent and flamboyant than an old hustler in his late sixties named Columbus Marion Joiner. Joiner had been telling everyone for ages that their piny hills and parched fields were floating atop a vast ocean of oil, and that he, Columbus Marion Joiner, was the one who would find it. As early as 1920, at sixty, he leased 320 acres of land in the southern part of the county between Henderson and Overton. Both villages were poor. Dirt roads ran through them out into the hilly farmland, whose tranquility was broken only by an occasional sawmill or cotton gin.

Joiner was born on a farm in Alabama on March 12, 1860. He worked on the family farm until he was seventeen, picking cotton, building fences, and cutting down trees. His sister taught him to read the Bible, the only book available in the house, and he taught himself to write by copying the Book of Genesis. Aside from seven weeks spent at the local schoolhouse, this was his only education. When he reached the age of seventeen he took off, venturing into the big world on his own in search of adventure and experience.

His nomadic life took him to Muscle Shoals Canal, Alabama, after having toured the South as far west as Texas, where he got married and opened a dry-goods store. From there he wandered to Tennessee; there he got himself elected to the lower house of the Tennessee legislature when he was twenty-nine. Eight years later, having had his fill of Tennessee politics, he joined his sister, who had married a Choctaw Indian on a reservation in Oklahoma. For a number of years he worked with the Indians, leasing their land to white farmers, and managed in the process to accumulate for himself some twelve thousand acres of Indian land worth about $200,000.

The depression of 1907 wiped him out. Broke again at age forty-seven, he drifted over to the oil fields in Oklahoma where he rounded up some oil leases in Seminole County. He hooked up with a mysterious stranger who called himself Dr. A. D. Lloyd. Lloyd's real name was Joseph Idelbert Durham, but he had thought it prudent to change it to avoid litigation by a number of women, all of whom claimed to be married to him. Lloyd had spent a good part of his life prospecting for gold in Alaska and Mexico, and had recently returned from an extended engagement on the road conducting Dr. Alonzo Durham's Great Medicine Show, which featured patented medicines he made himself from crude oil. Joiner and Durham, alias Lloyd, recognized immediately that some star-crossed aspect in their lives had destined them to find each other; the Lord God Almighty could only have created the two of them to meet one day and become partners. It was a perfect marriage of personality and talent, and they took to each other immediately like long-lost twins.

Joiner issued a glowing report on the oil potential of his land, citing "the nationally known geologist" Dr. A. D. Lloyd as his authority. With this tract in hand, Joiner went into the hinterlands to sell partnerships in his land to raise enough money to dig a well. His first well went down 3,150 feet before he ran out of money and was forced to abandon it; shortly afterward, the Empire Gas & Fuel Company drilled 200 feet deeper on a near-lying lease and discovered the huge Seminole oil field. Joiner's second well in Cement, Oklahoma, also came in dry only months before the Fortuna Oil Company tapped into another vast field in the same area.

In an effort to snatch some measure of success from the jaws of these two maddening failures, Joiner started to advertise himself as "the man who discovered the Seminole and Cement fields." He and Lloyd went to Texas where Joiner leased his 320-acre spread in Rusk County. They set up a base of operations in a tiny one-room office in the Praetorian Building in downtown Dallas and, once again, tried to raise some cash to sink a well on the land.

After another series of failures, Joiner was stricken with an attack of rheumatic fever, which ravaged his body and left him bent at the waist most of the time. With supreme effort, Joiner could straighten up long enough to have his picture taken before resuming his question-mark posture. In his youth he had been smallish, with a lean, wiry build, good looks, and a full shock of thick dark hair. The years had swelled his waist a bit and added a dusting of gray to his hair, but he was still a remarkably youthful and energetic man despite his crippling ailment. His friend and partner, the good doctor A. D. Lloyd, had a gargantuan physique, which fully matched his larger-than-life personality. Lloyd stood a full six feet and tipped the scales at over three hundred pounds. Although he said he was several years older than Joiner, he had a prodigious appetite for food, women, and a roaring good time. He moved his three-hundred-pound body with all the force of a rutting bull.

Ensconced in their tiny broom closet of an office in downtown Dallas, the two men found themselves with leases on 320 acres of land and less than $20 cash between them. With their backs flat up against the wall, they put their heads together and devised an ingenious scheme for producing some sorely needed cash: they scanned the obituary columns for news about the deaths of well-off men in the county, and then went calling on the widows, hat in hand, after a decent period of mourning had elapsed. The land he had leased near Henderson, Joiner told the widows, was floating on a vast sea of oil. His partner, the noted geologist Dr. A. D. Lloyd, would bear him out on that fact. For a reasonable investment, he would be willing to cut them in on oil royalties when their first well came in. By the fall of 1926, Joiner had solicited enough money to increase his block of oil leases to 5,000 acres. He was ready to make his move.

Meanwhile, in the town of Kilgore, a few miles north of Henderson, a merchant named J. Malcolm Crim visited a fortuneteller who told him, "You have a farm . . . bounded on the north and west by a creek. There is a railroad line running through it, and there is a big house on a hill. There is oil on your farm and someday you'll discover it. There is oil on other farms bordering yours. You should get that land if you can...."

Crim's mother, Lou Della Crim, had inherited just such a farm from her father, and he needed no further convincing when he left the fortuneteller's tent. By the summer of 1921 he had bought leases on over twenty thousand acres of land surrounding the farm. A few miles northeast, a real estate agent in the town of Longview was equally possessed by the notion that a vast reservoir of oil lay beneath the soil on the northwest edge of town. Hadn't his daddy all his life told the farmers of Longview that the oil was there? "It'll be brought up one of these days," he told them again and again. "It'll make you rich. If we don't get it, maybe my boy will," he added, patting his son, young Barney Skipper, on the head. "Won't you, boy?"

"Yes, sir," Barney answered.

He was not a boy to let down his daddy. And he never doubted his daddy's word

Columbus Marion Joiner put the noted geologist Dr. A.D. Lloyd to work tromping across the farmland between Henderson and Overton and sniffing for the exact spot to sink his first well. All decked out in his official geologist's outfit consisting of knee-high leather boots laced up to the top, khaki trousers tucked into the boots, a safari shirt that barely contained what had to be the most stupendous stomach ever seen in Rusk County, and a wide-brimmed Mexican sombrero worn at a jaunty angle on his head, Lloyd was an imposing sight as he strutted over the farmers' land.

With his insatiable appetite for food, whiskey, and available women, his legend spread instantaneously countywide. He was fond of inviting the farm children to trace the ridges in his skull with their fingers while he told them, "A Mexican bandit gave me that when I was fighting against Pancho Villa. Split my head like a watermelon with a four-foot sword."

Word spread that he was being pursued by six wives and was the father of at least two dozen children scattered throughout the western half of the country. Lloyd was the last one in the world to deny these rumors, since he was the best promoter of his own legend. Upon sitting down to a meal one day, a farmer's wife remarked after watching him shovel fried chicken into his mouth for the better part of an hour, "My God! He's going to eat the legs off the table!"

Gradually, Lloyd zeroed in on the farm of an attractive widow named Daisy Bradford, who owned a 975-acre spread smack in the middle of Joiner's 5,000 acres at the midway point between Henderson and Overton. It is not known whether the widow's charms and her reputation for setting a generous table were at least partially responsible for Lloyd's decision, or whether it was made strictly as a result of findings based on his geological research. But, whatever the reason, the widow Bradford was flattered to have her land selected as the site of Joiner's first well.

# 23.

ENCOURAGED BY THE DISCOVERY of oil in the Woodbine sand at Carey Lake, fifty miles southwest of Daisy Bradford's farm, on March 19, 1927, Joiner worked quickly to put his plan into operation. He mailed out hundreds of copies of a study titled "Geological, Topographical and Petroliferous Survey, Portion of Rusk County, Texas, Made for C. M. Joiner by A. D. Lloyd, Geologist and Petroleum Engineer" to prospective investors.

The report was unimpeachable as a formal geological document. Its language and format were precise, and it contained detailed descriptions of the anticlines, faults, and saline domes Lloyd had supposedly found, along with the statement that several major oil companies had paid unusually high prices for leases in the area. The only thing wrong with Lloyd's survey was that it was a work of fiction. Joiner's land contained no such geological formations as Lloyd described in precise language and detail, and no one had paid inordinate prices for leases in the area as was claimed. The report, however, was sent not to professionals, who would know better, but to a sucker list Joiner had put together, made up of widows, doctors, railway employees, postal clerks, and others who dreamed unrealistically of striking it rich overnight.

Joiner assembled a collection of rusted and abandoned old equipment and hired a driller named Tom M. Jones, who had previously worked in West Texas. When Jones got his first look at Joiner's equipment, he remarked to the old hustler, "This pipe isn't anything but a streak of rust."

Undaunted, Joiner patted him on the shoulder and replied, "You'll get it down, son. We're going to get us the well of the world."

Jones, as it turned out, was the only individual in the Joiner operation who had more than a rudimentary knowledge of the oil business, but not even he could keep Joiner's poor-boy equipment functioning for more than brief spurts of time. After several breakdowns and countless delays, Joiner was forced to abandon his well at a depth of just over a thousand feet.

Daisy Bradford, however, believed in the venture as much as Joiner did, having been won over apparently by the persuasive force of Dr. Lloyd's logic. She advanced the partners enough money to get them on their feet again, and Joiner quickly sold off a 500-acre patch of his lease to new investors in order to raise enough cash to sink another well. In April 1928 he started drilling a second well on Daisy's farm, this one a hundred feet away from the first, with a new driller named Uncle Bill Osborne in charge of the operation. Osborne drilled to more than twenty-five hundred feet but abandoned the well when the drill pipe broke off in the ground.

Again Joiner had to appeal to the postal clerks and widows and other citizens on his sucker list to form yet another syndicate for a new attempt to hit paydirt. On October 14, 1929, the Pure Oil Company brought in a successful well in Van Zandt County, sixty miles west of Daisy Bradford's farm. Joiner was more convinced than ever that the Woodbine sand ran beneath his own acreage, and it was just a question of time before he drilled down deep enough with decent equipment and tapped into the lode. He hired himself a new driller, a big, powerful, handsome man about forty named Ed Laster, to start a new well, the Daisy Bradford No. 3, a few hundred feet away from the second well.

After a series of delays because of broken equipment and lack of cash, Laster managed to drill to a depth of 2,600 feet. Just when all hope was nearly lost, the equipment was a disaster, and the money gone, Joiner showed up at the drilling site with a group of men whom he introduced to Laster as "some investors from Dallas."

"Show these gentlemen a core sample," he said authoritatively to Laster, winking at the same time.

Laster got the message and brought up a sample of earth from deep inside the well. Joiner made a great show of sniffing the lump of soil and examining it thoroughly. Examination completed, he intoned deeply to his driller, "It seems to me that you're nearing the Austin Chalk, Ed. The Woodbine can't be much farther down according to our geologist."

"That's right, sir," Laster said, going along with the charade. "I expect to hit the chalk any day now."

"Fine. Keep right on with the good work."

Laster shook his head and went on drilling as his hunched-over boss walked off with his prospects. He laughed loudly to himself, but it was Joiner who had the last laugh. By the following afternoon he had raised enough cash money to pay all the back wages he owed his men, including Ed Laster, and to round up some halfway decent drilling equipment.


While Joiner continued work on the Daisy Bradford No. 3, Ed Laster decided to do a little moonlighting of his own to help pay living expenses for himself and his family. He was contacted by scouts for some of the major oil companies that had taken an interest in the area. They had reasons of their own to believe that the Woodbine sand did indeed run through the earth in the area around Joiner's leases. It seemed that Lloyd's geological survey, contrived as it was, may have been right for all the wrong reasons.

Would Laster, the scouts wanted to know, keep them informed of any favorable developments on the Daisy Bradford No. 3? The majors wanted to hear about any good news as quickly as Joiner did. Laster would be nicely compensated for his services if he agreed. A bargain was made, and when Laster tapped into the Woodbine sand at 3,500 feet, precisely the depth that Lloyd had predicted he would find it, Laster gave samples of the soil to the majors as well as to Columbus Marion Joiner. In the first week of August 1930 the Mid-Kansas Oil & Gas Company quietly leased a spread of land for one dollar an acre alongside Joiner's land.


On September 5, 1930, a crowd of farmers, oil scouts, geologists, and assorted prospectors gathered in the field around the Daisy Bradford No. 3. Rumors had circulated quickly around the county that the Woodbine sand had been tapped in Joiner's third well, and they all wanted to be present for the testing. Laster lowered the rig deep inside the hole and within minutes the unmistakable smell of gas came bubbling up out of the wellhead. As Laster raised the rig with a load of earth from down below, the entire field suddenly began to vibrate. Seconds later a geyser of thick black liquid exploded from the earth, rocketing high into the air and drenching everyone present with a dark heavy shower. The gusher lasted only a minute before it subsided and quit, but the smell of oil was heavy in the air.

"What do you think, Laster?" someone asked.

"It ought to make a pretty good well," Laster replied, smiling over at his boss who was hunched up against a tree with a beatific smile across his face. The mob closed in around Joiner, shaking his hand, clapping him on the back, and offering congratulations. When the crowd thinned a bit, three men walked over to Joiner with their hands extended.

"Congratulations," said the leader of the trio, a tall, heavily built man smoking a long black cigar. "I'm Haroldson Lafayette Hunt from El Dorado. These are my associates, Mr. Lake and Mr. Miller."

Joiner studied the big man for a moment, then accepted his hand. "Thank you, boy, but it's not an oil well yet," he said to Arizona Slim.

# 24.

WHILE IN TEXAS LOOKING for a new deal, Arizona Slim got word from Frania that she was pregnant for the third time. He sent for her immediately and rented a house in Dallas for her and her two children. A few months later, on October 28, 1930, she gave birth to her third October baby, a pretty girl whom they named Helen. Slim himself was living in Tyler with his haberdasher friend and gambling consort, Pete Lake, and with an associate named M.M. Miller from his El Dorado oil business. Tyler was just a few miles northwest of Henderson, an easy commute to the Joiner oil well that had stirred up all the commotion. With Frania a hundred miles away in downtown Dallas, she was just close enough for him to visit when he felt like it, yet far enough for him to go about his business in peace and privacy.

Within weeks of the successful testing of Daisy Bradford No. 3, Rusk County was invaded by an army of strangers who came flocking to the area in their broken-down trucks and automobiles. It was a replay of the El Dorado oil-boom days, Texas-style. A makeshift village, immediately christened Joinerville, was erected along the road connecting Henderson and Tyler, and just outside Daisy Bradford's farm. Men rented cots for $2 or $3 a night in clapboard shacks on the side of the road. Food stalls and tumbledown sheds offering a variety of merchandise were thrown up overnight. The Just Right Hotel in Henderson stacked four or five men in each room at exorbitant prices. Thousands of eager prospectors and hustlers of assorted stripes descended on the area within weeks to be part of this latest excitement, and maybe find a way to make their fortunes while they were at it.

Now that the first hint of oil was discovered in Rusk County, the major oil companies and some local businessmen decided to take a closer look at maps of the area showing the lay of the land and various ownership rights. Land values could only skyrocket from this point on, and it was important to ascertain exactly who owned what. The nearest mapmaker was W. W. Zingery in Fort Worth, who suddenly found himself with more work than he could handle. Zingery had himself managed to acquire some rights on Joiner's leases when Joiner was out beating the bushes raising money to sink his wells. Taking a good look now at exactly what his investment entitled him to, he found that he owned four certificates with a face value of $100 apiece, each of which gave him a one-three-hundredth interest in the Daisy Bradford No. 3 well, as well as four acres of the 320 allocated by Joiner for this particular syndicate. Doing a little quick adding and dividing in his head, Zingery concluded that there should be a total of eighty certificates outstanding for the entire syndicate. After doing some detective work at the courthouse in Henderson, however, he discovered that there were actually hundreds of similar certificates on file. The crafty old devil had oversold his lease to raise as much cash as possible. He had sold the same rights to dozens of unsuspecting citizens.

Smelling a swindle, Zingery approached some of the others who had been taken, and they hired a lawyer, Tom Pollard of Tyler, to file a receivership against Joiner at the courthouse in Henderson. When he heard of the action, old man Joiner and his geologist, A. D. Lloyd, immediately contacted the local newspapers, including the *Courier-Times* of Tyler, to announce that they were being steamrolled by the major oil companies that wanted to gobble up all the land in the area now that oil had been found. The picture of the hunched-over seventy-year-old wildcatter and the lovable three-hundred-pound geologist at his side on the front pages tapped a vein of sympathy in the local farmers, who were paranoid about outsiders, particularly big business and big government, moving in on them in the first place. Joiner was lavishly praised as the "Daddy of the Rusk County Oil Field," a designation which bestowed the nickname Dad on him forevermore. Good old Dad Joiner was likened to Moses, by the editor of the *Courier-Times*, who was "led to the Promised Land, permitted to gaze upon its 'milk and honey,' and then denied the privilege of entering by a crowd of slick lawyers who sat back in palatial offices cooling their heels and waiting while old 'Dad' worked in the slime, muck, and mire of slush pits and sweated blood over his antiquated rig, down in the pines near Henderson...."

Dad and Doc. The heroes of the day—for a fleeting moment at least. The old wildcatter and his gargantuan geologist, consummate salesmen and survivors that they were, had managed to turn a near disaster into a public relations victory in round one. But Dad knew he would have to do some fancy footwork from here on. After all, it would be only a matter of time before his other suckers learned to add up numbers the same way Zingery did.

One of those now taking a closer interest in Joiner's leases was Arizona Slim. Slim had, of course, been following with keen interest the legal action pending against the old man. He began visiting the old man at his well site, making oil talk with him and sniffing around for an opening to make his move. The two men developed a fondness for each other despite Dad's insistence on addressing the younger man as boy. Slim had already developed a reputation as a connoisseur of the waitresses in the ramshackle cafes in Joinerville. The old man admired his easy way with women; he also recognized in Arizona Slim a supersalesman and operator on the same exalted level as himself. The tall man cut an imposing figure with his powerful body, his rugged good looks, an expensive cigar planted in the corner of his mouth, and a straw boater angled across his head.

Arizona Slim was equally impressed by this man who was the focal point of all the celebration in the county. Despite his seventy years and his bent body, Dad Joiner was remarkably energetic and bristling with life. His eyes were bright and alert, and his mind was honed to razor sharpness. Slim spent a good deal of time sparring verbally with the old wildcatter, but Joiner was a good match for him and gave away little. The one thing he couldn't hide too well from Slim, or anyone else for that matter, was the fact that he was strapped financially. It was also apparent that he was more worried about the lawsuit than he admitted publicly.

On October 3, a few weeks before Frania gave birth to Helen, crowds flooded into the field around the Daisy Bradford No. 3. The big farm was packed with old trucks, automobiles, and horse-drawn wagons. Several merchants set up refreshment stands, selling sandwiches, soda pop, white lightning, and pop-skull whiskey from the backs of their pickup trucks. It was a wild party, a celebration, with some ten thousand citizens from a dozen walks of life gathering on Daisy Bradford's farm for the official completion of the well. Since Dad Joiner had sold rights to the well to nearly everyone he had come into contact with, most of those present took a certain proprietary interest in what was going on.

For two full days and nights Laster drilled while the multitudes looked on, but there was no show of oil. Assisting him in the operation was a new man Joiner had hired, D. H.

Byrd, who had been nicknamed Dry Hole Byrd because of his initials, and also because of the fact that he had drilled fifty-six dry holes in a row before hitting two winners on the same day. Hour after hour the men worked their machinery as the mob looked on, eating, drinking, fighting, sleeping in their trucks or out in the grassy fields.

"Nothing yet." The word was passed among them. "Nothing yet." Late in the evening, on Sunday, October 5, their patience was rewarded. The earth trembled violently and a roaring gurgle rose up from somewhere down deep in the hole. And then the mob went berserk as a great black tower of oil exploded out of the wellhead high above the rig, fanning out above the farm, showering everyone with a heavy black rain. While the crowd danced and screamed and rolled on the ground, Dry Hole Byrd got out his gauge and measured the flow.

"She's flowing at the rate of 6,800 barrels a day," he said to Joiner.

"Sixty-eight hundred barrels! Unbelievable!" old Dad Joiner yelled. The old man had come through after all. As he said all along, he was going to get the well of the world.

A week later, disappointment set in with a vengeance. The great initial flow had subsided to a comparatively puny 250 barrels a day, and the oil was coming up in spurts, with eighteen- and twenty-hour intervals between them. The well of the world, it was beginning to appear, was not so grand after all.

Arizona Slim, however, had been doing some independent testing of his own. He had acquired three leases to the east of Dad Joiner's well, and one to the south, but he was becoming more and more convinced that the great underground ocean of oil lay further to the west of the Daisy Bradford No. 3, on land Joiner had leased.

"Let's see if we can buy him out," Slim suggested to Pete Lake.

"Buy him out yourself, why don't you?" Pete replied.

"If I can, will you take an interest in it?" Slim was worth a tidy sum in assets, but he was a bit shy of cash, as usual, to work the entire deal himself.

"Hell, yes!" Lake laughed. He had not come all the way to East Texas with his gambling friend to be left out in the cold.

"How much do you want?" asked Slim.

"I'll take a fourth. Count me in."

A few days later Arizona Slim started moving some of his key men, Jick Justiss, Charles Hardin, and Robert Johnson, over to Henderson from El Dorado.

At the same time, some of the larger oil companies, having sniffed the smell of oil and money in the air, were also taking greater interest in the region. J. Malcolm Crim, the gentleman who had acquired oil leases on over twenty thousand acres of land surrounding the Lou Della Crim farm after visiting the fortuneteller, was visited by two scouts from the Bateman Oil Company at his store in Kilgore. Crim had been frothing at the mouth to sink a well in his land, and this was his golden opportunity. He made a deal for Bateman Oil to drill on his leases for a percentage of the oil royalties. The site Bateman selected for the first well was precisely thirteen miles due north of the Daisy Bradford No. 3. On October 28, twenty-three days after Dad's well was completed and the day Frania delivered Helen in Dallas, the first well was spudded on the Lou Della Crim farm.

A few miles northeast in Longview, Barney Skipper, the

man who had promised his daddy that he would bring up the oil in the area if the farmers didn't, decided it was time to keep his promise. He contacted an independent oilman in Fort Worth named Johnny Farrell, and Farrell put together a syndicate consisting of Barney Skipper, himself, other independent oilmen, investors Walter Lechner, W. A. Moncrief, and Eddie Showers, and two equipment supply companies, the Seminole Tool & Supply Company and the Arkansas Fuel Oil Company.

"We'll be flying equipment in, a few days from now," Farrell informed Barney over the telephone.

"Fly? Hell, there ain't no airport around here," Skipper replied.

"We're flying in anyway," Farrell said and hung up.

True to his word, Farrell's plane circled overhead the day he said he would be there, and Skipper waved him in himself for a perfect landing on the Bevins farm just outside Longview. It was the first time Farrell had ever set eyes on the lay of the land. Skipper was fond of remarking afterward, "That man was going to land his plane if he had to set it down on top of a cow."

# 25.

ON THE DAY THE TRIAL was supposed to start, Judge R.T. Brown rapped his gavel for silence. "Where's the defendant?" he inquired of the defense attorney, Colonel Bob Jones.

"He's ill, your honor," Jones replied.

Judge Brown agreed to let the attorneys for the plaintiffs, W.W. Zingery and other certificate holders, state their basic complaints. When they finished, the judge rapped his gavel again and said, "I believe that when it takes a man three and a half years to find a baby, he ought to be able to rock it for a while. This hearing is postponed indefinitely."

The plaintiffs moved to file a new receivership in Dallas, where they thought they could get a more objective hearing. Dad himself was holed up in the Adolphus Hotel there, trying to keep as low a profile as he could. Hundreds of irate widows, postal clerks, and assorted investors were after his head, to say nothing of the process servers who were trying to hand him a piece of paper. With Dad on the lam, Arizona Slim sniffed the air and decided the timing was just right for him to move in for the kill. The old man was beginning to panic now and Slim had to get him when he was most vulnerable. He would either have to close a deal with him now or lose it forever.

While Slim and Pete Lake rented a room at the Baker Hotel in Dallas, Justiss, Hardin, and Johnson, whom Slim had moved over from El Dorado, were watching a well west of the

Daisy Bradford No. 3. The Deep Rock Oil Company had acquired a small lease a mile west of Daisy Bradford's farm on land completely surrounded by Dad Joiner's leases. Arizona Slim believed that the great sea of oil lay to the west of Daisy Bradford's farm, and that the testing of the Deep Rock well would be critical. So, while his men were observing progress on this well, Arizona Slim and Pete Lake invited Joiner to their room at the Baker Hotel.

"You're buried under all these lawsuits," Slim said to Dad Joiner. "I'm willing to buy you out lock, stock, and barrel, legal problems and all."

"You'd be buying a pig in a poke, boy."

"That's my risk. You walk away clean with cash in your pocket."

Joiner looked at Arizona Slim, then at Pete Lake. He thought the offer over and replied, "Sorry, boy. No deal."

November 26 was a raw, rainy day. The men out on the Deep Rock well west of Daisy Bradford's farm—the drillers, roughnecks, and observers—were huddled up against the damp cold as the drilling continued. Late in the afternoon, just as the light was fading from the cloudy sky, the drilling stopped and a core sample was lifted from deep down in the well. Slim's associate, Robert Johnson, moved closer and broke off a six-inch piece from the sixteen-foot-long core. He held the sample under his nose, then put a few grains of the soil on his tongue. Within minutes he was on the telephone to Charles Hardin, and at 4:30 in the afternoon Hardin called Arizona Slim at the Baker Hotel in Dallas.

"They've hit it," said Hardin. "The core barrel cut sixteen feet of material, and ten-and-a-half feet of it is Woodbine sand saturated with oil."

Arizona Slim displayed no emotion on the phone; across the

room Doc Joiner was deeply involved in conversation with Pete Lake. That morning a Dallas banker named E.R. Tennant had been appointed receiver for the various leases Joiner had sold out of his block, and the old man could feel his entire world, everything he had worked for all his life, closing in on him. Slim hung up and walked toward the two men. He was determined to close the deal. It was a now-or-never situation.

"Look, Dad," he said. "This is the way I see it. They've got you in a bind. You stand to lose everything you worked for. I'm offering you a way to walk off free and clear. I'm prepared to make you a good generous offer for your leases and take over all the legal mess. This way we both make out. You make a good profit on your leases and I get a chance to see what's in the ground. Otherwise, we all lose out in the end."

Joiner looked up at Arizona Slim for a long moment, then said as resolutely as he could, "I didn't come here to waste my time, boy. You come up with a fair bargain or we got no deal."

For the next four hours the men haggled in earnest. Joiner remained a tough adversary even though he was on the ropes. His attitude was that of a man who would rather lose everything than permit himself to come away with a bad deal just to salvage some small measure of success. At 8:30 that night, with their attorneys present, the two men affixed their signatures to an agreement whereby Arizona Slim would pay Dad Joiner $24,000 in cash, most of which came from Pete Lake, as a downpayment for the oil leases on Joiner's 5,000 acres, an additional $3,000 in cash as a downpayment on the 80-acre site that contained the Daisy Bradford No. 3, and a final $3,000 in cash as a downpayment on a separate 500-acre lease on the Bradford farm. In addition to the $30,000 in cash downpayments, Arizona Slim signed four different notes totaling $45,000, which were to be paid off over the next nine months. Slim also agreed to cut Joiner in for oil royalties up to

$1,260,000 from any oil production on the land. In return, Arizona Slim agreed to drill and develop the leases himself, and defend them against the barrage of lawsuits mounting in the nearby wings. In effect, by the time Joiner left his room at about nine that night, Arizona Slim had managed to wrap up a $1.3 million deal for Dad Joiner's leases for $30,000 in cash and a promise to pay off the rest. Since the thirty grand was put up by Pete Lake and two other partners, his net cost out of pocket was zero dollars.

"I do believe," Slim remarked to Lake when Joiner had left, "this is going to turn out to be the greatest business coup of my life."

Robert Johnson's nose and tongue served Arizona Slim well that rainy day at the Deep Rock well. Scarcely two days after Slim wrapped up his agreement with Dad Joiner in the Baker Hotel, news of the oil-soaked core which was taken from the Deep Rock well was circulated word-of-mouth throughout the county. On the strength of this news alone, Dad Joiner was approached by a major oil company that offered to buy his leases for $3.5 million. Alas, it was too late for the old man. The old con artist had been outconned by a craftier young hustler. Joiner immediately spread the word that he had been cheated out of his leases by a man who already knew what the land contained, and the *Dallas Morning News* ran a story to that effect.

"I hear that Hunt fellow really put one over on the old man," Ed Laster remarked to Dry Hole Byrd when the story was made public.

"I don't think anybody cheated the old man. I think Dad cheated himself," Byrd replied.

"I hear they locked him up in a hotel room with a bottle of pop skull and a bunch of floozies until he signed the agreement," Laster continued. "I hear they worked him over with floozies and whiskey until his brain got soft."

"Don't you believe none of it. Old Dad's too cagey for that. He likes his good times as well as the next man, but he don't let that get in the way of a business deal."

"Well, one way or another, I still think he had it coming to him. Just a case of one con man conning another, that's all there is to it."

The story about how Arizona Slim had conned old Dad Joiner out of his oil leases stirred the collective imagination almost as much as the news of the oil find itself. Testing continued at the Deep Rock well, and on December 13 oil came roaring out at a rate of three thousand barrels a day of heavy crude. This was the kind of well wildcatters dream about all their lives. It was rich and steady, with no sign of any letup. Just one week later Slim hooked the Daisy Bradford No. 3 to his own pipeline, which he had been building in anticipation of a major strike in the area, and started pumping oil to the loading rack at the railroad, where it was transported to the Sinclair refinery in Houston. Arizona Slim's Panola Pipeline Company was the first one ready to serve the area, and he signed an agreement with the Deep Rock Oil Company to transport oil from its big well. Within a week Inland Waterways Pipeline Company completed its own pipeline system. A new boom was in the making and speculators everywhere, independents and major companies alike, were scrambling fast to get in on the action.

# 26.

O N DECEMBER 14, 1930, THE Bateman Oil Company
drilled into the Woodbine sand at a depth of 3,629
feet on the Lou Della Crim farm, thirteen miles north of
Daisy Bradford No. 3. The well was completed on Sunday
morning, December 28, and by noon the oil was flowing at a
rate of twenty-two thousand barrels a day. J. Malcolm Crim's
fortuneteller had called it right. By Wednesday, three days
later, the population of Kilgore had swelled from seven
hundred sleepy souls to some ten thousand rampaging citizens crazed with oil fever.

At the same time, thirteen miles north of the Lou Della
Crim farm and twenty-six miles north of Daisy Bradford No.
3, Barney Skipper and his syndicate were drilling a hole on a
farm owned by F. K. Lathrop, just outside Longview. At one
o'clock in the afternoon on Monday, January 26, 1931, with
twenty thousand onlookers camped out on the Lathrop farm
and a sea of automobiles and wagons covering the landscape
for as far as the eye could see, the drill bit cut into the
Woodbine sand. The flow was measured at a rate of twenty
thousand barrels a day before the well was choked. Skipper's
well, the Lathrop No. 1, was evidently as big as the Lou Della
Crim well. Barney had not let down his daddy after all. He
had gone down into the ground and brought up the oil just as
he said he would.

Just two weeks later, John Farrell, W. A. Moncrief, and

Eddie Showers sold their interest in the well to the Yount-Lee Oil Company for the tidy sum of $3,270,000. What everyone assumed at this point was that Daisy Bradford No. 3, Deep Rock No. 1, Lou Della Crim No. 1, and Lathrop No. 1 had been drilled on four separate oil fields. No one dreamed, not even in his wildest imagination, that all these wells might be part of a single gargantuan underground sea of oil. Such a fanciful notion was too farfetched. An oil field that size would be, by far, the largest one ever discovered on the North American continent, and one of the largest ones found on the planet.

In early February 1931 Lyda was living in the three-story house in El Dorado; Frania was in a rented house in Dallas, to which she had moved a few months earlier; and Arizona Slim was approaching his forty-second birthday. Slim was fond of holding court at the Just Right Hotel in Henderson, where he ran an occasional poker game and also bet on baseball games in his spare time. He had won almost $3,000 on Connie Mack's Philadelphia Athletics in the 1930 World Series, and he enjoyed the sport even though it was not nearly so scientific a pastime as poker playing. His immediate concern, following his business coup with Dad Joiner, was coming up with additional cash to hit a big well of his own, bigger than the Daisy Bradford No. 3 and certainly bigger than a small well he had brought in just south of it. It was at this point that he met Leota Tucker, wife of a farmer named Walter Tucker, whose land near Kilgore was leased for a fortune after the completion of the Lou Della Crim No. 1.

"I can lend you some money to drill a well," Leota Tucker said when she ran into him in town one day, "for a percentage of the profits plus eight percent interest."

Arizona Slim tipped his hat and smiled at her. "That's just what I'm accustomed to paying, ma'am," he said.

"It's a deal then?"

"It's a fine deal, ma'am."

A short time later he offered to pay her back when he raised some money on his own, but Mrs. Tucker refused.

"I intend to keep you on the hook," she said. "Just keep paying my interest and drilling for oil. You're going to be very rich one day, and when you are, so will I."

Arizona Slim set up an office in Wright City, a tiny hamlet located not too far from Daisy Bradford's farm. From there he ran his pipeline operation, which turned out to be a stroke of genius now that successful wells were being developed all around him, and there he laid out his plan for developing the leases he had bought from Dad Joiner.

As new wells were drilled successfully on the farms to the west of Daisy Bradford No. 3, and also on the rolling fields and pasture lands stretching north above Lathrop No. 1 into the next county, the farmers and oilmen in the area began to realize that they were, indeed, sitting on one enormous sea of oil. The size of the field boggled the imagination. Everywhere they drilled, southwest of Daisy Bradford's farm in Cherokee County, as far to the west as Smith County, and far to the north as the Lathrop well in Upshur County, successful wells were being completed. The extent of the discovery was unprecedented. People who had bought leases cheaply on land they thought was on the outskirts of the major field discovered they were smack in the middle of the action. The distance between Daisy Bradford No. 3 and Lathrop No. 1 was twenty-six miles alone, and new wells were being brought in five miles north and south of them. This meant that the giant field had to run a good thirty-five miles, at least, north and south, and since Daisy Bradford No. 3 was apparently sitting on the eastern rim of the field, God only knew exactly how wide it was.

One unexpected development of all the fanfare was the instant fame that was bestowed upon the participants. Doc Lloyd held one press conference after another to announce that he was the one who made the original discovery. "I told Dad to drill two miles farther west," he said. "If he drilled where I told him to, he'd have gone down right in the middle of the fairway where the oil was thick and rich." Geologists picked over his report to reveal all the inaccuracies and outright fabrications it contained, but no one could deny that the oil was found exactly where he said it would be.

The immense, self-proclaimed petroleum engineer would eventually have made his fortune in East Texas, with all the other wildcatters, had an unexpected development not arisen from his overnight celebrity. Newspapers around the country published photographs of the three-hundred-pound geologist standing in front of the Daisy Bradford No. 3, surrounded by Dad Joiner, Arizona Slim, Ed Laster, and members of the crew, and he was recognized by not a few ladies as the man who had married them and then left them in the lurch. Not long thereafter a dozen or so women, some accompanied by offspring, detrained at Overton and inquired after the whereabouts of Dr. Lloyd. They, of course, knew him by different names, but there was no mistaking the likeness they had seen in the paper. No other man filled a pair of pants quite the way he did.

Before the ladies could call him to account, Doc Lloyd departed for safer parts. Exactly where, is not known. He was found in a Chicago hotel room ten years later, dead, just shy of his eighty-seventh birthday.

Arizona Slim formed the Hunt Production Company as the principal organization to develop his leases. He consolidated his organization, moving his lawyer J.B. McEntire, Pete Lake, Jick Justiss, Charley Hardin, and others from his El Dorado operation to key positions. He also contacted his brother Sherman, who had been a wanderer like Slim. Sherman was the brother who he felt was in many ways most like himself and whom he always wanted to know better. Slim offered him a place in the company. To his surprise and delight, Sherman accepted and moved his family to Tyler. Sherman knew as much about the oil business as Arizona Slim knew about writing Broadway musicals, but Slim was happy to have him around and put him on the payroll at $1,000 a month.

"Mr. Sherman," Pete Lake remarked to his colleagues when Arizona Slim wasn't around, "doesn't have to do anything for his money but draw breath."

"He's valuable to the boss in other ways," said Roy Lee, who managed office operations. "He spends most of his time placing horse bets for the boss. The way I hear it, he gambles almost as good as his kid brother."

Meanwhile, Arizona Slim began his drilling program in earnest, determined as he was to get the oil out of the ground and into his own pipelines faster than the others. He sank one well after another into the giant field and virtually every one came up a winner. The field was so vast that no time at all was wasted on exploration. All one needed was a rig capable of punching a 3,500-foot hole in the ground and he was sure to hit the rich oil-soaked layer of Woodbine sand. It was easier than shooting ducks in a pond if one owned a lease and had $25,000 to drill a well.

During the rest of 1931 and the following year, Arizona Slim managed to sink about nine hundred wells into the ground. The money flowed in by the millions. While the rest of the country was in the throes of perhaps the nastiest depression in the nation's history, the East Texas oilmen were raking in legal tender faster than they could spend it in ten lifetimes.

In 1932 Slim moved his headquarters to the Peoples National Bank Building in Tyler, the closest thing to a skyscraper the town had to offer. He also bought a huge nineteenth-century house on East Charnwood Street in Tyler for Lyda and the family. Lyda moved into the sprawling Mayfield House, which was named after the family who built it, and on August 2, 1932, gave birth to Lamar, the last of the six children she brought successfully into the world.

# 27.

THE STATUTE OF LIMITATIONS was to run out on November 25, 1932, exactly two years after Arizona Slim closed his deal with Dad Joiner. On November 24 Joiner visited Arizona Slim, who was laid up with a back injury, and the two men chatted for the better part of the afternoon. The subject of litigation lay heavily on Slim's mind, but throughout the course of their conversation the old man failed to raise the issue. Finally, as Dad got up to take his leave, Slim hoisted himself from his bed and walked the older man to the door. He decided to broach the subject himself.

"I believe there are those who are trying to get you to sue me," Slim said. "I hope you don't fall for that."

Dad looked up at the bigger man and said, "Boy, I'd never do a thing like that to you. I love you too much."

Then, with the tears welling in his eyes, Joiner turned away and left the room. Arizona Slim closed the door behind him and walked over to the phone. He called his lawyer, J.B. McEntire, and told him to come over at once.

"Joiner's going to sue me," he said, "and I want to secure my indebtedness. I should've done it a long time ago."

They spent most of the night writing up mortgages on his assets, with the loan secured by Continental Supply Company. With the papers properly signed and witnessed, McEntire filed them first thing in the morning, just as the doors were opening at the courthouse in Henderson. One hour later, Dad Joiner's lawyer filed a suit on behalf of his client, claiming that one Haroldson Lafayette Hunt had defrauded him out of his oil leases. Joiner could have put a lien on Slim's entire operation until the issue was resolved had Slim not filed his own papers ahead of time.

The old man's tears had tipped his hand.

The drilling continued at a frantic pace. Each individual operator was hell-bent on pumping the oil out of the ground as fast as he could since the Rule of Capture, based on an 1889 court decision, was still in effect. Rule of Capture held that the oil belonged to the one who got it out of the ground first, regardless of whose land it was under. Because of this, a dog-eat-dog atmosphere prevailed at the East Texas oil field, with each man working his rig as fast as he could to get the lion's share of the profits.

In 1932 there were almost four thousand working wells on the field, nine hundred of which belonged to Arizona Slim. Well over a hundred million barrels of oil had already been brought to the surface, and an estimated two billion barrels, a staggering figure by anyone's standards, still lay in the earth. It was clear to everyone involved that this kind of overproduction would only depress prices, especially since the country was already mired deep in a stubborn depression, and work to the disadvantage of the industry in general. Much as the oilmen, rugged individualists and entrepreneurs that they were, detested any form of government intervention in their affairs, many of them began to realize that some semblance of order was necessary.

Already, the waste was enormous. Great lakes of oil deteriorated in open pits because the oil couldn't be funneled into the pipelines fast enough. The refineries were operating full blast but still could not handle the overflow. Much of the oil caught fire during thunder and lightning storms, or else it evaporated and was lost forever. It ran off into streams and rivers, and polluted the countryside. Still the oilmen pumped; if they didn't, someone else would.

The oil had brought prosperity to the old dusty farm towns. Henderson, Overton, Tyler, Kilgore, Longview, and dozens of more obscure villages all had new schools, restaurants, hotels, shops, paved roads, and other amenities they had only dreamed about before. But this very prosperity and boom town atmosphere now threatened to overwhelm the entire area with overabundance. This irony was not lost on the oilmen themselves or on the authorities in government. More and more the eyes of a nation gripped by a devastating depression focused on the boom towns of East Texas, and on the contradictions they were breeding.

Gradually, the great individualists and free enterprisers in the oil industry began to clamor for government regulation of their own business. They didn't trust their competitors to cooperate with one another in an effort to conserve the oil and stabilize prices, which had begun to fluctuate wildly, primarily downward. W. S. Farish, the president of the Humble Oil & Refining Company, had previously been an outspoken critic of government interference in the marketplace but suddenly changed directions and called for state control of production and pricing. He was joined by E. W. Marland of Marland Oil and J. Edgar Pew of Sun Oil; other major oil companies and independent operators began to fall in line. Their efforts led to the creation of the Central Proration Committee, whose purpose was to limit the amount of oil that could be produced by any well each day. The limit proved unenforceable, however, and led to new efforts by the Texas Railroad Commission, which despite its name was the regulatory body with jurisdiction over the oil industry, to impose new ceilings on oil production a little later.

Even with these proration limits in effect, the price of oil continued to fall; there was simply an overabundance on the market. From $2.29 a barrel in 1926, the price dropped to $1.10 in 1930, and then to $.50 a barrel in 1931, the year Lathrop No.1 was brought in. Times were getting tougher throughout the country, and the markets were drying up. The oilmen were making overnight fortunes even with the lowering prices, but feared that the intense competition would squeeze them all if it continued much longer. By the time Franklin Roosevelt was elected president of the United States in 1932, most of them had hopped aboard the bandwagon yelping for proration to save their own skins. Among those sounding the clarion call for government control of the oil industry was that most rugged and adventurous of individualists, Arizona Slim.

One who refused to go along with the cry for proration and more government control of the industry was Carl Estes, the fiery editor of the *Tyler Courier-Times*, who had written the article defending Dad Joiner when he was being sued by Zingery and others who had invested in the old man's well. Estes sensed a battle of monumental dimensions shaping up between the "big boys" who favored proration to monopolize the industry, and the "little guy," lone wildcatters like Dad Joiner, who would be legally barred from competition against the established operators if proration took effect.

"I love a good fight more than a hog loves slop," Estes remarked to a friend, and then sat down at his typewriter and pounded out a series of denunciations of the "monopolistic companies," which advocated proration "as a means of holding up the price of oil.... Has the time arrived," Estes continued, "when the 'big boys' of the oil industry can tell the people of Texas who may produce oil, when they may produce oil, and what oil prices should be? We say NO."

But, as it turned out, Estes was a voice howling against the wind. Lined up against him were some of the richest and most powerful men in the county, as well as an army of lawyers and politicians only too happy to oblige the oilmen if regulation was what they wanted.

At a special hearing conducted by the Texas Railroad Commission, while Robert Penn, an advocate of proration was making a point, Estes, who was hunched over with pain because of stomach ulcers, struggled to his feet, waved a crutch at Penn, and started to scream, "Come on, you son of a bitch, and I'll knock your brains out!" Despite his spirited opposition, however, the forces for proration won out. By the time the meeting adjourned, new quotas were set for oil production, stricter than the ones which had been set earlier. Only time would tell if the commission could make them stick.

While Arizona Slim, the largest independent operator in the field, was joining forces with the major companies, trying to create a more powerful state agency, the Oil and Gas Conservation Commission, to replace the relatively ineffective Texas Railroad Commission, Dad Joiner was proceeding with plans of his own. His lawsuit against Slim hinged on two issues: first, Slim had bribed the driller of the Deep Rock well with $20,000 to get a piece of the core material before anyone else did; and, second, Slim withheld this information from him while they were negotiating in the hotel room that day. Had he, Dad Joiner, been privy to the favorable development at Deep Rock, he would have been able to sell his leases for a lot more money to someone else. This was the substance of the case as it went before the court.

On the witness stand, Arizona Slim denied that he had paid Frank Foster, the driller for the Deep Rock well, $20,000 for privileged information. The money was a consideration for something else, he said.

"What else?" asked Fred Weeks, Joiner's attorney.

"For a lease I wanted to buy from him. Later on I decided against it."

"Still, you gave him the same amount of notes without buying the lease that you were going to give him for the lease. Is that right?"

"Well, I had already signed the notes," said Slim.

"But, what exactly did you sign those two $10,000 notes for?"

"I told you, for the lease and also to settle some claims he was making against me."

"What kind of claims are you talking about?" Weeks pressed.

"I owed him a commission on a deal that had not been consummated yet."

"And did you feel his claims against you had any merit?"

"No, sir. None whatsoever."

"As a matter of fact, you knew they didn't, didn't you, Mr. Hunt?"

"I was sure he couldn't collect in court."

"You didn't value that claim of his at five cents, did you?"

"I didn't value any of his claims as having any merit," said Arizona Slim.

"You did value the fact that he let your man have that core that night, didn't you?"

"I've always been appreciative of all the information he furnished us from that well, and all the other wells he was drilling."

"Yes, and you paid him those two $10,000 notes as a token of your appreciation, didn't you?"

"No, sir," answered Arizona Slim.

Realizing that his testimony was weak and ambiguous at best, and that he was in serious danger of having to return a good piece of his recently acquired fortune to Dad Joiner, Slim placed a phone call to one of his top employees after he left the witness stand and instructed him to pay a private visit to the old man immediately. He also gave him explicit instructions on exactly what to say to Joiner when he saw him. The following day, just as the court was to reopen proceedings, Dad Joiner startled the assemblage, with the exception of Slim, when he marched into the courtroom and read a statement to the judge. After a brief preamble, the statement read:

"Since the suit was filed, I have made a thorough investigation and have determined to my satisfaction that the allegations of fraud in my petition are not true in fact. After making such investigation, I reached the conclusion, and hold to that conclusion now, that I was not deceived or defrauded in any manner...."

Dad Joiner asked that his claim against Arizona Slim be dropped, and his request was accepted by the judge. A great roar of shock and surprise arose in the courtroom. As the judge tried vainly to gavel the crowd to silence, reporters were racing to the corridor to phone the news to their papers. Outside the courtroom a heavy snow descended on the county, covering the farms and rolling hillside with a thick white blanket. The air was cold and raw, and the heavy flakes kept falling. It was the first heavy snowfall East Texas had seen in over thirty years.

News of the Joiner suit against Haroldson Lafayette Hunt was the talk of East Texas for weeks afterward. At the Just Right Hotel in Henderson they talked of little else.

"How do you think he got to the old man?" one local asked another.

"I hear it had something to do with that Hardin fella," the second replied, "the one who was out at the well that day and got a sample of the core."

"I heard that story. Some say he was supposed to be a witness against Hunt, that Joiner bought him off and turned him against his boss. I don't buy it myself, though."

"No, it don't sound exactly right to me neither. Had to be something more than that, something bigger."

"I think it had something to do with that young girl old Dad wants to marry, girl young enough to be his grand-daughter."

"Sounds more like it if you ask me. I think Hunt got wind of it and threatened to spill the beans on exactly what went on in that hotel room that day."

"You mean with the floozies and whiskey and all?"

"Yep. Sounds like plain old blackmail to me. Threatened to spill the beans to the young girl about the floozies."

"Still, he must've sweetened the pot for old Dad too. Made it worth his while to drop the case."

"That's it, I reckon. Blackmail and a little sweetener. Gave Dad a cash advance on some of those oil royalties and offered to forget about what went on that day if old Dad dropped the case. What do you think?"

"That's the only thing that makes any sense to me. Had to be something along those lines I'd say."

On September 8, 1933, Dad Joiner went to Juarez, Mexico,

with his twenty-five-year-old secretary, Dea England, where he divorced his wife of fifty-two years and married the young woman. The old man was seventy-three years old. The wedding took a few people by surprise, but not those who knew Dad Joiner well, including Arizona Slim.

By this time Slim had been the defendant in over two hundred fifty lawsuits brought against him by people who had invested in Joiner's leases. Slim was able to defend each case successfully. With all these legal problems finally behind him, his fortune was now secure. The threat of anyone attaching his oil profits, now soaring into the tens of millions, was behind. He was in his early forties and need never worry about money again.

# 28.

PRESIDENT FRANKLIN DELANO ROOSEVELT had barely finished taking his oath of office when he received a petition from the North Texas Oil & Gas Association, a lobby group formed by the major oil companies and larger independents, calling for federal regulation of their industry. The new president was formulating the National Industrial Recovery Act, his grand design for overhauling the ailing economy, and was only too happy to be of service. Arizona Slim and his confederates had already succeeded in getting a law passed making it a felony for any producer to exceed the limit set by the Texas Railroad Commission, but some operators got around this law by shipping their excess oil, hot oil it was called, out of state. President Roosevelt responded immediately by signing a proclamation banning hot oil from interstate commerce. To enforce his edict, he shipped fifty federal agents to the East Texas oil fields with the authority to impound any hot oil heading across state lines.

Still, the overproduction continued and hot oil found its way to out-of-state markets. Agents were bribed; others, unfamiliar with the oil business, found it impossible to determine exactly how much oil was being pumped from the ground in the first place. One of those found violating the law which he himself was instrumental in getting passed was Arizona Slim. When he was fined $49,000 for his transgression, he asserted that some of his employees were stealing oil from him and selling it on their own. At this point there were 13,512 wells in the huge East Texas field, 390 were in the process of being drilled, and 94 new ones were in the planning stage. Of this number the major companies and larger independents such as Arizona Slim owned over eight thousand, and the smaller wildcatters, who opposed any kind of proration limits, owned the rest.

Determined to end all illegal trafficking in hot oil, Franklin Roosevelt appointed two men to oversee the operations of the fifty federal agents and to enforce his proclamation. One was J. Howard Marshall, a young lawyer who was special assistant to the attorney general, and the other was Tom Kelliher, a former FBI agent who had helped in the investigations of John Dillinger, Pretty Boy Floyd, and Machine Gun Kelly. Marshall and Kelliher were given what amounted to dictatorial power to make sure no one exceeded the production limits in the East Texas field.

Also frothing at the mouth to nationalize the oil industry was Harold Ickes, Roosevelt's secretary of the interior, who envisioned himself in the role of an omnipotent oil czar. Ickes was, in fact, so enthusiastic about his job that some of the oilmen who had been begging for government intervention, most notably Arizona Slim, started to worry that maybe they had pleaded their case a bit too strongly.

After all, proration was supposed to benefit the established oil producers while they maintained control of their own industry. What they wanted from Washington was a kind of semifree enterprise, for their industry only, designed to keep competition from eating into their profits. And now, irony of ironies, Uncle Sam was giving them a bit more than they bargained for. Harold Ickes and his lieutenants, Marshall and Kelliher, were coming on like flaming socialists. Arizona Slim took an immediate dislike to this Ickes fellow, and made a vow that one day he would find a way to get him. And one day, later on, he did get him, but in a way that had nothing whatever to do with the oil business.

Arizona Slim continued to expand his operation. The Hunt Production Company acquired new leases throughout the area, and the Penrod Drilling Company was formed to do the drilling for his own wells and for some of the major companies. His Panola Pipeline Company carried much of the oil in the area to the refineries.

While Arizona Slim, brother Sherman, and partner Pete Lake were patronizing the bookies in Tyler, betting on baseball games, horse races, and other sporting events, Slim passed a company rule that none of his employees was allowed to gamble.

"They shouldn't be wasting their hard-earned money during a depression," he explained.

The rule applied only selectively, or so it appeared to Slim's employees, who not infrequently observed Sherman handicapping horses at his desk. At the same time, Arizona Slim passed another rule, this one forbidding his employees to drink. The help again noticed apparent exceptions.

"I notice Mr. Hunt's rules don't apply to Mr. Sherman or Pete Lake," a secretary said one day.

"Mr. Sherman keeps a bottle in his file cabinet," another replied, "and I've seen him and Mr. Lake nipping on it more than once."

"Mr. Hunt says his doctor prescribed it for his brother."

"Well, if you ask me, I don't think anyone ever had to prescribe a drink for Sherman Hunt."

"Still and all, these are hard times and jobs are hard to come by. Mr. Hunt may be a hypocrite, but at least he pays his help on time."

Money from his various enterprises was coming in by the

tens of millions, and with these easy profits, Arizona Slim found that he needed to spend less time tending to business. Through his brother Sherman he had developed a passion for horse races, a passion every bit as intense as the one he had had for poker. He, Sherman, and Lake started traveling to the big tracks around the country: Saratoga and Belmont in the summer, the Fair Grounds in New Orleans during the winter. There he bet thousands of dollars at a time on a race. To help Sherman dope the horses even better, Slim hired two full-time statisticians, one with a degree from MIT, and set them up with special telephone lines in an office next to his and Sherman's. Good old Mr. Sherman might not have known much about the oil business, but he and his younger brother were birds of a feather in the area that most interested them.

With all his preoccupation with the fight for proration, and the gallivanting it necessitated, as well as the daily demands created by his ever-expanding oil and pipeline business, Arizona Slim had little if any time for either of his families. Lyda had long ago accepted her fate, and her relationship with her husband had regressed to a rather formal and distant politeness when they were together. But Frania was entirely different. She was not a resourceful or independent woman to begin with, and her loneliness during Franklin's absences had turned into a hard bitterness and nagging resentment.

After his own move to Texas, Franklin had begun to lose interest in his Frania. The infatuation of the make-believe world of Florida had worn thin shortly after he had moved her to Shreveport, and her constant demands for more attention only served to drive him even further away. Still, she was the mother of his children, the blonde and lovely conduit of his genes, and he honored his obligation to her. There were times when he was with her when they were almost able to recapture something of their Florida days, and when he thought that maybe, just maybe, they could make their musical come true after all. Frania still appealed to him as a woman much more than Lyda ever did; she was still fair and lovely, and a warm and loving bedmate when things were going right for them. So they tried one more time, after the strain of the past few years, to bring their love back to life. He returned to live with her briefly after Christmas 1933 and—wouldn't you know it?—Frania presented her Franklin with yet another October baby, her fourth, this one called Hugh, which he later changed to Hue, on October 14, 1934.

Some things never change after all.

Perhaps he could have kept his double life going indefinitely. But Arizona Slim had been a gambling man all his life, and he knew the odds were bound to work against him sooner or later. He didn't know exactly where or when or how it would happen, but it was inevitable that one of his wives would eventually find out about the other. He just hoped it would happen later rather than sooner.

Actually, he had gotten away with it longer than he thought he would. Had he been asked to put money on it in the beginning, he never would have bet that it would take Frania nine years and four babies to find out about his first family. It was too much of a long shot, and Arizona Slim always preferred tighter odds than that.

It was ironic, in a way, that it was his oldest son, Hassie, who did him in. Hassie, his namesake, was, of all his children, causing him the most trouble. Just a few weeks before she gave birth to Hugh, Frania picked up a morning newspaper and saw a picture of her Franklin in front of an oil well and identified as Mr. H. L. Hunt of Tyler. That was bad enough, surely, but even that could have been explained. After all, it wouldn't be the first time a newspaper got somebody's name wrong, and Franklin's business was closer to Tyler than to Dallas. But when the sixteen-year-old boy next to him was identified as Mr. H. L. Hunt's oldest son, H. L. Hunt, Jr., that was just too much. No newspaper reporter in the world could have screwed up a story that much.

That Frania was able to deliver a normal, healthy baby after making this discovery was testimony to her strong constitution. If Arizona Slim wanted a woman who was genetically sound as the mother of his second family, he had certainly chosen well. Frania restrained her hysteria until after the baby was born, and then unleashed the full fury of her rage. Whatever love she still harbored for her Franklin, whatever hope she still entertained that her marriage might somehow be made to work, all of it had been thoroughly annihilated by a brief caption under a photograph in a daily newspaper.

For his part, Arizona Slim felt relief more than he felt any other emotion. He had known for years that this marriage, this musical, was never going to work. Certainly, after Helen was born and Frania insisted that he move in with them in Dallas, he knew he was unable and unwilling to give her what she wanted. The brief reconciliation and the attempt to patch things up with a fourth child had been wishful thinking at best. When the blush of rekindled infatuation gave way to the reality of pregnancy and the practical details of encroaching childbirth, Arizona Slim resumed his routine of wandering and disappearing for weeks and months at a time. No, he had known for years that this marriage was doomed, that, as bad as it was, his home with Lyda and the kids was his bedrock, the place he belonged to, if indeed it could be said he belonged to any one place. The great revelation, the uncovering of his secret double life, was therefore more of a relief than anything else for him. The odds had worked, as sooner or later they had to.

When Frania packed up all her belongings, and moved

with her children to Nassau County on Long Island, just east of New York City, Arizona Slim promised her that she never need worry about money or a place to live for her and the children.

"I'll make sure you're taken care of," he said.

"You bet you will, Mr. H. L. Hunt or whatever your name is," she cried. "You'll pay plenty for what you did, believe me."

With Lyda, all pretense at cordiality was forever lost. The barest civility was all that remained.

"Give this to Mr. Hunt," Lyda would say to Margaret when she had something to pass on to him.

"Tell Mrs. Hunt I have to go on a business trip for a couple of weeks," Arizona Slim would say, when delivering a message to his wife.

From that moment on, they ceased addressing each other by their first names.


If all the deception was taking its toll on Lyda, Frania, and their offspring, it was leaving an indelible mark on Slim's oldest boy, his namesake, Hassie. Hassie had locked horns with him right from the beginning. The boy was like him in so many ways; he was the image of his father physically, and had his strong will and stubborn determination. Besides, he had a preternatural intelligence that bordered on the psychic; he was possessed of what many people are fond of calling a sixth sense. The boy did, however, have one tragic flaw: he was determined, above everything else, to please his father and make his father love and be proud of him. With a father like Arizona Slim, alas, this was all but impossible.

During his father's lengthy absences when a growing child, Hassie would be seized by fits of fury and uncontrollable violence more horrible to witness than the most severe forms of epilepsy. The boy would froth and rage through the house, screaming and attacking everything in his path. Slim's attempts to deal with this when he was home were ineffective at best. Later on, as the boy grew larger, his fury was directed more specifically against his father. And now, at seventeen years of age and as tall and strong as a man, he was at the point of being nearly able to overpower the forty-six-year-old Slim.

To make matters even worse, Arizona Slim tried to suppress his son's wildness rather than to find a more productive outlet for it. Hassie was powerful and bristling with frustrated energy, as his father had been in his life, but Arizona Slim refused to let him play football in high school, which was a natural sport for him.

"Football causes kidney damage and I won't hear of it," Slim said on more than one occasion.

Arizona Slim had started to develop some exotic notions about health, medicine, and food, but mixed in with this was his own mania for protecting his firstborn son, his namesake, his clone as it were, against any form of injury. He could not supply Hassie with love and attention, two things the boy craved most from him, but he was, paradoxically, obsessed with the idea of reliving his life through Hassie, obsessed with bringing Hassie up to be a duplicate of himself. So football was out for Hassie, and so was anything else that might injure him in any way. Meanwhile, Hassie was crushed by his father's absences, and was devastated by his inability to do anything at all worthy of his father's approval. He simply was not perfect enough for his old man.

By the time Frania uncovered Arizona Slim's double existence, things had already gotten out of hand between him and Hassie. The physical confrontations were taking place more and more frequently, and Hassie's size was making them increasingly dangerous for both father and son. It was at this time that Slim decided to ship Hassie off to Culver Military Academy, against Lyda's wishes.

"Tell Mrs. Hunt the boy needs the discipline," he said to Margaret. "It'll help make a man of him. Help tame that wildness and recklessness in him."

Lyda relented because she had to. In any disagreement or test of wills, Arizona Slim always got his way.

# 29.

THE YEAR 1935 PUT the icing on the cake for Slim and his considerable fortune. The production of hot oil had already slowed to a trickle, thanks to Tom Kelliher, J. Howard Marshall, and a company of Texas Rangers whose salaries were paid by Arizona Slim, Craig Cullinan, and several other rich independent oilmen. Slim and his fellow free enterprisers may have resented the heavy socialistic hand of Washington intruding into their affairs, but they didn't mind regulating the marketplace with an iron fist so long as the fist was theirs. By banding together and helping Franklin Roosevelt defray the considerable cost of enforcing proration in the East Texas oil fields, Arizona Slim and his confederates were able, in effect, to regulate their own industry in a way that suited them best.

Their ultimate victory came early in 1935, when the Supreme Court handed down a decision curtailing the power of Harold Ickes and furthering the interests of the oilmen. In essence, the decision read by Chief Justice Charles Evans Hughes said that the federal government had overstepped its authority in enforcing proration in the oil industry:

"It is no answer to insist that deleterious consequences follow the transportation of 'hot oil'—oil exceeding state allowances. The Congress did not prohibit that transportation. The Congress did not undertake to say that the transportation of that oil was unfair competition. The president was not required to ascertain and proclaim the conditions prevailing in the industry which made the prohibition necessary...."

With this decision from the highest court in the land in place, the path was clear for the oilmen to get a proration law passed that was more to their own liking. This was accomplished within days when Tom Connally, the senior senator from Texas, who was acting for Arizona Slim and the other oilmen, placed a call to J. Howard Marshall.

"Can you write a law that conforms to the Supreme Court decision?" Connally asked.

"I sure can." Marshall said, only too happy to oblige.

"How long will it take?"

"Give me forty-eight hours."

"Let me have it when it's ready, son."

Two days later Connally conferred with Senator Albert Gore of Oklahoma, who was equally anxious to pass a law favorable to the oilmen in his own state, and on February 16, 1935, President Roosevelt signed the Connally Hot Oil Act into law. The signing took place one day before Arizona Slim's forty-sixth birthday, and he could hardly have wished for a finer present. The new law pretty much legalized the status quo by imposing controls on the production, transportation, storage, and handling of crude oil, and thus protected the interests of the existing majors and large independents, and restricted competition from the smaller wildcatters. This was Arizona Slim's first adventure into political combat. He found the taste of victory much to his liking.

The year was also marked by a series of lawsuits pitting various members of the Joiner family against one another following the old man's marriage to the young woman,

Arizona Slim against Gulf Oil when Gulf drilled wells on leases that belonged to Slim, and various plaintiffs against Barney Skipper after Lathrop No. 1 came in. Judge R.T. Brown was kept so busy in his little courtroom that he remarked whimsically from the bench, "Not even the facts can settle a lawsuit as quickly and as thoroughly as a dry hole."

The simple fact was, the number of lawsuits increased in direct proportion to the number of producing wells in the area. It was testimony to Arizona Slim's developing talent for legal infighting that he had yet to lose a case in court. Having all his life successfully tested his skills in the marketplace and at the gambling tables, doing so by his wits alone, he now had also learned successfully how to bypass the perils of competition and manipulate the system to his own advantage.

Nineteen thirty-five was also the year that Arizona Slim decided to take some necessary steps to protect the interests of Lyda and her children against litigation which he knew would be forthcoming from Frania. He had made a handsome settlement with her, anxious as he was to make sure that the children he had with her would be well provided for, but she was still in a position to cause him trouble, particularly as she came to understand the full extent of his growing fortune.

So, just before the end of 1935, he had his lawyer draw up six trusts, one for each of his children by Lyda. Each child received shares in a new corporation, Placid Oil Company, which owned most of his producing wells in Arkansas and Louisiana, and shares in Penrod Drilling, Panola Pipeline, and Hunt Production. Arizona Slim's penchant for giving his companies six-letter names beginning with the letter *P* was a subject of great amusement among his employees and others who knew him.

"Mr. Hunt is probably just superstitious," one clerk suggested.

"The word profit starts with a *P* and has six letters," added another. "As everyone knows, that's his favorite word."

"You're both wrong," said a third. "Knowing him he's probably naming them after some trollop he's keeping on the side. Somebody whose name starts with a *P*." They all guffawed.

Whatever the case, Arizona Slim had divested himself of a good piece of his assets and put them in the names of his six children by Lyda, a move that ensured their interests against any litigation from Frania and her four offspring.

When Hassie returned from Culver Military Academy, Slim decided to give him a job with Penrod Drilling, selling the company's drilling facilities to other oil companies. Hassie, always eager to prove himself to his father, threw himself into this unexpected position of responsibility with all the energy and enthusiasm he had at his disposal. With Arizona Slim quietly looking over his shoulder to see if his number-one son was up to snuff, Hassie arrived at the office early and started placing phone calls to the other producers in the area.

On one of his first appointments, he went up to Longview to call on J. Edgar Pew, the founder of the Sun Oil Company. After Hassie made his sales pitch in the older man's office, Pew got up from his desk and walked over to the young man, placing his hand on Hassie's shoulder. "I'm impressed, young man," said Pew. "Very impressed. I have to let you know, however, that two other drilling contractors will be bidding against you. Business is business. The best bid will get the contract. It's as simple as that."

Three days later Pew received a bid by mail from Hassie and, to his own relief, it was the lowest of the three. Pew was a friend of Arizona Slim, having worked cheek-by-jowl with him in the fight for proration, and he had been hoping he could see his way clear toward helping Slim's son. He notified Hassie at once that Penrod would get the contract, then sat back in his chair filled with a feeling of satisfaction. The next day his secretary stuck her head into his office and informed him that there was a call for him.

"Who is it?" asked Pew.

"It's Mr. Lee from Mr. Hunt's office. Mr. Hunt senior."

Pew picked up the receiver and listened in shock as Roy Lee said, "Sir, I've just been on the phone with Mr. Hunt. He asked me to tell you that his son's bid was too low and it should be withdrawn immediately."

Pew, for once, was speechless as he held the receiver in his hand.

"Sir?" Lee broke the awkward silence.

"Yes, yes, I heard you," Pew said, snapping back to business. "Tell Mr. Hunt I'm sorry, but I will, of course, honor his request."

Pew returned the receiver to the cradle and shook his head sadly. "What gets into that man?" he asked himself rhetorically. "What a way to raise a boy and expect him to stand on his own two feet."

Hassie flew into another of his uncontrollable rages when he learned of his father's action, and Slim had all he could do to restrain him. It was, perhaps, the most vicious confrontation between the two Slim's associates had yet witnessed. When it was over, when Hassie had drained himself of his fury and bitter frustration, Arizona Slim dealt the boy a final crushing blow with the remark, "Maybe you should visit some of those poker parlors I've been telling you about, and learn to sharpen your wits a bit."

Hassie was beaten. The young man was simply no match for his ruthless and experienced father and his iron will. Slim decided that his oldest son was not quite ready for business yet, so, despite his own contempt for formal education, he enrolled

Hassie in the University of Texas, where he hoped they would "drum some sense into his head."

Not long after his arrival at the university, Hassie exhibited signs of strangeness, obvious to professor and student alike. There was no question about his intelligence, but Hassie was either not interested in or incapable of applying his mind to his studies. He spent much of his time building his own radio transmitter and then, instead of confining himself to the amateur frequencies, he started jamming commercial programs he didn't like, or else cutting in on them with his own editorial comments while they were broadcasting live. Understandably, the university officials frowned upon these unscheduled extracurricular activities and decided that Hassie should test his talents elsewhere. It was only Arizona Slim's persuasiveness and the considerable power of his purse that allowed Hassie to continue as a student.

When Hassie was not occupied with his impromptu broadcasts, he started acquiring oil leases on his own, without his father's blessing, in an effort to prove to Slim, once and for all, that he was capable of succeeding at something. Slim was at first annoyed by his son's assumption of authority. But when his geologists informed him that Hassie's leases had potential, and when one well, then others were brought in successfully on them, Arizona Slim remarked to one of his associates, but never openly to Hassie himself, the one who most needed to hear it, "The boy seems to have some kind of a sixth sense, a genius almost, for sniffing out oil. It's hard to explain. He just seems to know where it is."

So Arizona Slim did put Hassie to work for him after all, sniffing out oil with that preternatural gift of his. Hassie, in turn, received a good measure of satisfaction knowing that, finally, he was able to be of use in the family business. But he never did get that one thing he needed and craved the most: a word of praise from Arizona Slim.

With all the millions of dollars that were rolling in from his various enterprises, Arizona Slim was still not content to sit back and rest on his laurels. Money, after all, had never been anything more to him than a means of assuming even greater risk and broadening his field of operation. When he suggested to Pete Lake that they expand their area of interest to the fields in West Texas and in other states, Lake decided to beg off.

"Hell, I'm already as rich as I ever want to be," Lake said. "It seems to me I'm ready to sit back and take it easy for a change."

Sitting back and taking it easy was an emotional and psychological impossibility for Arizona Slim, as Lyda discovered on more than one occasion during the early years of their marriage. At this point, with their ambitions clearly taking them in opposite directions, it was time to go their separate ways. In October 1936 the assets of Hunt Production Company were divided into two distinct entities: Hunt Oil Company and P. G. Lake, Inc. In essence, Slim bought out his long-time associate from the Arkansas days for a total of $5 million—$1 million in cash and the balance in producing wells and undeveloped leases. Since Lake's interest in Hunt Production had amounted to twenty percent, Slim's share of this company alone was worth $20 million. Add to that the assets of Penrod Drilling, Panola Pipeline, Placid Oil, and some of his smaller enterprises, and Arizona Slim was already worth a total of about $100 million.

Clearly, his motivation for wanting to expand his activities to other areas could not have been money. He already had more legal tender flowing in each week than he could possibly spend. No, Arizona Slim was driven, as he had been all his life, by his need to keep on proving himself, his obsession to keep his life in motion by seeking new challenges. One of his first acts after buying out Pete Lake was to acquire a refinery. In doing so he demonstrated, once again, that he was capable of fighting a little dirty if he must to get something he wanted.

Rather than build a refinery of his own, he decided it would be easier to acquire one already in existence. The one he had his eye on was the Excelsior Refining Company, which he had been supplying with his own oil. Excelsior was located in the southern part of Rusk County alongside land owned by Slim. One day the partners who owned Excelsior received a call from Arizona Slim, who startled them by declaring, "I'm interested in buying a piece of your refinery."

After conferring briefly with each other, the partners informed Slim that they had no interest whatever in selling a part of their business.

"I'm wondering if that might not be a hasty decision," Slim said slowly. "After all, I am your major supplier. And, since I own the land right next to you, there's nothing to stop me from building my own refinery and competing with you."

The partners allowed that Mr. Hunt just might have a point, so, after putting their heads together for another moment or two, they offered to let him buy a one-third share.

"I was thinking more like half," Slim countered. "Half for me and you boys retain twenty-five percent apiece. Just put a fair price on the deal and get back to me."

The partners figured, what the hell, why not be outrageous, we've got nothing to lose. So when they told Mr. Hunt that a one-half interest in their plant was worth, gag, $150,000, he astonished them by replying immediately, "Done. Have your lawyers draw up a contract and get a copy over to me."

Just like that. No bargaining, no dickering. They had the feeling after he hung up that he wouldn't have batted an eye had they asked for half a million; he was determined to have his way and money was no object. When Arizona Slim suggested a few weeks later that they change the name of the refinery—Excelsior just didn't do anything for him—the partners were agreeable. Hell, they could not have cared less what the place was called, so long as it continued to make money for them. Arizona Slim found a name with six letters that started with *P*, and he rechristened his new company Parade Gasoline.

Again his employees nodded to one another knowingly, and snickered behind his back.

# 30.

THE HAMLET OF LONDON had a single main street and about a hundred inhabitants in the days before the oil boom. When oil was discovered in the hills around the town, the population grew, new roads were built, and the village expanded. Another hamlet developed a few miles away; called New London, it sat along the highway running north from London to Kilgore.

Oil money brought prosperity to the area, one evidence of which was the sprawling million-dollar campus that the residents built for their children. By 1937 there were almost a thousand students at one level or another in the New London Consolidated School District, which some said was the wealthiest in the country.

March 18, 1937, started normally for the people of New London and their children. The winter cold was mostly gone, but the air was still damp and raw. In another month or so the warm weather would descend on the country, but not today.

At three in the afternoon the parents began to anticipate the return of their children, who were soon to be released from school. Ten minutes later, at precisely 3:10, the village was rocked by an enormous explosion that could be heard for miles around. The center of the blast was the main building on the New London campus, which was blown to bits, leaving only a rubbish heap. Children were sent flying through the air, their bodies smashed and battered beyond recognition.

Parents jumped into their cars and trucks and started toward the school, expecting the worst. Their expectations were not disappointed, for the final toll in lost human lives was horrendous. By the time the dust settled and the bodies were counted, 280 children and 14 adults had lost their lives in the explosion.

The offices of Hunt Oil Company resembled bedlam for the rest of the afternoon and late into the night. Virtually every employee with children in the New London district had lost someone. Since many of the bodies were impossible to identify, it had to be determined by process of elimination whose children were lost. Bodies, and parts of bodies, were laid out on the sidewalks and on the grass as officials tried to match them up with parents whose children had been killed. Roy Lee, Arizona Slim's office manager and general right-hand man, worked through the night, assigning corpses to various employees and making funeral arrangements.

The following morning, Arizona Slim came in early and formed a delegation of his key employees to visit different homes with him that day. He and Roy Lee broke them up into twos and threes and prepared an itinerary for each group. Slim climbed into his big Buick with Lyda, his brother Sherman and his wife, and his sisters Nettie, still single, and Rose Hunt Taylor; both sisters were down for a visit. Off they went over the wet, bumpy roads to visit the homes of his victimized employees outside town. At one of his first stops his secretary was busy washing dishes for the bereaved parents, and a young office worker named Virgil was also in attendance. Arizona Slim walked over to the father, who was preparing to load his son's body into the back of a panel truck.

"Where are you taking your boy?" asked Slim.

"Back to Junction City, sir. Back home where the family is."

Slim grabbed one end of the casket and helped his employee carry it out to the truck. When the latch was secured tight, he pulled a thick wad of bills from his pocket, peeled off a few from the outside, and stuck them into the man's pocket.

"You'll probably be able to use this," he said and walked off.

He repeated this performance throughout the day. At one house he stopped in, the mother approached him as he walked through the front door and clutched his arm. Pointing toward the unrecognizable remains of a dead child in the coffin across the room, the woman suddenly grew hysterical and started to scream, "That is not my boy, it's not him. I refuse to accept that as my boy."

Disengaging himself slowly, Arizona Slim paid his respects, left some money with the parents, and proceeded to the next house on his list.

When the initial impact of the tragedy subsided, the townspeople themselves exploded in a rage, calling for an investigation to determine the cause of the explosion. In the confusion and simmering demand for justice which threatened to get uglier by the minute, Governor James V. Allred declared a state of martial law and assigned state troopers to help the local police maintain order. Within weeks there were three separate entities conducting their own investigation of the accident: a military court of inquiry, appointed by the state; and the U.S. Bureau of Mines and the Department of Agriculture, of the federal government.

The military court determined that no one was at fault, but both federal agencies concluded that gas had escaped from lines or fittings beneath the building, and was ignited by sparks from an electric switch. The people of New London, however, were not satisfied with such general conclusions; they wanted vengeance for their children's deaths, and that meant zeroing in on something even more specific.

Additional detective work revealed that W. C. Shaw, the

school superintendent, had discontinued service with United Gas Company several months before the accident and tapped into a pipeline owned by Parade Gasoline Company, whose name had recently been changed from Excelsior Refining. United Gas was costing the school system $3,000 a year and Shaw saw a chance to obtain gas for nothing by hooking into Parade's pipeline. Shaw admitted this was true, but added in his own defense, "I acted with the knowledge and consent of most of the members of the school board."

The superintendent maintained that various churches in the area had done the same thing, and that it was common practice for many homes and businesses to get free gas that way.

"Besides," Shaw continued, "I discussed this arrangement with several Parade officials, and they indicated to me that they had no objection."

"Did they give you specific approval to tap into their gasline?" Shaw was asked.

"Not exactly. But I got at least tacit approval. They more or less agreed to look the other way."

Shaw argued that this kind of tapping did not cost Parade Gasoline anything since the gas that was being siphoned off was casinghead gas, which came up in the casing of the well and would ordinarily have been burned off in flares at the wellhead. Rather than let the gas go to waste in this fashion, many oil companies, including Parade, allowed certain consumers to tap into it before it was burned off, for little or no money. It was common knowledge that casinghead gas was extremely volatile, containing as it did so much liquid, but people used it anyway for cooking and heating because it was virtually free.

Superintendent Shaw had lost a son of his own in the explosion, as well as several nephews, but the townspeople had located a scapegoat and they weren't about to permit their sympathies to dampen their passion for vengeance. They forced him to resign and then brought thirty lawsuits against him, the other members of the school board, and Parade Gasoline.

Once again Judge R. T. Brown found himself presiding over an emotion-filled courtroom. In this instance, however, there would be no dry holes to mitigate the passion of the plaintiffs. No, this was the most difficult case he had yet to hear; and certainly he would not be called upon to judge in ten lifetimes a case fraught with such an emotional set of circumstances. Finally, after months of weighing the evidence, Judge Brown brought in his verdict.

"Not guilty," he said wearily from his chair. "None of the defendants can be held responsible for the series of events which led to the loss of so many human lives that day."

A victory of sorts was granted by the state legislature to the people of New London while the trial was in progress. A law was passed prohibiting the use of casinghead gas in Texas schools, and requiring that all gas sold to the public be injected with a distinctive odor so that people could recognize leaks that occurred in the future. It was a small victory, indeed, but no law or legal verdict in the world could have brought those 294 victims back to life. At least, users of gas henceforth would have a way of recognizing the volatile substance when it was loose in the air.

And the townspeople did have their religion and their fear of God to fall back on in the end. The explosion was God's way, they would say for years afterward, of punishing them for their sinfulness and greed during the oil-boom days. Fear of the Lord, it seems, is the mightiest pacifier of all.

# 31.

I T WAS TIME TO MOVE on again. The wheel of time was
rolling endlessly on, and Arizona Slim was again itchy
for new fields of interest. His fortune was now secure and the
battle of East Texas was over and won. His wells were in place,
pumping oil into his pipelines from deep in the earth. Money
poured in effortlessly, more money than ten families could
reasonably spend in a dozen lifetimes.

The oilmen moved from the grubby oil-boom towns of East
Texas to the nearest metropolis the state had to offer, bustling
Dallas. By the end of the 1930s Dallas had succeeded Tulsa as
the oil capital of the Southwest. Tulsa was loaded with oil and
money, but nobody else was as rich as the oilmen who made
Dallas their home.

The symbol of the new wealth was the flying red horse high
above the Magnolia Building in downtown Dallas. Visible
from thirty miles away, the winged stallion flew defiantly atop
the tallest building in the city, six thousand pounds of blazing
metal, illuminated at night by eleven hundred feet of neon
tubing.

It was only natural that sooner or later Arizona Slim would
make Dallas his base of operations. He located a huge,
sprawling house on ten acres of land sloping down to White
Rock Lake, in the eastern part of Dallas. The house was a
copy of Washington's Mount Vernon, but in true Texas

style it had been built twice as large as the original. The house sat on top of a hill, and on warm evenings one could sit in the wicker chairs on the six-columned portico and watch the moonlight ripple softly on the surface of the lake. Arizona Slim also moved his business headquarters to Dallas, to the First National Bank Building, where he occupied a corner office overlooking the city.

More and more, Hassie was assuming the role of chief scout for new oil fields. His talent was uncanny. Nobody could explain exactly how he did it, but the young man had an unerring gift for locating new oil deposits. He simply pointed and there they were.

On Hassie's suggestion, Arizona Slim expanded into the Cotton Valley field in northwest Louisiana. Slim was at first reluctant to drill there. The field had produced oil at shallow depths in the 1920s, and everyone thought it had been tapped out. Hassie insisted, however, that much more oil lay deeper in the earth, so Slim finally acceded. Sure enough, Hassie was right again, as always. He always insisted he was right, and then would proceed to prove it in a way that defied logic. He seemed to *know* things intuitively. Slim drilled into the Cotton Valley field and hit a large pocket of oil at precisely the depth Hassie said he would.

Gradually Hassie branched out on his own. He was possessed by an insatiable need to get out from beneath his father's wing and become his own man. He acquired his own leases, drilled his own wells, and developed a business independent of his father's. No longer was he content merely to help his father expand the family enterprises; he needed to prove that he could be more successful than the man who brought him into the world and gave him his looks and his name.

"That Mr. Hassie is two people at the same time," a

secretary remarked one day. "One Mr. Hassie is so calm and quiet, and the other one is possessed. He'll never be happy until he gets to be a bigger boss than his daddy."

Hassie was determined to be his own man in name as well. Before reaching his twenty-first birthday the young man, who felt as though he would never be truly free as long as he was referred to as Haroldson Lafayette Hunt III, had his name legally changed to Hassie. This was his ultimate act of defiance, the move which signaled unequivocally that he had no intention of living his life as a mere surrogate for his father.

Even with this change, however, Arizona Slim found himself curiously dependent on his son's business sense, and, oddly enough, Hassie continued to lean on his father's leadership qualities to keep order in his own affairs. Besides his ability to locate oil, Hassie had an intuitive sense which Slim found invaluable, but he was chaotic as far as the administration of his business was concerned. Bills were never paid on time, the million details of efficiently running an office seemed beyond his grasp, and his personal behavior was eccentric, to put it mildly. Walking down a street in Jackson, Mississippi, with a friend one day, he passed an automobile showroom. Hassie took one look in the window, suddenly bent down and picked up a rock, and hurled it through the glass. When the staff emptied out of the place and came running up to him, he told them politely, "See that car over there. I want to buy it." He entered the showroom with them, paid for the window with cash, and signed an agreement to buy the car.

Around the office he was equally unpredictable. Sometimes he would stare for hours into space without saying a word; one day he might be impeccably dressed in a suit and tie, and the next day be in old work clothes that looked as though he had slept in them. He was fond of disappearing for weeks at a time with a pack of cronies, whom he treated to endless rounds of parties; his bills for liquor, women, and hotels were astronomical. Such disorder in his business and personal activities, to say nothing of his eerie mental processes, disturbed Arizona Slim immensely. But Slim was as powerless in his dealings with Hassie as he was successful in manipulating others and getting them to do his bidding. Hassie delighted in infuriating his father, and in taking him head-on in one-on-one competition. Rather than cooperate with Slim when he was acquiring oil leases in Mississippi, Hassie went off on his own and struck oil before his father did, an accomplishment that amused their employees no end but enraged Arizona Slim. Together they drilled successfully in central Louisiana—in the Nebo, Olla, and Little Creek fields in Webster Parish—and added considerably to the family's growing fortune.

Notwithstanding, as much as father and son antagonized each other, they also became more and more inseparable as Hassie approached his twenty-first birthday. Ironically, as their competition intensified, Hassie started to enjoy a closeness with his father that he had yearned for throughout his youth. The more their rivalry developed, the more they were bound to each other. Their relationship was not so much that of father and son as that of a symbiotic love-hate struggle destined to destroy one of them. They resisted each other and needed each other simultaneously. They traveled everywhere together on business: to Germany, where they traded oil for German steel pipe after the invasion of Poland; to California, where they arranged a deal to sell oil to Japan after that country had invaded China. In this they were not unique; many American businessmen at the time continued to trade with Nazi Germany and imperialist Japan, and were opposed to getting involved in any conflict with them.

More often than not, Arizona Slim preferred minimizing Hassie's peculiarities to acknowledging them to his employees. Striding into the office one day, he assembled his staff and announced, "Today I want you all to concentrate on organizing my son's files and taking care of any unfinished business. He's off on a business trip and I'd like everything in order before he returns."

"Hassie may be a genius when it comes to finding oil, but he sure can't run an orderly business," one man said when Slim had left them.

"If that was his only failing, there'd be no problem at all," replied a colleague. "It's Mr. Hassie's strangeness the boss can't face up to."

"Well, sometimes it's easier to look the other way than to face the truth in your own mirror. Mr. Hunt sees what he wants to see. It's less painful that way."

In 1941 Frania announced unexpectedly that she wanted to marry an old friend of Slim's, John Lee, whom she had been seeing during the few years of their separation. Arizona Slim was only too happy to agree to a proper divorce to tidy up this unfinished piece of business in his own life. In April of that year he set up four trusts, one each for Howard, Haroldina, Helen, and Hue—his children by Frania—by way of settling up with her. Slim was especially fond of Helen, a pretty, vivacious replica of her mother, but had remained in contact with all of them over the years. With their divorce now official, Frania married John Lee and the children legally took his name.

Meanwhile, European war clouds were drifting closer to our shores. Franklin D. Roosevelt had asked for a selective-service bill to draft young American men in the event of war, and Congress enacted it into law in 1940. Opposition to American participation in the war against the Axis powers was growing on different fronts. At Brown University, during Peace Week in 1940, the Socialist candidate for president of the United States, Norman Thomas, delivered a ringing attack against the war to a large crowd of cheering students.

As a squadron of Army Air Corps planes flew overhead on maneuvers, Thomas suddenly pointed skyward and shouted, "Look at them! You could be up there soon bombing helpless women and children."

Thomas told the students that the United States, by entering the war, "would not save European democracy. The United States would have to wage war on totalitarian terms, and have fascism at home under another name." The war, he said, would end in the destruction of civilization.

In the spring of 1940 Hitler's blitzkrieg rolled across western Europe, crushing an unprepared France with the Wehrmacht's tanks and troops. Soon, the powers in Washington were saying, the British Isles would be the only barrier between the United States and Adolf Hitler's drive for world conquest. Hitler's propagandists responded by declaring, "America is ours! National Socialism alone is destined to liberate the American people from their ruling clique."

Registration for the new draft, for American men between twenty-one and thirty-six, was scheduled to start on October 16, 1940. As the day approached, the debate between the forces of isolationism and those favoring intervention grew more and more heated. Kingman Brewster, Jr., the young student editor of the *Yale Daily News*, published an article in the *Atlantic Monthly*. In it he stated, "We of the ivied walls and cloistered walks are in agreement with the great majority of Americans of all ages in choosing a course of nonintervention."

Groups favoring American involvement in the conflict protested the shipment of scrap metal to Japan on the grounds that it might be returned in "the dead or maimed bodies of U.S. servicemen." In February 1941, while Arizona Slim was negotiating his divorce from Frania Tye, the American Student Union opposed the lend-lease bill, which provided assistance for Britain and others defending against the Axis powers. "Spend money for schools—not for battleships!" was its warcry.

But the military draft was already in effect, and when it came up for renewal in August 1941, it squeaked through Congress by a margin of one vote. By autumn the isolationists, the America First Committee under the sponsorship of aviator and hero Charles Lindbergh, were losing to the advocates of direct American action in the war against Nazism and fascism. And then came December 7 and the Japanese bombs on the American fleet at Pearl Harbor, and the debate was over. The American people were stunned and outraged; the attack crystallized public opinion as no words, no debate, no editorial ever could have. The United States of America had no choice but to enter the war and defend its honor and freedom.

Down there in Dallas, that great American city with the flying red horse and where all the oilmen had moved after making their fortunes in the vast East Texas oil fields, Arizona Slim was not happy about the prospects of war. Hassie was now twenty-two and eligible for the draft. One way or another, Slim would have to find a way to keep him out.

# Book VI

# The Propagandist

# 32.

A S THE LARGEST INDEPENDENT oil producer in the world, with more oil reserves than all the Axis nations put together, Arizona Slim, one might reasonably assume, was in a position to do something about keeping Hassie out of World War II. After all, the lifeblood of the country was the gasoline, diesel fuel, and oil that flowed into the tanks and airplanes and warships the Allies needed to make the world safe for democracy again, and that lifeblood was something that Slim produced in monumental quantities. Not surprisingly, therefore, Hassie Hunt was stationed at the Carleton Hotel in Washington, D.C., while millions of the nation's young men were being shipped off to kill or be killed in the jungles of the South Pacific or the gentle farmlands of Europe.

Unlike most of his compatriots, Hassie Hunt was spared the tedious grind of having to work his way up through the ranks. He was commissioned immediately as a second lieutenant in the Army Corps of Engineers, and assigned to a special position as an adviser to the Chinese nationalist government of Chiang Kai-shek.

Most American soldiers would have given their left hand to be spared the grisly hell of combat and to enjoy the good life in the nation's capital city, but this was not the case with young Hassie. As a successful oilman in his own right, he had been on the verge of finally slipping a step beyond his father's shadow, and now, with one masterstroke of power and influence, Slim had managed to tuck him safely under his wing again. Hassie had the choice of running off to war as an ordinary dogface, defying his father in an ultimate life-and-death situation, but he elected instead to accept Slim's haven from the perils of war. That acceptance proved to be his final surrender to the will of his father.

While the sons of ordinary Americans were slaughtered and maimed on the battlefields of Europe and the Pacific, the children of the rich and influential amused themselves with a never-ending round of parties near the banks of the Potomac. The women of the nation had been left behind as their men went off to war, and many gravitated to Washington, where jobs in the various agencies servicing the war effort were plentiful. The young men who remained behind, the sons of the rich like Hassie who attended the parties in their fitted uniforms with the gold and silver bars gleaming on their shoulders, had their pick of the lonely young women who outnumbered them many times over. The variety of females was enhanced by the Chinese nationalist government, which staffed its embassy heavily with nubile young beauties from the Asian mainland. Willing young females have always been one of the earth's most readily accepted forms of currency, and currency was required to purchase power and influence from the authorities who mattered in the capital city of the United States of America.

Most young men thrived in this teeming paradise for healthy young males with money and time on their hands, but Hassie did not. Paradise had the opposite effect on him. Returning to his room at the Carleton drunk one night, after an evening of partying at the Chinese embassy, Arizona Slim's oldest son suddenly flew into a violent rage, screaming at the top of his lungs and smashing furniture into the walls. When hotel personnel came up to determine the cause of the disturbance, they found the room in a shambles and the twenty-two-year-old man, still in uniform, standing across the room near the window with a wild look in his eyes.

"I've been betrayed!" he screamed at them. "They've betrayed me!"

The management sent for reinforcements as Hassie continued his incoherent tirade.

"Betrayed by the Rockefellers, betrayed by my father's enemies, they're all out to get me!"

As security guards approached him cautiously, he broke out with a new round of invective: "Get them off my back, get them away from me! They're all around me, everywhere, they're coming to get me!"

Well, they did come to get him, authorities from the United States Army, and they shipped the distraught young man to an army hospital on Lake Ponchartrain in Louisiana for observation. Hassie was still safe from the perils of combat, but the devils within had finally seized control of him. He continued to babble incomprehensibly, and when his father came to visit him at the military hospital, he flew at Slim in a mad rush, trying to attack him physically before he was restrained by the guards.

"The boy's too high-spirited, too sensitive," Slim said, trying to explain away Hassie's behavior to Lyda and the rest of the children. "He's always been too sensitive and reckless. Why, there's nothing wrong with the genes in that boy. He comes from the finest stock. He'll be all right once they tone him down a bit, you'll see."

Staring at her father with hate in her eyes, Margaret, the firstborn of all his children, hissed at him slowly, "You destroyed Hassie, nobody but you. You've gotten away with a kind of murder and it's time you faced up to that."

Visibly shaken for the first time in his life, Slim managed to mutter weakly, "Why, he'll get better, don't worry. I'll spend all my money, if I have to, to put Hassie back together again. I'll find a way."

Hadn't Slim all his life accomplished everything he set out to do? Hadn't he mastered the best gamblers in the country at the poker tables, pitted his muscles against the toughest trees the forests had to offer, tested his mental skills against seasoned traders and come up a winner? And hadn't he outsmarted the most cunning oil hustlers in the business and gone on to make more money than most human beings could dream of making in a hundred lifetimes? Of course he had.

And if he had to find a way to put Hassie back together, to make him whole again, why, he would do that too. There was nothing in the world he couldn't do once he set his mind to it.

Just you wait and see.

While Hassie was getting the best care money could buy in the hospital on Lake Ponchartrain, Arizona Slim was discovering that World War II wasn't so bad after all. The demand for petroleum products soared astronomically as the war continued, and this increased demand drove up prices faster than any proration law could possibly have done. And since the tax laws were such—what with oil-depletion allowances and all—that oilmen could get off almost scot-free from having to pay any taxes whatever, Slim began to realize that maybe he had been a trifle hasty in opposing American intervention before the attack on Pearl Harbor.

The biggest problem he had to face now was spending his money fast enough on additional exploration to avoid paying taxes on it. After consulting with his accountant one day, he strode into one of his branch offices in Midland, Texas, and announced, "I want you people to go out and spend $4 million by the end of the month on new oil leases."

"But, sir. Mr. Hunt, sir," the agent on the premises

protested. "There aren't $40 worth of worthwhile leases available anywhere around here anymore."

"Don't argue with me, boy. Just go out and spend that $4 million on leases. And, when you get them, I want you to go ahead and drill on them. That's a direct order."

For the next two weeks the agent put every available body he could find to work, scouting up leases for Arizona Slim before the month ran out. When that was accomplished, he had derricks erected on all this unpromising new land and started drilling for oil. To his astonishment, oil was discovered on one of the first wells. Thinking that Arizona Slim was some kind of a genius, or a divinely inspired oilhound, he got on the phone at once to report the good news to his boss.

"Oil you say? Damn it, boy," Slim responded with one of the only profanities anyone had ever heard him utter, "there wasn't supposed to be any oil there. That means more money I got to spend before the revenue man gets it. Go out and get me some more leases and make sure it's all rock this time."

Slim opened a new office in Shreveport and sent his scouts into the backwoods and swamplands of Louisiana to acquire vast tracts of land as quickly as they could. He bought up large amounts of acreage in the Florida panhandle, cotton plantations in Mississippi, where he moved his sister Florence and her husband, and other stretches of wide-open land in states as far away as Montana.

"It's the policy of my organization," he instructed his scouts, "to acquire land and leases everywhere. Don't worry about title clearances or the suitability for oil prospecting. Just buy it up and I'll take care of the rest."

The money rolled in faster than ever during the war years. No matter how much land he bought and how far he expanded his fields of operation, his cash kept growing faster than he could possibly spend it.

In 1942 he passed his fifty-third birthday. He was still a vigorous man, albeit thickening slowly through the middle and thinning across his reddish-brown head. A sharp, conscientious dresser in his youth, he had allowed a certain carelessness bordering on indifference to enter into his choice of clothes. His suits had always been well chosen, but there were times now when he tended to throw together a jacket and pair of trousers from different outfits, and that usually gave him a slightly seedy appearance. He was rarely without a cigar, lit or unlit, between his fingers or in his mouth, although the quality of them had deteriorated slightly as his wealth increased. As his fortune became secure and his success mounted, he grew indifferent to the appearance of success.

His thickening girth and indifference to attire did not affect his attitude toward members of the opposite sex, however. He was in Shreveport tending to affairs in his new office, now headquarters for his oil interests beyond the East Texas field. Walking into the office one morning, he felt as though he were suddenly struck by lightning. Sitting behind a typewriter, diligently pecking away at some report, was a pretty young secretary who could have been the twin sister of Frania Tye. She was the image of beautiful young Frania as she looked almost twenty years before in that real estate office in Tampa.

This lovely young creature was still a child. Perhaps not even twenty yet? She might have been Shirley Temple's older sister, a young Betty Grable starting out in her first musical, or Virginia Mayo lighting up the silver screen with her glowing blonde beauty. She did, in fact, bear a striking resemblance to Jane Powell, who in ten years would become one of America's darlings on the strength of her freshly scrubbed loveliness and her golden voice.

Arizona Slim, fifty-three-year-old multimillionaire oilman, was again thunderstruck by a vision straight out of his fantasies. Ruth Ray was stamped in the same mold that

Hollywood musical queens were coined in. She was vibrant and full of life; wholesome as a freshly picked peach; and wore her thick wavy blonde hair swept away to the side, the way they did in the movies. She had round apple-dumpling cheeks, shiny white teeth, and laughing blue eyes, which closed like a Dresden doll's every time she smiled; and a smile that was wholesome, carefree, and uniquely American. This lovely little doll, reminiscent of a pinup queen straight out of a happy-go-lucky Hollywood musical extravaganza, caught Arizona Slim's eye in a way no one else had since his early days with Frania. She was a musical come true, the dream girl who had been missing in his life for far too long.

Yes, Ruth Ray would be a perfect conduit for his genes, just the girl to bring another new Hassie into the world. The young starlet was flattered by her boss's attentions and his generosity. He put her on a pedestal; treated her like something special, not like just another southern poor-girl secretary pecking out a meager living on a typewriter.

Ruth Ray had dreams and fantasies too, dreams of meeting Mr. Right some day, who would take her away from all this, someone who would treat her like a princess and buy her pretty things to wear.

Arizona Slim did just that. He set her up in a nice modern apartment in Shreveport and bought her frilly things that made her look even more like Betty Grable and Virginia Mayo than she naturally did. And Ruth Ray gave Slim what he wanted in return. She loved him up good and was there when he wanted her. And she gave him a baby boy, not another Hassie exactly, but a handsome healthy boy who would grow up to look a little bit like his daddy at least. And one year later she presented him with a round, bouncing baby girl, the image of her mother, whom they christened June. The boy was given the last name of his mother, Ray, and was called Ray-Ray until he was old enough to resent it.

The year 1942 was significant for Arizona Slim on a wholly different level as well. J. B. McEntire, his lawyer and long-time associate from the El Dorado days, walked onto a golf course one day and was stricken by a heart attack. McEntire fell toward the immaculate green earth and was dead before he hit the ground. To replace him, Arizona Slim hired an East Texas politician who had been an ally of his during the proration fight and the hot-oil restrictions. Sidney Latham had served in the state legislature in the 1930s and during the war years was secretary of state under Governor Coke Stevenson. All in all, Sidney Latham would be of great service as a high-ranking member of Slim's organization.

Until this time, Arizona Slim's political orientation had been unformed at best. He had a vague notion that Calvin Coolidge was, perhaps, the greatest American president who ever lived, but this traced primarily to the fact that Coolidge had been in office during the 1920s, the booming decade when Slim first started to acquire some money. His memories of the man and the time were fond ones for a very real reason. Slim's distaste for the Roosevelt administration, most particularly for Harold Ickes, was likewise based on highly personal considerations: Ickes had attempted to overregulate an industry that Slim himself, along with his cronies, wanted to control. As an individualist, a free enterpriser in practice before the 1930s, and a risk-taker all his life, Arizona Slim had an instinctive bias toward the capitalist system, which enabled him to accumulate his immense fortune, but he had never been a philosophical man, and he had never bothered to formulate his biases into a cohesive political ideology. He was a man of action, not ideas. Slim also had some rather quixotic attitudes about race and ethnic background, about genes and biological superiority, but until this time his covert prejudices had not been shaped into a virulent philosophy of hatred and bigotry. It was all there under the surface, bubbling like a vast pool of oil waiting to be pumped to the surface by an expert driller.

Sidney Latham entered Arizona Slim's life precisely when he was most vulnerable to such exploitation. The simple truth was, Arizona Slim had run out of worlds to conquer. Poker, farming, land speculation, oil, women—Slim had taken them all on and emerged victorious. No more frontiers remained for him, no more challenges except that one mysterious area in which he had battled successfully a few years before, the world of politics. And Sidney Latham was nothing if he was not a political man.

Every breath Latham took, every word he uttered, was colored with his own brand of harsh and rigid conservatism. Sidney Latham was a devout Christian fundamentalist who believed that just about everybody who lived beyond the borders of Texas was joined in a vast conspiracy to impose atheistic communism on planet Earth. The man had views on everything, and most of them had to do with the worldwide communist conspiracy. Ask him what he thought of Jews, atheists, and people half a shade darker than he was, and he would tell you in no uncertain detail.

If Latham had one abiding goal in life, aside from ridding the world of the hordes of humanity whom he regarded as communist sympathizers, it was to become governor of Texas. In Arizona Slim he saw a benefactor who had the wherewithal to finance that dream. If only he could find a way of getting through to him. Slim had the right basic instincts. Churning away inside him were the makings of a fine Christian anticommunist like himself. Latham's challenge was to find a way to bring all these rumblings to the surface, to give them shape and direction, to impose on them an ideology.

It would be a formidable task indeed, but one, Latham thought, not beyond his considerable talent for political persuasion.

# 33.

G AMBLING," SAID ARIZONA SLIM, "is unpatriotic. The government needs all our resources in the war effort, and it's not right for people to fritter away their hard-earned dollars and waste their time gambling."

He ordered his brother Sherman to have their special phone lines removed from the office in Dallas, and he put the two statisticians to work on more constructive projects like keeping tabs on his oil reserves and tax liabilities. But when during the war Arizona Slim linked gambling activity to a lack of patriotism, he was referring to the masses, employees who worked for him, underlings, hoi polloi, members of the herd. People like himself with money to burn were in a special class. Bromides did not apply to them. So, as a further contribution to America's efforts in the war, he had the ostensible trappings of his gambling interests removed from public view. The least he could do was set a good example. From now on, as long as the war was on, he would place his bets quietly through a bookie he knew, an old friend of Al Capone's, in Terre Haute, Indiana. The war demanded sacrifices from everyone.

At the same time, his next order or priority was, somehow or other, to find a way to put Hassie back together again, to straighten the boy out once and for all. His oldest son still was in command of a hard, cunning logic a good part of the time, and had an encyclopedic grasp of the facts and figures relating to their various oil ventures. These fleeting moments of sanity and genius, however, made Hassie's bouts of lunacy and rampaging violence all the more difficult for his father to accept. Visiting his son at the hospital on Lake Ponchartrain one day, Hassie suddenly looked up at his father and said, "You know, sir, that together we have more oil reserves than all the Axis nations put together."

Startled to hear a statement like this coming from Hassie at this stage of his mental deterioration, Slim studied the young man for a moment and replied, "Are you sure? How about Rumania and their big Ploesti field?"

"I'm including Rumania," Hassie said with finality. The case was closed. Hassie left no room for argument and Slim had no doubt in his mind that his son knew what he was talking about.

Counterbalanced against this display of calculating clarity was Hassie's ability to explode in terrifying rage and physical violence. Arizona Slim was more determined than ever to make his oldest son healthy again. Didn't the boy have the finest genes stamped into his character? Didn't he come from the best stock both mentally and physically? His unpredictability, his high-spiritedness, had to be caused by some sort of a temporary imbalance within Hassie's system. Perhaps it was chemical, perhaps due to improper diet. His son couldn't possibly be deranged, couldn't possibly be a crazy person. Lunacy was a sign of genetic deficiency, of biological inferiority. The boy needed a good stiff talking to by someone outside the family, or, failing that, a good shock to his system to jolt him back to solid ground again.

When a tour of various facilities in different parts of the country failed to have any effect on Hassie, Arizona Slim decided to bring him to a modern institution in Andover, Massachusetts, about fifteen miles north of Boston. This new place was experimenting with all the latest techniques to make people mentally well again, and it was said that they were getting immediate results. That's exactly what Slim was looking for, an instant cure. After all, Hassie had been acting strangely for a long time now, too long for his own good, and it was high time he straightened out. Slim was an impatient man, a man of action, and this situation had been dragging on long enough.

At the hospital in Andover, they treated Hassie with all the newest methods. They strapped him onto a table and sent electric shock currents rippling through his body. They brought him to a different room; there a doctor lifted his eyelids and stuck a metal scalpel into his brain, severing the prefrontal lobe from the rest of the organ. This was a new miracle cure called a prefrontal lobotomy, the doctors told Arizona Slim, and they were getting marvelous results with it on everyone.

When the doctors finished slicing Hassie's brain and riddling his body with electric currents, they told Slim he could bring his boy home to Dallas again; Hassie would be just fine from now on. So Slim brought his oldest boy, his namesake, home again. But Hassie was far from being all right when he went home to Dallas. The latest miracle cures certainly made the young man different from what he was before, but no one in his right mind could say that Hassie was now normal.

One of the first things Hassie did was to tie his shoes together and wear them around his neck like a scarf instead of putting them on his feet.

"They help me see more clearly this way," he said.

At dinner, he sat three feet from the table and ate his food from a tray in his lap.

"The table's charged with electricity. Don't touch it. You'll get a shock," he instructed his family.

"It must be the poisons in our food," Arizona Slim

explained to Lyda and the other children. "The Jews and the international communist conspiracy are out to destroy us without firing a bullet. They're poisoning our food and our water. It's all part of the plot."

"Perhaps you've been listening to Sidney Latham a bit too much," Lyda retorted, her way of rebuking her husband. She wasn't buying her husband's theory for a moment. But the younger boys, particularly Bunker and Herbert, listened to their father with rapt attention. Jews. Communists. Atheists. Food. Water. Out to destroy the American way through subversion. They didn't bother to ask their daddy why they all weren't as crazy as Hassie, since they all ate the same food.

Hassie did show some improvement in one area after leaving the clinic in Massachusetts. Although his general behavior was, perhaps, more bizarre than ever before, he was now less inclined to fly off into rages as long as Arizona Slim satisfied his basic appetites and as long as no one asked him a direct question. His appetite for women increased to a point where he had to have them around all the time, had to have their sexual favors on a moment's notice, whenever he felt the urge. And Hassie felt it often. When he couldn't get it when he demanded it, he was inclined to charge about his room in the huge house on White Rock Lake in luxurious East Dallas, banging his head against the wall, flinging his shoes through windows, and busting his lamps and other furniture. So Arizona Slim hired a staff of women whom he dressed up like nurses in sparkling clean, virginal white uniforms, and kept them on call around the clock. The "nurses" were just what the doctor ordered for Arizona Slim's high-spirited boy. As long as they catered to his needs, when he needed them, in his big comfortable room overlooking the great blue lake, Hassie would behave himself and leave his furniture in one piece.

The other thing that invariably triggered a temper tantrum in Hassie was requiring him to make a decision of any kind.

[219]

For example, asking him to decide how he felt on a particular day—"How are you, Hassie?"—was enough to send war clouds swirling through his severed brain. But as long as one couched the language so as not to require a direct decision—"I was wondering how Hassie felt today"—he could get along with the brooding and tormented young man perfectly well.

"It must be the food," Arizona Slim said over and over as Bunker and Herbert listened intently. "The food and the water. Must have caused a chemical imbalance in his system. None of us are safe from the communists and their sympathizers."

Slim's oldest daughter, Margaret, also listened to her father's monologues but, unlike her younger brothers, was not in the least impressed. She, more than anyone else, stood her ground against him and was not afraid to speak her mind.

"You did it to him," she said firmly. "You're the one who did it to Hassie, and it's time you faced up to it."

# 34.

H E WAS A STRANGE AND brilliant man. What great
dreams thundered in that man's skull," remarked
Arizona Slim, almost eloquently, when he learned about Doc
Lloyd's death in Chicago. After the invasion of East Texas by
a platoon of women, all claiming to be Lloyd's wives, the
blustering three-hundred-pound self-styled geologist retreated
to parts unknown. He doubtless continued seeking that ever-
elusive fortune, until he wound up in a flea-bag hotel in
Chicago ten years later. Here his enormous body resisted.
Swollen with mountains of food and oceans of whiskey, his
frame could bear up no longer. He died in 1941, flat broke, his
condition for most of his hard-driving, adventurous life. He
was almost eighty-seven years old.

Dad Joiner was also a bit shy of his eighty-seventh birthday
when he died in Dallas in 1947. He had continued his
obsessive search for another giant oil field on the scale of East
Texas right up to his last days, but without success. Although
he was not quite as destitute as his old partner, Doc Lloyd,
neither did he have a fraction of what he could have made had
he not signed away his leases to Arizona Slim that fateful day.
The old man had gotten the royalties he was entitled to,
amounting to well over a million dollars, but most of that was
used in his search for a new strike of his own in places like
Morris, Titus, and Pecos counties. His last try, in Comanche
County, finally broke him. Arizona Slim looked on as they

laid his bones to rest in Dallas, and felt the old stirrings of fondness for the old con man who had been one of his main adversaries a little more than a decade ago.

"I remember the earthy beauty of the old man's language," Slim remarked to one of his aides. "I'll miss the old devil."

World War II came to a close. As the Allied powers carved up the wreckage of Europe into jigsaw pieces which all could endure but none enjoy, life in the United States of America returned more or less to normal. Normal for Arizona Slim meant gambling activity, which he renewed on a scale truly regal, even by his lofty standards. He thought nothing of wagering hundreds of thousands of dollars on the outcome of a single baseball game. In addition to the horses, poker, and baseball games he was so fond of, he expanded his betting activities to include football and gin rummy.

Walking into his bookie's office in Miami one day after the war, he sat down in his usual chair and watched the tote board list the odds for the day's races at the track. His old acquaintances were quick to notice the seediness and eccentricity that had become an integral part of his demeanor. His blue trousers were two shades lighter than his baggy dark-blue suit jacket, which draped across his considerable girth like a rumpled old tent. The top of his head was almost barren of hair, and what remained was rapidly turning to a wispy gray. His floppy white socks hung down loosely over his ankles, and his rundown black shoes hadn't seen a coat of polish for two years. In his hand he carried a brown bag filled with nuts and various kinds of dried fruit, which he continually popped into his mouth as he studied the day's odds. Finally, his decision made, he strode over to the window and placed his bets. This was a good day, indeed, for Arizona Slim. When he left the premises later that afternoon, his bag of nuts and fruit depleted and his third cigar of the day smoked down to a gray stub, he had winnings amounting to a shade over a million dollars stuffed inside his pockets.

In 1948 Arizona Slim became a public figure for the first time in his life. Until now he had been raking in his tens of millions of dollars in relative obscurity, known to friends and acquaintances and to certain figures in government, but unknown to the public at large. He had continued his political battles behind the scenes. He supported, for instance, a bill limiting an American president to two terms in office for the simple reason that his old nemesis, Harold Ickes, opposed the measure; he thereby took his pound of revenge out of Ickes' political hide on an issue that had nothing whatever to do with their proration fight a decade earlier. Notwithstanding this and his other battles, and notwithstanding the power and influence that were his, Arizona Slim had remained a private person.

All that changed in 1948. The April issues of both *Fortune* and *Life* ran articles on America's super rich, identifying one "Haralson" (the misspelling was theirs) Lafayette Hunt as the richest man in the country. Using figures supplied by an associate of Sidney Latham's, the magazines estimated Slim's income to be $1 million a week and his total assets to be around $263 million. Like everything else about Sidney Latham, these figures were, if anything, a shade on the conservative side. To determine the exact extent of Arizona Slim's fortunes would have required a regiment of accountants and statisticians since his vast empire included, in addition to some of the largest oil reserves in the world, vast tracts of land in Texas, Louisiana, Arkansas, Florida, Mississippi, Montana, Wyoming, North Dakota, and probably a few other states Slim had forgotten about.

[223]

At any rate, the publicity served to force Arizona Slim out of his private kingdom and into the pedestrian world at large. He basked easily in the spotlight, somewhat flattered by all the unexpected attention he was receiving, and he gave the first interview of his life to Frank Tolbert of the *Dallas Morning News.* Slim had been tutored well by Latham for the occasion, and he used the forum of a public interview to expound the ideas that had been forming in his head during the war years.

"I've always attempted to maintain a nonalcoholic and noncommunistic organization," said Arizona Slim. He did not mention the international Jewish banking conspiracy as being primarily responsible for softening America's brains with alcohol to make the job of conquest easier for the communists, but such views were already being disseminated by Latham in several right-wing journals he controlled.

When asked directly by Tolbert about his political inclinations, Slim allowed that "General Douglas MacArthur is my first choice for president."

On the subject of money, Arizona Slim remarked ingenuously that money was never all that important to him; taking the gamble was his big motivation, and he coined a folksy aphorism that was to become something of a trademark as the years rolled by: "Money as money is nothing. It's just something to make bookkeeping convenient."

After the interview with Tolbert, he elaborated on this theme a bit more: "Anyone who has $200,000 can live as well as I do. The total amount of my money is not all that important."

More and more, money and politics were becoming intertwined in Slim's life. With Sidney Latham's blessing, he decided to put his newfound fame to use by going public, giving talks to civic and business clubs around the country.

"I never spoke publicly before," he said, "because I did not know how and I was afraid to try to speak. But I think we're so far gone that everyone is going to have to do everything he can to dispel the people's apathy. I think we are being taken over by the communists."

In his own mind, patriotism and profits had become synonymous. "Everything I do, I do for profit," said Arizona Slim. "Patriotism and free enterprise are one and the same thing."

As he spread his message at banquets and conventions from one end of the country to the other, his political adversaries, those whom he was denouncing publicly as Reds and communist sympathizers and subversives, observed him with growing alarm.

"If he had more flair and imagination," said one newspaper editor who had known him for years, "if he weren't basically such a damned hick, Hunt could be one of the most dangerous men in America."

His obsession with food also became increasingly mixed up with his politics, convinced as he was that Jews and communists were out to poison our food and water, as well as soften the brains of American youth with alcohol. Walter Lechner, one of the early pioneers of the East Texas oil field back in the early 1930s, lunched with Slim in his office after the war and received the shock of his life. He had known Arizona Slim as a hard-living, hard-driving roustabout with unlimited appetites. Lechner himself was used to dining sumptuously, knocking back a shot or two of good sour-mash whiskey before diving into a feast of prime ribs of beef running freely with blood.

When he and a mutual friend walked into Slim's office in Dallas they were greeted, not by the strapping, handsome, dapper man they had known fifteen years before, but by a rotund, disheveled eccentric in an ill-matching, badly fitting suit who looked like anything but a multimillionaire Texas oilman. Slim greeted his guests warmly, and proceeded to seat them around his desk as he heated some broth on a hotplate in the corner. He spread their lunch out on paper plates: dried figs, raw carrots and sliced onions, almonds and pecans, and peanut butter spread on whole wheat bread and dark crackers. Alongside their plates stood paper cups filled with freshly squeezed apple juice.

"These vegetables are all mine," said Arizona Slim. "I grew them myself on my farm in Dallas. Nothing but natural whole food. No poisons or other subversive ingredients to worry about."

The three men reminisced about the old days in East Texas, before any of them drilled into the rich Woodbine sand and became millionaires. After chatting for a good part of the afternoon, the two guests shook Arizona Slim's hand and got up to take their leave.

Outside Slim's office, Lechner's friend started to laugh and asked him, "Well, how did you like the food today?"

Lechner stared at his friend in surprise, speechless for a long moment, and then broke into a roaring laugh of his own.

"Hell," he bellowed, "it's a diet I ought to have been on myself for twenty years!"

But some things did not change. Slim was still determined to make his musical come true, and he continued his relationship with Ruth Ray, with whom he lived from time to time in her Shreveport apartment. In 1949 she presented him with their third child, a beautiful apple dumpling of a baby girl whom they named Helen, and one year later she delivered another girl, named Swanee. Fifteen children Arizona Slim had fathered, fourteen had survived.

Ruth Ray remained the great love of his life, the one woman whom he revered more than any other on earth. Since Ruth knew about Lyda and his other children, she did not make demands on him the way Frania had, nagging him incessantly about more attention. Slim visited Ruth as often as he could. Indeed, he wanted to be with her as much as possible, and she was happy and content with the affection he showed her.

The situation was not nearly so idyllic on the homestead in Dallas, however. His frustration over Hassie grew worse when it became obvious that his "strangeness" would not go away, and he turned to his second-oldest son, Bunker, as a potential replacement. But Bunker simply was not a suitable substitute in Slim's eyes. For one thing, the young man was rather chubby and nearsighted, and did not look at all like his father and older brother. Worse than his physical drawbacks, however, was the fact that his number-two son was a bit plodding and dimwitted by Slim's standards. As loony as Hassie was, he at least had a sharp and quick native intelligence and an uncanny ability to locate oil. Bunker seemed slow and witless, and Arizona Slim made no bones about telling him so in plain language.

"Stupid, boy. That's what you are, stupid. It's the only word for you. I can't believe you've got my genes in you."

During his first years working full-time for the Hunt Oil Company, Bunker did nothing to disprove his father's assessment of him. After he used up $11 million of his own trust money to drill one dry hole after another, Arizona Slim came storming into the office one day, screaming at the top of his lungs, "The boy's an idiot. I can find more oil with a road map than he can with a whole platoon of geologists. His brother Hassie's a towering genius compared to him."

And $250 million later, with the assets in his trust fund all but wiped out, Bunker had yet to strike a drop of oil. Humbly, his pride swallowed up inside him like a great dry lump, he had to suffer the further humiliation of asking his father for a loan to keep on trying. Later he would finally succeed, in Libya, as it turned out, but not before he heard Arizona Slim scream at him on numerous occasions, "Get out of my sight, you dimwit. Your younger brothers have more sense in their feet than you have in your whole body. Herbert and Lamar are my true sons. You're not fit to be my heir."

Bunker had no choice but to suffer it all in silence. One day he would prove his father wrong and go on to surpass all his brothers, but that day was well off in the future.

# 35.

**K**ARL MARX WAS A JEW," said Dr. Frederick C. Schwarz from the podium at an anticommunist rally in Dallas. "Like most Jews, he was short and ugly, lazy and slovenly, and he had no desire to go out and work for a living. But he was also possessed of a keen intelligence, a superior evil intelligence like most Jews are, and his mission was to destroy all of Christian civilization by whatever evolutionary means he could employ."

Fred Schwarz's Christian Anti-Communist Crusade was only one of the extreme right-wing propaganda groups Sidney Latham sponsored as the decade drew to a close. Others were sprouting throughout the country, all of them echoing more or less the same general theme. The anticommunist fervor sweeping the nation was institutionalized officially as an agency of the federal government in the form of the House Committee on Un-American Activities, and Richard Arens, who served on its staff, was hired by Sidney Latham as a special adviser to Arizona Slim.

The most influential figure to be introduced to Slim by Sidney Latham at this time, however, was a former FBI man named Dan Smoot. Smoot was a tall, powerfully built, ruggedly handsome man who had managed to avoid fighting in World War II because of colorblindness and fallen arches. But these defects were not sufficient to keep Smoot from

[229]

defending America from communism as an agent in the subversive activities squad of the FBI.

Smoot developed his philosophy early in life. "The communists, the socialists, and the liberals are burrowing in, softening up the United States for the final Red takeover," he said. "As philosophies of government, modern liberalism, communism, and fascism are all essentially the same."

Smoot set himself up as a self-styled expert on communist infiltration. Because of his former role as a "spy" for the FBI, as well as his dynamic presence on the speaker's platform, he was extremely successful in attracting a growing army of followers and financial contributors to his cause.

When Smoot resigned from the FBI in June 1951, after nine years of service, Latham invited him to visit Dallas and meet Arizona Slim. At their meeting, Dan Smoot shook Slim's hand firmly and said in his evangelical, fire-breathing style, "I wondered, when I was a member of the FBI commie squad, why those who oppose communism were vilified and slandered. I learned the reason. It was because people were blindly following the philosophy of the New Deal, which stands for the total transfer of power from the individual to the federal government under the claim of using the power beneficently. The philosophy of the New Deal is also the basic philosophy of communism, fascism, and Nazism."

After their meeting, Arizona Slim remarked to Latham, "I like the man's style. He's forceful and dynamic. And he's telling the truth."

Slim agreed to put up the money to create an organization named Facts Forum, which was a network of radio and TV programs, a monthly magazine called *Facts Forum News*, and a publishing division to distribute anticommunist pamphlets and the works of well-known patriots like Senator Joseph McCarthy. Dan Smoot was hired as the commentator for the weekly half-hour broadcasts, which were aired over three hundred fifty radio stations and eighty television stations across the country. Smoot was also named editor of the magazine and publishing division.

Almost immediately, Smoot clashed with his new boss over a sensitive political issue. Smoot, with all his inflammatory political rhetoric, believed ardently in the cause of democracy.

"Democracy," said Smoot on one of his broadcasts, "is a political outgrowth of the teachings of Jesus Christ. Christianity is essential to the creation of our democracy. We in Facts Forum know that American democracy is still the most nearly perfect expression ever made by man in legal and political terms of a basic ideal of Christianity."

When Slim heard this broadcast he was outraged. Through Latham he instructed Smoot that democracy was the handiwork of the devil himself, and was just a phony liberal form of watered-down communism. "In an ideal society," said Arizona Slim, "the more taxes you pay, the more votes you get. If you accept government help because you are poor or sick, you cannot vote at all, and you are denied an old-age pension."

Dan Smoot was not a stupid man. He knew who was supplying the butter for his toast, and was quick to recognize the error of his ways. Shortly after this encounter, he went back on the air again and proclaimed, "One of the best indications of how far we in the United States have slipped is the wide contemporary use by practically all our intellectual and political leaders of the word 'democracy' to designate our system. The Founding Fathers knew, and Jefferson said in specific terms, that a democracy is the most evil kind of government possible."

A bit later, he elaborated on the theme. "Democracy always degenerates into tyranny. The majority is not blessed with morality or wisdom. The Founding Fathers knew this. They knew that a dictatorship of the majority is not constitutional government."

[231]

Arizona Slim didn't mind paying others to disseminate his message for him, but as long as he was paying the bills, he was going to be damned sure they got the message right.

When the workload increased to a point where Smoot could no longer handle it all himself, he hired a zealous young right-wing speechwriter named Karl Hess to help him edit the magazine. Hess, not yet thirty, was a burly man with wavy black hair who would rather be fishing when he was not pounding the typewriter to help further the anticommunist cause. Later on he would surface as one of Barry Goldwater's chief speechwriters, and later still, he would shock the entire conservative world with his announcement that he could no longer support the war in Vietnam and was joining the New Left anarchist revolution. In 1950, however, he was a dedicated and unsmiling anticommunist with a typewriter for hire.

Arizona Slim took an immediate liking to his new employee and invited Hess to spend a few days with him in Dallas so they could get to know each other a little better. As the two men were chatting in Slim's office on the corner of the seventh floor of the Mercantile Bank Building, Slim summoned a member of his staff and instructed him to go out and buy him a new car. The aide returned a short time later and announced that he had purchased a brand-new Cadillac, which was waiting for him downstairs.

Slim drove Hess around the city, pointing out various sights as the two of them discussed politics for the rest of the afternoon. The next morning Arizona Slim returned to his office and called for the assistant who had bought the car the day before.

"I don't like that big car you bought me," he scolded him.

"Go out and buy me a smaller one. What kind of a car do you drive?" he suddenly asked Hess.

"Why, uh, a Chevrolet, sir. A small Chevrolet," answered Hess.

"That's good enough for me then. Go out and buy me a Chevrolet."

"Yes, sir," the aide trembled, nearly scraping the floor beneath him. "Just tell me where you parked the Cadillac and I'll take it back and bring you a Chevrolet."

"Parked the Cadillac?" said Arizona Slim. "Why, I honestly don't remember. Never mind the Cadillac. Just go out and buy me a Chevrolet."

Later that day, touring the oil fields with Hess in his new Chevrolet, Slim stopped at a well about an hour's drive from Dallas. Slim had made an appointment to meet one of his geologists at the site, but the geologist arrived late and kept Slim waiting. When the geologist drove up nearly half an hour later in his brand-new Cadillac, Arizona Slim was fuming visibly. Before the man could utter a word of excuse for his late arrival, Slim walked over to the car and asked him loudly, "What kind of a car is that you're driving?"

"Why, it's a Cadillac, sir."

"You're obviously suffering from some sort of a character deficiency," said Arizona Slim. "I want you off this job at once. You're fired."

Arizona Slim told Karl Hess about the visionary plan he had to subdivide some of his real estate into five-hundred-acre farms and put some of the country's unemployed youth to work on them.

"I'll build barracks on the farms and train the kids to farm the land. It'll be my own private Civilian Conservation Corps. The healthiest thinking today is done on medium-sized farms all around the country. I've already told Sidney Latham to draw up the plans for it. Why, we'll grow natural food without any poisons in it. We'll create a regular army of anti-communist farmers who'll grow up to be decent patriotic Americans."

The idea never did fructify, however. It sounded a trifle bizarre even for Sidney Latham's impassioned tastes, and Slim's daughter Margaret dismissed the option contemptuously when she learned of it.

"What difference will it make," she said, "what kind of good healthy food you grow, if those nasty communists take over and eat it all?"

It was inevitable that two men as opinionated and individualistic as Slim and Hess would eventually lock horns. When they did, it was over something as trivial as the proper label to put on their mutually shared political philosophy.

"The magazine will do more to further the conservative cause than any other forum in the country," Hess said to Slim one day.

The older man stopped dead in his tracks and glared at his young protégé.

"Don't call me conservative, boy," Slim said, biting off each word as though he were speaking to a child. "There's not a conservative bone in my whole body. *Constructive* is what I am. I believe in action and I like positive, constructive action embodying the best independent and middle-class values. Conservative is just the opposite of what I am."

But Hess insisted on using the word *conservative* in his writings for the magazine, so Slim decided to get even with the strong-headed young upstart in one of the most constructive ways he could think of. When introducing Hess to a group of his associates on several occasions, Slim said, "I'd like you to meet a young colleague of mine, a prominent anti-Semite from New York, Karl Hess."

"I think you got it wrong," Hess corrected his boss in

private later on. "I think you meant to say anticommunist, not anti-Semite, when you introduced me."

Slim roared with laughter, clapped Hess on the back, and said, "Did I make that slip of the tongue again? Why, everybody knows you're not an anti-Semite, boy. To prove it we're going to have a party for that anticommunist rabbi from Maryland and I'm going to let you be master of ceremonies."

And so he sponsored a huge dinner for the anticommunist rabbi from the east. And while the young Karl Hess held sway at the rostrum, Arizona Slim leaned back in his chair, puffed on his long green cigar, and quaked silently with laughter.

Finally their disagreements went beyond the joking stage. Hess refused to knuckle under, and his insubordination destroyed what was left of Slim's patience with him.

"Stop arguing with me, boy!" Slim screamed at him one day. "I'm richer than you are and therefore smarter. So be quiet and listen to your betters for a change!"

At this point in their relationship, Hess had no choice but to pack up his belongings and take his leave.

"It's a bit disconcerting," Hess said in parting, "to work for a man who reminds you, as a conclusive end to any argument, that he is rich and therefore right. It's a pity. I think you have it in you to be something more than just another anti-communist."

Devin Garrity, who would later establish a right-wing publishing house named Devin-Adair, was another fellow traveler on the right who went to work for Arizona Slim at the time. Garrity selected books for publication under the Facts Forum umbrella, and was invited to join Slim on a plane flight from Dallas to New York in 1951. Garrity was assigned the task of calling ahead to make sure Slim's favorite suite would be vacant for his arrival that evening, but it so happened that the Waldorf-Astoria had booked the king and queen of Greece into the suite on the same day.

Recognizing the pecking order of influence regarding European and American-style aristocracy, the Waldorf management decided to find the king and queen suitable accommodations in another suite. Their departure from the rooms was so hasty that, when Arizona Slim and his entourage arrived shortly afterward, a bouquet of flowers belonging to the royal couple was still there. Taking obvious delight in his power to displace foreign royalty, Slim looked at the flowers and then winked at Devin Garrity and said, "Wasn't that nice of the king and queen to leave their flowers for us?"

# 36.

**L**OOK HERE, HAROLDSON," said Jake Hamon, a Dallas oilman and the only living person who addressed Slim by his proper name, "this isn't right. I'm going to drill this well and I want $2,500 dry-hole money."

Hamon owned 2,500 acres of land in Louisiana alongside a spread of land owned by Slim. Hamon wanted to drill a well on a site bridging their properties and expected Slim to contribute $2,500 to the drilling costs in the event the well should come up dry. When Slim had failed to deliver the money, Hamon barged into his office and demanded payment. Slim stared at Hamon, whom he had known for years, then said slowly, "I saw you playing gin rummy at the club the other day with Ed Landreth, and you were playing for a dollar a point."

Startled by this unexpected turn in the conversation, Hamon stammered, "Why, yes, I didn't want to, and I just played him one game. I normally play for a penny a point, maybe a nickel."

"Well," said Slim, "you got to play me a couple of games of gin at a dollar a point."

Jake Hamon had seen Arizona Slim in action at the poker table on a number of occasions and was not eager to tangle with him on that level. Still, gin rummy was a relatively new game for Slim, one which he was trying his best to master as well as he had poker. Besides, Hamon was trapped. He was an oilman, a risk-taker. If he refused to gamble with Slim, Slim would give him his money contemptuously and tell everyone he knew what a yellow-belly Hamon was. It was a question of honor.

Arizona Slim broke out a deck of cards and the two men played for a dollar a point right there at Slim's desk. Slim took him quickly for $800 in the first game, and then they played a second.

"I meld," said Hamon when it was apparent he had lost the second game as well. He turned his discard face down and Slim reached over and put his hand on Hamon's cards.

"Don't show me your hand and I'll tell you what you got," said Slim. He then proceeded to name every card in Hamon's hand as his friend looked on in horror.

"Damn you, Haroldson. You're inhuman!" Hamon turned visibly red. When they added up the points, Slim had won $1,100 more, for a total of $1,900.

Slim settled back in his chair and chuckled to himself. "How much did I owe you when you came in here?" he asked.

"Twenty-five hundred dollars," said Hamon miserably.

Arizona Slim reached into his side pocket, pulled out a wad of bills, and pushed $600 across the desk toward Hamon.

"Here's the rest then," said Slim.

The two men stared at each other in silence for the better part of a minute, then simultaneously broke into peals of laughter. When he left Slim's office later that afternoon, Jake Hamon felt as though he had just been dealing with the devil himself.


"General Douglas MacArthur is my number-one choice for president of the United States," said Arizona Slim as he dealt the cards to himself and Senator McCarthy. It was April

1952 and the two men were playing a round of gin rummy in Joseph McCarthy's hotel suite in Dallas.

"Do you honestly think he's got a chance of getting the nomination?" asked McCarthy.

"I've never contributed anything to a candidate unless I thought he had an awfully good chance of winning," Slim replied.

The senator had taken off his suit jacket and tie, and was sitting across from Slim in shirtsleeves as he studied his hand. Arizona Slim was dressed in his usual attire—an ill-matching baggy blue suit and white socks—and was puffing on the ever-present cigar. Since the senator was also a heavy smoker, thick tendrils of blue-gray smoke coiled throughout the room.

"I'm getting up a meeting at the Waldorf in a couple of weeks with MacArthur, Lucius Clay, Herbert Hoover, and Ike. The idea is to get Ike to back out and throw his support to the good general," said Slim.

"I'd like to see you pull it off more than anything else in the world," said McCarthy.

"If Ike backs out it's in the bag. MacArthur's going to be the next president of this country, you wait and see."

When the photographers arrived for a picture-taking session a short while later, they found the two men locked in an earnest game of gin. McCarthy got up to knot his tie and put on his jacket, and then he and Arizona Slim were all smiles as the cameras clicked away at Slim pinning a button on Joe McCarthy's lapel. The button read: GENERAL DOUGLAS MACARTHUR FOR PRESIDENT.

When Arizona Slim arrived at his favorite suite in the Waldorf-Astoria in May 1952, his guests had already arrived. It was a bright and sunny day, and the traffic on Park Avenue in front of the hotel was bumper to bumper from the ramp at Grand Central all the way up to 59th Street, where it suddenly thinned out. The Republican party's convention was due to be held in Chicago just a couple of months later, and there was little time to waste.

Slim shook hands warmly with Generals Dwight D. Eisenhower, Douglas MacArthur, and Lucius Clay, all of whom were dressed in civilian clothes, and Herbert Hoover, former president of the United States. Of all the men present at the meeting, Slim felt an almost spiritual affinity with MacArthur. Aside from the fact that the general's politics were most closely aligned with his own, there was about MacArthur a man-of-destiny quality, a quality Slim felt belonged to himself as well. They were both men of destiny, Slim thought, special human beings placed on the good earth to fulfill a holy mission. MacArthur had led American men in battle and captured the imagination of the entire world, and Slim had risen from poverty to riches and supplied a lion's share of the energy that was needed to destroy the nation's enemies.

Of course, General Dwight David Eisenhower had played no small role in bringing the Nazis to heel, but he lacked the dramatic flair, the chosen-man-of-the-hour flamboyance that MacArthur had. Besides, Ike was too pedestrian, too plebeian, and too boring when you got right down to it. His mind was as uncomplicated as a bright red apple, which he resembled somewhat with that bulbous bald head of his. He exuded an essence of moderation and compromise, which Slim found repugnant. No, Ike was clearly not the man to lead America during this crucial hour of its life-and-death struggle against international communism.

With Herbert Hoover, a pliant and affable man who was so much like Ike in many ways, playing the role of mediator, Arizona Slim and Lucius Clay put their case before Eisenhower.

Douglas MacArthur would be the candidate, they argued, with the best chance of beating the Democrats in the fall. While he, Eisenhower, was a beloved and popular war hero, Douglas MacArthur had captured the public imagination like no one else with the possible exception of George Patton. He, Ike, was young and could afford to sit back, lend his support to MacArthur, and succeed MacArthur four or eight years later. Between the two of them, they could ensure a Republican reign for the next sixteen years. MacArthur's age would soon be working against him; he was seventy-two years of age, ten years older than Eisenhower, and this would be his last chance for the presidency.

Eisenhower sat back and listened to it all in silence. Buried deep inside him, hidden beneath the jovial, easygoing, somewhat slow-witted exterior, was a fighting man with a will of iron. People seemed to forget just how stubborn and strong-willed he had been throughout his career as a military officer. The press liked to portray him as a lovable fuddy-duddy, a benevolent fumbler, everybody's favorite uncle, not too bright, someone you could count on not to do anything rash or stupid in a crisis. Hadn't he been living in the shadows of more flamboyant men like MacArthur and Patton all his life? The public loved military men who swaggered and cursed, who gave them something to cheer about and someone to idolize in time of war, great actors as well as military tacticians who commanded the international stage for a brief glorious moment in history. Such men, however, do not necessarily make good civilian leaders in times of peace. Such men, with their ravening egos and craving for action, could be downright dangerous when the world gets too boring for their tastes.

Yes, General Dwight D. Eisenhower had been living in the shadows of men like MacArthur all his life, and here was his chance to emerge from those shadows and become just the man the people needed and wanted in the aftermath of the war. He did not entertain the notion of revenge; it was too petty for such an occasion. But there was an element of sweetness to the fact that he now had a chance, at last, to deny the biggest prize of all to his old nemesis, and, maybe, just maybe, snatch it for himself. All these years he had kept his own counsel, bided his time, waiting in the shadows, keeping the peace as was his custom, and now his moment had come. No, he was not going to abandon it without a fight. If they were going to take it from him, they would have to do it without his help.

At the end of the meeting, Ike smiled broadly, warmly, shook hands all around, and thanked them for sharing their ideas. He promised them nothing and did not give them what they were looking for. Arizona Slim knew he had a fight on his hands.

# 37.

IT WAS A HOT, HUMID day in July when the train left the station in Dallas bound for the Republican convention in Chicago. On the train with Slim were Jake Hamon, his oilman friend whom he had bested a short while back in gin rummy, and other members of the American Petroleum Institute, also headed for the convention in Chicago. The men lit up their cigars and cigarettes and got up a game of poker as the train rolled northward across the sprawling country. Slim sat back, chomping on a cigar of his own, chuckling to himself as he observed his colleagues playing cards. After a couple of hours had gone by, one of the players started badgering Slim to get into the game.

"You don't know what you're asking for," said Jake Hamon, who was prepared to fold for good if Arizona Slim joined the game. "Haroldson over here can play rings around all of us."

"I hear he's lost his touch," the other man baited. "I hear he hasn't played in years because he got a little rusty."

"You all play like babies," said Arizona Slim. "I know too much to play with you. I know how cards run. I remember cards."

"Come on, Hunt. Get in the game," some of the others said, feeling courageous after nipping on bourbon for the past two hours. After a little more of this, Slim grew visibly annoyed and started to relent.

"Well, all right," he said. "But remember. When you play with me, you play for keeps."

Arizona Slim started to win big right from the start. He played forcefully, unsmilingly, with a single-mindedness he hadn't shown in years. The money meant nothing to a man who bet $300,000 on a single baseball game. His ego and reputation were at stake in this game, and that meant more to him than anything else. He had been goaded, and once he decided to take the bait, teaching these men a good lesson was more important to him than taking their money. By the time the train had sped halfway across the width of the country, the oilmen were wishing that Chicago was only minutes away instead of another few hours distant. Jake Hamon sat back and enjoyed the spectacle; he had dropped out the minute Slim entered the game, not caring what kind of a yellow-belly the others thought him.

Hours later the train chugged into the Chicago station. Slim had drained his fellow players of all their available cash, and the man who had started badgering him to get into the game in the first place, presented Slim with his check for $24,000 to cover the balance of his debt. The men had managed to put away several gallons of bourbon on their journey, but every last one of them was cold sober by the time the train arrived.

At the Republican convention in Chicago, there were two delegations from Texas, one of them pledged to General Dwight D. Eisenhower and the other to Senator Robert Taft of Ohio. Arizona Slim had positioned himself so that he was a delegate on both slates. His primary goal, of course, was to deny the candidacy to both men and secure it for Douglas MacArthur.

At two o'clock in the morning of the day the first ballot was to be taken, Slim was on the phone with Senator Taft to discuss strategy.

"It appears, senator," said Slim, "that the trend is going away from you toward Eisenhower."

"I'm afraid you're right, sir. My people are telling me the same thing."

"The question is, do you want to see Dwight Eisenhower become the next president of the United States?"

"I'm prepared to lend my support to Douglas MacArthur under certain conditions. I suggest we have our staffs get together to discuss this further at eight o'clock."

Barely able to conceal his delight in his new role of kingmaker, Slim called his MacArthur for President Committee to action. "Get ready," he instructed his troops, "for an eight o'clock meeting with the senator. I think we're going to make us a deal."

At six o'clock in the morning, two hours before the scheduled meeting, the phone rang once again in Slim's suite. The caller was a top aide to Senator Taft.

"The senator has decided," said he, "to wait until after the first ballot before taking any action."

But, but, but, protested Arizona Slim. No, sorry, the senator could not be disturbed now. He had a busy night and would be unavailable until after the first ballot.

It was with a sense of great foreboding that Arizona Slim entered the convention hall that evening. Taft would not even get on the telephone with him throughout the entire day. Slim was convinced, crafty negotiator that he had been all his life, that the Eisenhower people had gotten to him, and that Taft had worked a deal with Ike instead of him. Slim felt it in his bones.

And so it came to pass that General Dwight David Eisenhower became the Republican presidential candidate in 1952, and went on to win the election in November against the

Democratic nominee, Adlai Stevenson. When "Mr. Republican," Senator Robert Taft, became a close, influential adviser to President Eisenhower during the first few months of the new administration, Slim was convinced that he had been right.

"I came within two hours of making MacArthur president," Slim lamented to his associates for years afterward. It was his first major defeat since he had achieved his big success in life. It was a bitter pill for him to swallow. "Just two hours," he said over and over. Just two hours away from changing the course of history.

# 38.

EVERY GENERATION SEEMS TO produce its own fabulous figure in lofty gambling," Damon Runyon had written in one of his columns. "As Nick the Greek has been used to connote high rolling for years and before him Pittsburgh Phil Smith, now it is Ray Ryan. He plays the highest gin rummy of any man since the game was invented."

Arizona Slim had played poker against Nick the Greek in New Orleans and had beaten him, and he knew Ray Ryan from years of kicking around the oil fields. He had never gambled against Ryan since gin was not his game, but as Ryan received more and more publicity as one of the great gamblers of the time, Slim's ego was piqued. If he had beaten Nick the Greek, who was supposed to be the best a generation earlier, he was sure he could beat this Ryan fellow as well at his own game. After all, Arizona Slim was the best all-round gambler there ever was, even if Damon Runyon had never picked up on the fact.

Ray Ryan was a tall, handsome man with straight dark hair combed back flat on his head. He was irrepressible and enthusiastic, whether flat broke or flush with cash, whether hustling for an oil lease in Texas or planning to decimate someone's bank account in a game of gin rummy. He was quick to flash his movie-star smile, quick to charm his adversaries, quick to insinuate himself into the confidence of a skeptic. In short, he was a consummate con man.

When Arizona Slim thought he had learned the game of gin rummy as well as any other man alive, he called up Ray Ryan and challenged him to a game. Ryan was busy at the time, winning money left and right in the midst of a hot streak, and was reluctant to break his stride to satisfy Slim's ego. The rejection infuriated Slim. He was a man who had come within two hours of altering the course of history, and was not accustomed to being dismissed in such an offhand fashion. Through a mutual friend, Slim learned that Ryan had booked passage on a luxury liner that was to cross the Atlantic. Slim bought a ticket on the same ship, and once aboard, he cornered Ryan and renewed his earlier challenge.

"I took this trip to relax," said Ryan, "not to work. Why don't we save it till I get back?"

"I'll make it worth your while," said Slim. "Just name the stakes."

Hoping to get rid of him once and for all, Ryan named an outrageous figure, one that would have moved any normal human being to flee for cover.

"If you want to play me," said Ryan, "you got to play me for ten dollars a point."

With stakes like that, $30,000 could change hands in a single game. Slim didn't hesitate for a moment. "Let's play," he said. He had come aboard to beat a legend at his own game.

The week-long crossing was a marathon, around-the-clock gin rummy game between Arizona Slim and Ray Ryan. Slim quickly discovered that, with all his countdown and memory powers, he still had much to learn about the game of gin rummy. He learned a lesson that week—poker was different from gin, and success at one does not guarantee success at the other. It was a costly lesson indeed. When the two men stepped ashore on the coast of England, Ray Ryan was $243,000 richer. Ryan had won not only much of Slim's money, but his respect as well. Arizona Slim admired and respected a man who could beat him at anything.

"I'd like you to meet Jimmy Snyder, otherwise known as Jimmy the Greek," Ray Ryan said to Arizona Slim.

Slim picked up the receiver and said hello to Jimmy the Greek, who was in his room at the Savoy Plaza in New York City. The two men chatted amiably, taking each other's measure over the long-distance wire. In the course of their conversation, Slim mentioned casually that he had just quit smoking since he had figured out that peeling the wrappers off his cigars had cost him $380,000 over the years; that's how valuable his time was. He also reflected on how he had gotten his first stake in the oil business, winning a man's leases with three queens over two pair.

The two men agreed to bet $50,000 a game on Saturday afternoon football games. On Saturday mornings they would call a bookie joint in Chicago to get the line for the day, then would each select three teams, giving or taking points according to the official spread. Unknown to Arizona Slim, Ray Ryan had gotten chummy with a secretary in Slim's office who informed him that her boss had a habit of jotting down his selections for the week on a notepad on his desk. The girl agreed to tell Ryan what the choices were, then Jimmy the Greek would place a heavy side bet on Slim's selections to narrow the odds at the bookmaker.

As the weeks rolled by and Slim's losses to Jimmy the Greek began to mount, he called his opponent up one day and said, "Young man, I think we should delete the Southeastern Conference. My area of expertise is the Southwest Conference and you have the advantage over me."

"Well, sir," said Jimmy the Greek, after thinking it over

for a moment, "that's your prerogative. But if we delete the Southeastern Conference, I think we should delete another conference of my choice."

"That would be fair," said Slim.

"All right, then. We'll delete the Southwest Conference."

Slim was quiet for a moment as he thought over the deal. SMU, his favorite team, was in the Southwest Conference. He would never be able to bet on SMU again.

"No, young man. We'll let it go as it is," he said.

By the time the Kefauver hearings, which were called to investigate the role of organized crime in gambling, got under way, Jimmy the Greek and his pal Ray Ryan had taken Arizona Slim for the grand sum of $600,000 in their weekly football bets. Slim couldn't figure out exactly why they had been so lucky while his track record was so dismal, but he was sure they had a con going on between them. They curtailed their activity during the hearings, but Slim had to have some kind of action somewhere, so he contacted a bookie he knew in Chicago named Johnny Drew, who was connected to the Al Capone gang. Drew, once fined for running a crooked craps game at an Elks convention, controlled most of the gambling activity in Chicago and Las Vegas.

Slim suddenly hit a hot streak while placing bets through Drew, and ran his winnings up close to $1 million. When he tried to collect, however, Drew told him to take a walk. Since Drew was under investigation at the time, there was little Slim could do to make him pay up. His biggest worry was that his own name might turn up if the authorities seized Drew's records.

With all this going on, Slim's phone rang in his Dallas office one morning. Jimmy the Greek was on the line. "You still owe me seventy grand from those last games we bet on," said the Greek.

Arizona Slim, still fuming about being stiffed by Johnny

Drew, and still vaguely suspicious that Jimmy the Greek and Ryan had somehow rigged the odds against him in their weekly bets, saw a chance to get a measure of revenge.

"Why don't you get the money from Johnny Drew," said Slim. "He still owes me."

"H. L., you know Johnny isn't going to pay me," pleaded Jimmy the Greek.

"Well, Jimmy, you know I've always fulfilled my obligations. But I got screwed by Drew and I'm not going to pay."

"In a way I can't blame you. But it really isn't fair to put your problems on me. If someone didn't pay me, and I laid off some of your bets, I'd still be responsible to you."

"I'll think about it," said Arizona Slim.

"I wouldn't ask if I didn't need it," Jimmy the Greek said, trying to play on the older man's sympathy.

"I realize that," said Slim.

When he put the receiver onto its cradle, Jimmy the Greek knew that he had gotten the last nickel he would ever see from Arizona Slim. The oilman's voice was cold as ice; his mind was made up. Slim couldn't do anything about Johnny Drew, but he was determined to take a pound of revenge out of the hide of Jimmy the Greek.

# 39.

DESPITE HIS EXPANSION INTO the world of far-right politics, and the time he spent on his oil business and gambling activities, the prime concern of Slim's life remained his firstborn son, Hassie.

Nothing seemed to work. Shock treatments, prefrontal lobotomies, psychiatric counseling, special round-the-clock "nurses" to cater to Hassie's considerable appetites—all had failed to restore his son. Still, Arizona Slim refused to accept defeat. There simply had to be a solution to Hassie's problems. There was no good reason why his son should not function like a normal human being. He came from the finest stock; was composed of the best genes. Something had gotten scrambled somewhere, some chemical foulup, perhaps, or some dietary disorder. Slim was determined to get to the bottom of it once and for all.

He contacted Jeane Dixon, the astrologer and prophet, whose politics were as conservative as his own. Dixon flew to Dallas at Slim's request and stayed in his Mount Vernon home. Here she talked to Hassie and observed him up close. The key to Hassie's mind, Slim was convinced, lay in his almost supernatural ability to locate oil. This talent was a special gift, a divine riddle thought Slim, and whoever could understand it fully would uncover the final solution to Hassie's strangeness. If Jeane Dixon succeeded, said Arizona

Slim, he was prepared to make a considerable cash donation to the children's charity the prophet had organized.

After several meetings with Hassie, however, Jeane Dixon was no closer to resolving his inner turmoil than any of the other therapists before her. Arizona Slim was devastated. Jeane Dixon was his final ace; he had a gut feeling that she was the one who would finally get through to Hassie; if she couldn't, no one could. And now she too had failed. What was he to do? Was Hassie irrevocably lost? There had to be a way.

The answer was in the genes. Somehow or other they had gotten scrambled inside Hassie. No other explanation was possible. Slim didn't entertain for a moment the notion, indeed, was incapable of accepting it, that he may have caused the boy some psychological damage in his youth with his chronic absences from home and his treatment of his son. No, the answer was genetic. The genes were the best and it was simply a question of sorting them out and putting them in the right order.

If this couldn't be done with the present Hassie, why then he would create a new, a perfect Hassie to take his place. Not just another son; he already had enough of those, ranging from the bumbling Bunker to his sharper, more dependable brothers, Herbert and Lamar. It was not another son he needed, but, rather, a replica of himself, as Hassie was, with all the genes straightened out inside. The word *clone* was not in use yet, but that's exactly what Arizona Slim was looking for, a clone to replace the imperfect model he had brought into the world.

And what better place to find the ideal conduit for his genes, the perfect host mother to deliver a miniature version of himself, than Germany, which had experimented the most with creating perfect human beings? Not that there was anything wrong with Ruth Ray. He still worshipped his apple-dumpling pinup queen, the star of his musicals, but she had already given him a son, Ray, who was a fine, strapping, handsome boy, but not the new Hassie he was looking for. Perhaps a perfect German Aryan would be more suitable. It all had to be done on a scientific basis.

And so, Arizona Slim dispatched one of his most trusted assistants to the land of blue-eyed blondes with the authority to offer $1 million to a suitable host mother, high IQ and all the proper physical attributes, who was willing to be artificially inseminated. Perhaps he would use Hassie's sperm, and if that failed, would try it with his own. It all remained questionable, however, when his assistant returned from Germany without a suitable female. Not one creature, possessing all the lofty characteristics Slim had insisted on, would agree to the experiment.

Momentarily at an impasse, but not totally daunted, Arizona Slim resolved to continue the search on more familiar terrain. "Keep your eye out for someone suitable in our own organization," he instructed his aide. "If she has everything else I'm looking for, I'm willing to settle for brown eyes."

While Arizona Slim continued his search for a perfect Hassie, one with all the genes sorted out properly, his name finally surfaced on a far more mundane level. In the aftermath of the Kefauver hearings, federal agents raided a bookie joint located over a restaurant in Terre Haute, Indiana, and among the names they discovered in the bookie's slips was none other than that of one H. L. Hunt.

Slim was subpoenaed by a federal grand jury in Indianapolis which was investigating interstate gambling, but on the day he was supposed to appear he suddenly became ill with a mysterious throat ailment. As reporters converged at the hospital, they were greeted by two of his doctors, who stated that their famous patient was suffering from throat polyps and might have to undergo an operation. In a bedside interview, to which Slim finally consented, he told the reporters in a raspy voice that he knew nothing whatsoever about any gambling operation.

"I did a little gambling in the past," he said, "but I gave it up a year ago. Besides, my reputation in that field has been greatly exaggerated. If you play a little bridge, gin, or bingo, then you are about as much of a gambler as I am."

Slim later asserted that he was too involved in the fight for freedom to give much thought to gambling any more. He did admit, however, that following his huge gin rummy loss to Ray Ryan aboard ship, he had hired Oswald Jacoby, a championship bridge player and the author of a widely read book on gin rummy, to teach him the game a little better.

"But Jacoby was overrated," said Arizona Slim. "He taught me everything he knew, and I still didn't learn that much."

More and more, Arizona Slim grew obsessed with the idea that communists were out to destroy the free, Christian world by poisoning our food and water. He got friendly with Dr. Joe D. Nichols, a rather single-minded MD from Texas who had served as the president of Natural Food Associates. Nichols, a fanatic on the subject, advised Slim to "eat natural, poison-free food grown on fertile soil," and to eat it "fresh, not overcooked."

Slim expanded his garden on the grounds around his Mount Vernon home, growing vegetables and fruit, which he insisted on eating raw or slightly steamed, along with a generous helping of whole-grain bread and nuts. He abstained from sugar and used only honey as a sweetener. In adopting such a diet, he was the mirror-image of the generation of back-to-nature advocates that came along twenty years later, the main difference lying in the fact that whereas Arizona Slim swore his food was being poisoned by communists, the latter-day faddists maintain they are being victimized by corporate America.

Slim's home became a magnet for a clique of right-wing celebrities in the film industry. On several occasions he hosted such luminaries as actors John Wayne and Adolph Menjou, director and visionary Walt Disney, and General Albert Wedemeyer, who was quick to support anything with an anticommunist label on it.

The quaint combination of natural-food faddism and right-wing politics gave Slim the idea of a new organization. HLH Products would be a food company; it would grow and market a broad array of products, ranging from collard greens to a curious antacid and vitamin concoction called Gastro-Majic, which Slim regarded as a divine elixir, nothing less than the elusive Fountain of Youth. So enamored was he of this product that he adopted a strategy which he referred to as "patriotic advertising," in an attempt to sell Gastro-Majic to the rest of the country. He put ads in every right-wing publication he could find and went on the air himself to pitch the divine elixir.

"Hello, I am H. L. Hunt," he said on radio, "the world's richest man, and these are Gastro-Majic, which I make, so they must be good. Try some."

He erected on the front lawn of his house a huge billboard advertising Gastro-Majic, but when several neighbors complained, the city council ordered him to take it down. He immediately put up a smaller one on a vacant lot adjoining his property; his neighbors apparently found that one less offensive. Arizona Slim also pasted Gastro-Majic stickers on his seventh-floor office window facing outward; presumably the birds could see them as they flew by. He pasted bumperstickers on his old small car, a Ford now, and he requested that his employees do the same. Most of them complied once it was learned that their boss had a habit of touring the company parking lot below the building to check up on them. Displayed prominently on his desk were a miniature American flag, a display sign for Gastro-Majic such as you would find in a local drugstore, and a letter from a satisfied customer stating that Gastro-Majic had cured him of gas "which lay like a lump in my stomach for two years...."

Lyda and the family put up with these idiosyncrasies, but wondered whether he was getting senile as he approached his sixty-fifth birthday, an age when most human beings are preparing to settle down to a quiet retirement. But Arizona Slim was busier now than ever, dividing his time equally among his various oil and real estate operations, Facts Forum and the dissemination of his rapidly evolving political philosophy, gambling, and most recently his natural-food business.

"You know, Haroldson," Jake Hamon said to him one day, "you'd accomplish a lot more if you spent your money on civic things, or gave it away to charity or a worthy cause, instead of spending it on these right-wing organizations of yours."

Slim stared at Hamon with a stony look in his eyes, then walked away; he was not accustomed to being lectured to, and did not take it kindly.

Early in 1955, with his various enterprises operating on all cylinders, and his own health as strong as it had ever been, Lyda suddenly suffered a stroke. It came without warning. One minute she had been Arizona Slim's quiet, long-suffering, agonizingly patient wife, attending church without her husband and tending to household chores; the next minute she was stricken low, her brain and body paralyzed by a massive stroke.

Stepping out of character for once in his life, Arizona Slim chartered a DC-6, loaded it up with the immobilized Lyda and all their children, including Hassie, and flew her to the Mayo Clinic in Rochester, Minnesota. Slim was a man who invariably flew tourist since he didn't think first class was worth the extra money. On this occasion, however, spurred on perhaps by a dollop of guilt, he treated Lyda to a journey worthy of the billionaire American sultan that he was. Alas, it was a grand gesture lost on the unconscious Lyda. Not even the high-priced medical talent at the Mayo could save her. She died within days, leaving an estate worth $3 million in assets and over $5 million in liabilities, an arrangement that had been created for its tax advantages.

Lyda was put to rest in the dark-red earth near their Dallas home. Slim waited a suitable period of time before making his musical come true. He did not marry Ruth Ray until two years later, November 1957. His new bride looked a good thirty years younger than he. The official word that was circulated was that Slim would adopt her four young children from a previous marriage.

Ruth was such an attractive, voluptuous, infinitely obliging young woman, it was easy for Slim's associates to see how he would have been captivated by her. But adopt her four children from an earlier marriage? It seemed too sweeping a gesture by a man not known for his generosity. Perhaps the old devil was mellowing in his old age, the public speculated. Perhaps he was human after all, despite his hard-line politics and his eccentricities.

The truth about Ruth Ray's children would not surface till some time afterward. For the moment at least, the secret was theirs.

# 40.

T HE LIBERAL MIND," WROTE William F. Buckley in
an essay for *Facts Forum News*, "is the product of the
swollen and irrepressible stream fed for so many years by the
waters of rationalism, positivism, Marxism and utopianism."

Arizona Slim had nothing but praise for his newest writer's
political philosophy, but he tried to teach the eager youngster
a thing or two about writing style.

"You use too many big words," he said to the Yalie from
Connecticut. He lamented further, "Except that I am slow, I
am the best writer I know."

Despite William Buckley's shortcomings as a literary
stylist, however, "Facts Forum" was reaching an ever-
expanding market under the guidance of Dan Smoot, Jean
Kerr, a legislative assistant to Senator Joseph McCarthy who
was soon to become his wife, and Robert E. Lee, another close
friend of the anticommunist senator. It was the combined
research talents of Jean Kerr and Robert E. Lee that produced
Joe McCarthy's famous list of 205 hard-core communists who
had allegedly infiltrated the highest levels of the United States
government. Using the list for his background material, Dan
Smoot went on the air and weaved an intricate scenario,
linking John Foster Dulles, his brother Allen, who was
director of the Central Intelligence Agency, and J. Edgar
Hoover to the international communist conspiracy.

Robert E. Lee got himself appointed to the Federal

Communications Commission under the sponsorship of Senator McCarthy. At the confirmation hearings it was pointed out that Lee's only prior communications experience was his association with "Facts Forum." Lee replied, "I feel that too much experience can sometimes be a handicap."

The senators conducting the hearing were won over by Lee's impeccable logic and appointed him to the commission, whereupon Arizona Slim decided to hold a party in his honor at his home in Dallas. For the occasion, popular singing star Pat Boone, famous for his white buck shoes, charcoal gray pants, red sweaters, and overall clean-cut image, was flown in from Hollywood to serenade the guests.

Slim was so fired up over the growing success of his organization that he appointed an advisory board composed of General Wedemeyer, who would later become an adviser to the John Birch Society when it was formed in 1958; Norman Vincent Peale, the power-of-positive-thinking minister who would warn, in 1960, against the perils of electing a Roman Catholic to the White House; General Robert Wood, who believed that Adlai Stevenson was a communist agent; and actor John Wayne, who stood foursquare behind Joseph McCarthy and his secret list of 205 communists.

But all good things come to an end sooner or later, and the existence of "Facts Forum" was threatened by an internal conflict between Dan Smoot and Arizona Slim over the format for the show. To maintain his tax-exempt status, Slim attempted to give the appearance of political balance on his programs by presenting both sides of any political question. He made Smoot, on the air, first present the procommunist or proliberal point of view and then refute it with a hard-hitting anticommunist message. Smoot grew tired of the charade and informed Slim, on more than one occasion, that the show would be more forceful if they broadcast only their point of view. Beating the tax man, however, was more important to

Slim than anything else, including the dread communist menace, and he refused to go along with Smoot's suggestions.

Finally, Smoot was given an unexpected assist by the authorities in Washington, who decided to take a closer look at "Facts Forum" and its tax status. At another hearing along the banks of the Potomac, Senator Mike Monroney decided that "Facts Forum" was "neither fact nor forum," but a partisan political program promoting a conservative cause. Congressman Wayne Hays agreed, declaring that Slim's organization gave "both sides of the same side, and no more merited tax-exemption than the A & P."

And so another subtle irony came to roost in Slim's affairs; the hated federal government, that hotbed of communist infiltration, was able to accomplish with one wave of its magisterial hand something that all of Dan Smoot's anti-communist logic had failed to produce. By lifting Slim's tax exemption, the feds induced him not only to change his format, but also to disband the organization altogether in favor of a newer, more forthright one. Smoot had won in a sense, but Arizona Slim, typically, would deny him any semblance of personal victory. In 1957 he replaced "Facts Forum" with "Life Line" and gave Smoot a permanent leave of absence. Smoot went off on his own to present the facts his own way, the anticommunist way, without the pretense of political balance, with the "Dan Smoot Report." In a few years the "Dan Smoot Report" would receive a five-star rating, the highest rating, from Robert Welch, the founder of the John Birch Society.

"The 'Dan Smoot Report,'" said Robert Welch, "is just right for putting in doctors' and dentists' waiting rooms."

"'Life Line,'" said Arizona Slim, "is only trying to present one side—the Constructive viewpoint. That's in public affairs.

[261]

It's also a part-time religious program. So it has a double-barreled appeal."

Under the influence of his lovely young wife, Ruth, Arizona Slim decided to give "Life Line" a religious as well as a political tone. Ruth took her religion seriously and induced her husband to hire a who's who of fundamentalist Protestant ministers to help in the war against international communism. His new board of advisers included several reverends: James Dobbs, who was fond of running for Congress between his "Life Line" sermons; Wayne Poucher, a Church of Christ minister and an ally of Senator Strom Thurmond; George Benson, president of the Church of Christ college in Searcy, Arkansas; and Dr. Barrett Batsell Baxter, head of the Bible department at a Church of Christ school in Nashville, Tennessee. One lay minister refused to join, however. Singing star Pat Boone resisted Slim's exhortations to join his illustrious group even after Slim threatened to have his friend Cecil B. DeMille blackball Boone from the movies. But Boone prevailed, and went on to make one forgettable movie after another.

With his new organization now fleshed out with fire-breathing ministers, Arizona Slim, who had not been inside a church except for his various marriages and a few other special occasions, immediately locked horns with the Rev. Wayne Poucher, the most outspoken member of the group. Slim tried to set the tone for "Life Line" at the outset.

"The battle for freedom," said Arizona Slim, "is a battle between communism and the profit motive system."

Poucher didn't particularly care for anyone, not even the world's richest man, putting words into his mouth. To Slim he replied, "Your life expectancy on this earth is almost used up, so you better believe the battle for freedom is not a battle between free enterprise, the profit motive system, democracy—or whatever name we might call it—and communism, but it is a battle between good, which is God, and evil, which is Satan, for the hearts and minds of men."

It is hard to say what offended Slim more: the criticism of Slim's political orientation and priorities, or the suggestion that he was mortal. After all, hadn't the Reverend Mr. Poucher ever heard of Gastro-Majic? Arizona Slim decided to straighten his minister out once and for all with free advice on every subject he could think of. He bombarded Poucher with scores of memos on on how Poucher might improve his "Life Line" radio sermons.

"It is completely inadvisable," said Slim, "that 'Life Line' string along with a white-supremacy group, but 'Life Line' would not want to declare war on them or espouse the opposition to a white-supremacy group. 'Life Line' is not anti-Semite, but inasmuch as there will be practically no Jews who fail to fight 'Life Line,' 'Life Line' is not due to carry the torch for them."

A short time later, Slim decided to switch tracks on Poucher to keep him on his toes. He suggested that Poucher praise a well-known Jew on the air because "'Life Line' would be given the credit of extolling and memorializing a Jew."

More important to Slim than anything else, perhaps, was his mission to get Poucher to link evil with communism, and godliness with the profit motive. All Poucher ever wanted to talk about was religion, and, to Slim's mounting frustration, rarely broached the pet subject of economics.

"Write a script," he instructed Poucher, "showing how rich people are turned into communists through the conspiracy of providing them with socialist nurses, socialist playmates, and finally through conspiracy-planned marriages and, for those not available for marriage, lovers." In this message, Slim also wanted Poucher to include the statement that socialists "will not overlook the proper approach to win the senile rich."

[263]

The feisty Poucher, who never wanted for words when he needed them, was so flabbergasted by this suggestion that he could merely stare at his benefactor, speechless, his jaw slack.

Still determined to make Poucher talk about profits on the air, Slim decided to incorporate the profit motive into the show. "The Bible is a bestseller," he informed Poucher, "so somebody must be buying Bibles." Why shouldn't we offer Bibles on the air, autographed by Poucher, with a "Life Line" broadcast schedule pasted inside the front cover? "We could sell and deliver it at twice the cost and delivery charge we have to pay," said Arizona Slim.

But Poucher put his foot down here. The idea of treating sacred objects as mere trinkets to be peddled for profit on the air was outrageous to him. "The material which comes with the Bible will lead some to believe it is bound in leather. Of course it is not," he replied. He didn't think the package was worth anywhere near the money Slim wanted for it, and he refused to ask for it.

Still, Slim persisted. "Then how about printing 'Life Line' bumperstickers for five cents each and selling them two for a quarter?" Slim inquired.

Poucher sighed, threw up his hands, and decided that the best course of action against Arizona Slim was no action at all; simply ignore the daffy old bird. "Working for him is a running battle against heavy odds," Poucher confided to a friend.

But Slim was relentless. His days were now increasingly occupied in his corner office in the Mercantile Bank Building with dictating rapid-fire memos to a battery of secretaries. Five or six a day were sent to Poucher alone, while scores of others flew off in all directions to politicians and business leaders, giving them advice on how to run the world.

"I have a horror of running other people's lives," he wrote to the Reverend Wayne Poucher, "but you should make an effort to improve your diction on the air."

On another occasion he told him to "stop jazzing up the hymns."

Again, "Don't quote Norman Vincent Peale by name as he appears to be on the wrong side of the fence about three-fourths of the time."

And again, "Five percent of the preachers in the country are dedicated communists."

And yet again, "I am dubious about your quoting Billy Graham. On the other hand it may be good. I am sure that he will be trying to cut your throat, and if you have made a favorable quote mentioning his name he may then be branded as an ingrate."

On the subject of politics he wrote Poucher, "Please do not approach political action by talking about anyone voting! Should the listeners of 'Life Line' become educated and aroused in a two-year period, they can be depended on to vote and vote right without hazarding our situation by talking to them about it."

And once more on religion, "I was struck that you went pretty strong when you urged your listeners to support 'their minister, their priest, and their rabbi.' I think it would fit better should you admonish them to support and cooperate with the 'spiritual advisers in their church.'"

When Arizona Slim visited the Reverend Wayne Poucher at his home in Washington, D.C., Poucher decided that this was as good a time as any other to make a God-fearing Christian out of the indefatigable memo writer. It was Poucher's custom to read the Bible every evening when the children were put to bed.

"Would you like to join us?" Poucher asked his guest.

Somewhat taken aback, Slim replied, "I would, but I'm a better observer than a participant."

Poucher pulled a chair up to the children's bedside for Arizona Slim, then he and the rest of his family knelt around the bed as the reverend read from the Bible and offered prayer.

Within minutes, Slim slid from his straight-back chair and took his place on his knees alongside the others. When the devotions were over and everyone stood up, Poucher turned to Slim and noticed that his face was streaming with tears. Taking this as a sign that the Lord had worked a miracle of sorts in Slim's soul, Poucher decided to convert Slim to his church before the night was out. He drove him back to his hotel, then spent another couple of hours with Slim discussing the work of God and the salvation of the soul. As he was getting ready to say goodnight, Poucher looked directly into Slim's eyes and told him, "I would like to take you back to the church building with me and baptize you."

Hesitating for a moment, his eyes still glistening with tears, Slim thought over Poucher's proposal and said, "Wayne, I want to, but I have been an evil person and I don't feel I can ask God to forgive me until I have lived better for a little while longer."


It was at roughly the same time that Arizona Slim met a different kind of crusader, though no less fervent than the Reverend Mr. Poucher. He was invited by Robert Welch, a fervent anticommunist from Massachusetts who believed that President Eisenhower was a willing agent of the international communist conspiracy, to come to Indianapolis in December 1958. There was to be a meeting, at a motel, of dedicated patriots from all over the country to talk about forming a new organization, which would be called the John Birch Society.

Arizona Slim had met Welch before but, despite the similarity of their political views, had decided against lending Welch any financial support. He likewise politely declined to attend the meeting in Indianapolis. When mutual friends of the two men learned of their inability to work together, they were confused and frustrated. The anticommunist cause would be far more effective if they could all pool their resources and work together, they reasoned. Slim's rejection of Robert Welch had nothing whatever to do with any disparity in their political beliefs, however; the reason was far more personal than that, as those close to the oilman later found out. "I kind of felt Welch should have joined me," said Slim.

And so the communist conspiracy continued unchecked because of a simple question of ego.

# 41.

WHAT THE HELL IS the matter? Are you slipping?. I see you rated today in the second-string list. Now get on the ball and get back in the top bracket where you belong, us Hunts don't recognize any second-raters."

Arizona Slim read the letter over and over in his corner office overlooking downtown Dallas and laughed wildly to himself. He called in several secretaries and some of his top aides and had them read the letter, then he assigned one of them to go out and have several thousand copies made for his own personal use. The letter was signed by a garage owner from Nebraska, also named Hunt, who had read in *Life* magazine that J. Paul Getty had surpassed Slim as the world's richest man; Slim had been relegated to second spot.

When the article was published, Getty denied its findings and claimed that Slim was, far and away, richer than he was. "In terms of extraordinary, independent wealth, there is only one man, H. L. Hunt," said J. Paul Getty.

Arizona Slim was so taken with the letter that he sent copies of it to people all over the world, and when he visited Kuwait at the beginning of 1958 he carried copies with him to show the sheiks that he wasn't so rich after all.

Saudi Arabia had already granted a drilling concession to Japan, but another one was available in the neutral zone administered by Saudi Arabia and Kuwait. Slim had for some time wanted to expand his oil interests into the Middle East and saw this as a golden opportunity to gain a foothold in the region. Slim arrived with his entourage and they were put up at the government guesthouse.

"The sheik and I will get on very well together," said Slim, "as long as he doesn't offer me any sheep's eyeballs or other Arabian delicacies."

Apparently no one attempted to alter his dietary habits; he stayed for several months, negotiating for valuable offshore drilling rights in competition with the Japanese and other interested parties. After months of intense discussions, Slim learned that the Japanese had won out, and he returned to the United States scarcely able to hide his bitterness.

"The grand vizier was bribed by those wily Orientals," he explained. "Sheik Fuad, who is half Ethiopian, accepted a bribe."

Later on, when Sheik Fuad was found dead in the desert, Slim speculated that the Japanese probably murdered him so they wouldn't have to pay him any more money. But an oil analyst in New York offered a more mundane explanation after studying the terms of the deal.

"You've got to have someplace to sell your oil," he said. "The Japanese could promise a market—their own country—which Hunt couldn't do."

The Japanese had also offered the Kuwaitis more generous terms than Slim did, and they offered to include Kuwait in the operations of the venture, which Slim refused to do. Despite the cold black-and-white, nuts-and-bolts terms of the agreement, however, Arizona Slim refused to accept the fact that he had, quite simply, been outbid. For the rest of his life he blamed his defeat on a sinister plot between wily Orientals and half-Ethiopian bribe-takers.


Back home in Dallas Slim's pretty young wife, Ruth, was managing to accomplish with her Jane Powell smile something that all the fire-and-brimstone preachers in the country had so far failed to do; she was making something of a believer out of her curmudgeonly husband.

Ruth had started attending the First Baptist Church in Dallas. It was the largest Baptist church in the world, with a budget of $1.5 million, and featured such ecclesiastical superstars as the Reverend Billy Graham among its ministry. The pastor of the First Baptist Church was the Reverend Dr. W. A. Criswell, a handsome, forceful, pulpit-pounding orator from the old school, who was already something of a legend in Dallas circles despite his young years.

With Ruth's quiet, never-nagging, yet persistent enticements, Arizona Slim finally agreed to attend the church with her and their children. If Slim was a sucker for anything, it was for a man with an oratorical flourish, a dramatic style, particularly if that man's politics were just so. Unlike Wayne Poucher, Criswell had no reservations about mixing politics and economics with his religion; in point of fact, he was, if anything, even more fanatical on the subject than Slim was.

When Dr. Criswell fairly bellowed from the pulpit, "I am a conservative in theology, a conservative in sociology, a conservative in politics, and you can tell it from my sermons. If I had a liberal hair in my head, I would pluck it out," Arizona Slim knew he had finally found the promised land, even though he would have preferred that the good reverend with the resonant voice substitute the word *constructive* for *conservative*. No matter. It was a small concession he was willing to make for Criswell, if not for Karl Hess, who erred on the matter before him. Arizona Slim was swept away, and Ruth could hardly contain her delight at her husband's late conversion. Yes, Slim had found religion in the seventieth year of his life, after all the decades of rambling and gambling, of womanizing and hustling, of fathering children inside and outside marriage, of making fortunes and losing them before ascending to the towering heights of unprecedented wealth.

On the first Sunday in 1960, a month before his seventy-first birthday, Arizona Slim, Ruth, and all four of their children were baptized together at the First Baptist Church in Dallas by the Reverend Dr. Criswell.

The ways of the Lord are not always easy to comprehend.

With the coming together of Criswell and Arizona Slim, it was inevitable that sooner or later they would combine their considerable energies and talents for proselytizing, and take on the communist menace together. During two full terms of the Eisenhower administration, Slim had come to the conclusion that the baldheaded former general was nothing short of a disaster.

"Except that he got rid of a few perverts in government," said Slim, "Eisenhower is no good. He is the worst president, the most harmful president we ever had. He's so popular he doesn't have to do anything people ask him to do."

One of the things Arizona Slim had asked the Eisenhower administration to do for him was to lease him some offshore oil tracts at bargain-basement prices, a request which was repeatedly turned down. This development may or may not have had something to do with Slim's assessment of Ike's performance in office. When Eisenhower's people had approached Slim for a campaign donation several years before, and the oilman sent them off with a paltry $5,000, Ike's disappointment in Slim made their feelings mutual.

Now the year was 1960, and a new presidential race was getting under way. Arizona Slim's favorite candidate this time around was Lyndon Johnson of Texas. While Johnson was not quite the man of the century that General MacArthur had been in his day, he was infinitely superior to John F. Kennedy, who was trying to take the Democratic nomination away from him, and he was head and shoulders above that "bad egg" Richard Nixon, who had never "gone to bat" for Slim throughout the eight years of his vice presidency under Eisenhower.

The Reverend W. A. Criswell was just as opposed to a Kennedy presidency as Slim was, and he said so in no uncertain terms from the pulpit of his church.

"The election of a Catholic as president would mean the end of religious liberty in America," Criswell intoned one Sunday morning as the campaign got under way.

His religion, as well as the fact that Kennedy had already gone on record as being in favor of reviewing oil-depletion allowances, was enough for Arizona Slim.

"I am in favor of depletion allowances for all natural resources," said Slim, "but without the depletion allowance for oil we are utterly ruined."

At his own expense, Slim printed up 200,000 copies of Criswell's sermon and mailed them to influential people all over the country. But the reaction was not as he anticipated. Instead of igniting a spark of fear of the papist menace that threatened America, Slim triggered a backlash against the injection of religion and an atmosphere of hate into a political campaign. Commentators and editorial writers throughout the nation grew indignant, and reporters descended on Dallas to interview the progenitor of the fear campaign. Arizona Slim went into hiding. Nowhere could the richest, or second-richest, man in the world be located.

"Come out, Big Daddy, Wherever You Are," headlined one newspaper.

Arizona Slim did surface eventually, only to announce that he had been not hiding, as everyone claimed, but writing a novel that would soon be published. Yes, he admitted, he did pay for the distribution of the Criswell leaflet.

"But I only did it," he said, "to help out poor Lyndon."

Any assistance from Slim at this point was tantamount to

receiving the kiss of death, and he ran into a wall of ice when he attempted to insinuate himself into the Johnson forces at the Democratic convention in Los Angeles. Arizona Slim wandered from room to room, looking for somebody to talk to. He finally accosted Jake Jacobson, an assistant to Price Daniel, the governor of Texas, who was headquartered next to the Lyndon Johnson suite. Jacobson spoke to him briefly, then followed him next door and observed as the Johnson people pointedly ignored the big shambling man with the old rumpled suit and the floppy bowtie. After several minutes of hanging around with no one to talk to, Arizona Slim contented himself with wandering alone through the corridors of the hotel, slipping "Life Line" pamphlets under the doors.

"What the hell," Jacobson thought. "Here's a man with all that money who can't get anybody to talk to him."

When the convention was over and Lyndon Johnson had accepted second spot on the Kennedy ticket, Arizona Slim bombarded him with a barrage of memos on how to conduct himself during the campaign.

"Lyndon could have had the presidential nomination," said Arizona Slim, "but he made every known mistake."

Four days before the election, Slim held a press conference to announce that he was officially supporting the Kennedy-Johnson ticket, and the chairman of the National Democratic Party, Henry (Scoop) Jackson, immediately called a press conference of his own to repudiate Slim's endorsement. He also refused financial aid from the oilman, which Slim hadn't offered in any case. The old man was generous with his memos and advice, but not with his pocketbook.

"I decided to vote for Kennedy," said Arizona Slim, "since I admire his father Joe Kennedy, who is a good businessman. I refuse to believe that any son of Joe Kennedy can be a liberal."

# 42.

AFTER ALL THE YEARS of dreaming, of setting music and lyrics down on paper, of attempting to transform his fantasies into the reality of a Broadway extravaganza, Arizona Slim had still failed to make his musical come to life.

His marriage to Ruth was as fine a one as any man could hope for. She was his all-American sweetheart, and would always remain so. She was the smiling, bubbly, vivacious star of his musical fantasies, and always would be. But real life was not enough for Arizona Slim. The ritual of bringing up yet another family, of running a household, of attending services at the Reverend Dr. Criswell's church was just fine as far as it went. But it was not the culmination of everything he had been searching for in life. It was too mundane, too real. It was not utopia.

If Arizona Slim could not make utopia come to life in the form of a musical production, then he would find another way to do it. And so he did, in 1960, shortly after John F. Kennedy took the election from that "bad egg" Richard Nixon, as Slim called him. Slim had not been kidding when he said he had gone into seclusion to complete a novel. He brought the novel, which he named *Alpaca*, into print at his own expense toward the end of the campaign year. The book was published as a paperback, under the imprint of the H.L. Hunt Publishing Co., for fifty cents a copy.

"I got the idea for the novel," said Slim, "on a trip to South

America in 1956. I hadn't seen a stable government in all the months I spent down there, and I began to wonder if a person could supply a constitution so that they could govern themselves."

Arizona Slim supplied a curious constitution, indeed, for the citizens in his make-believe country of Alpaca. Voting, it stated, would be based on the amount of taxes an individual paid each year. Anyone receiving welfare payments from the government would not be permitted to vote at all. Those paying high taxes might get as many as five or ten votes. The great masses in between, including government officials who turn back part of their income to the government treasury, would receive a lesser amount of votes on a complicated, graduated scale. When one reviewer wrote a satirical review, praising Slim tongue-in-cheek for having created the perfect "fascist democracy," Slim wrote him a letter stating, "You are the only one who really understood what I was getting at."

The novel also contained a love story, of sorts, between the main character, who resembled the author at an earlier age, and a beautiful opera singer named Mara. Was Mara purely fictitious or closely drawn from real life? Speculation on this question became more than mere titillation when it was learned that the great French soprano Lily Pons, who was still an attractive woman at fifty-six, had recently taken up residence in Dallas under Slim's sponsorship.

"I admire her and we're just friends," Slim replied to reporters who questioned him about a possible romantic liaison.

He had become more and more interested in opera, not to mention opera singers, in recent years, he said, and to prove it he was going to stage a performance of *The Barber of Seville* at the Music Hall on the Dallas Fair Grounds at his own expense.

The big night arrived and the crowds came swarming out to

the Fair Grounds in record numbers. Culture had come to Dallas, and none other than Arizona Slim was responsible for bringing it there. The performance went smoothly and the crowd loved the great extravaganza, yelling "Bravo!" and "Brava!" and applauding enthusiastically. At intermission the entire cast, overwhelmed by the uncharacteristic generosity from this latter-day patron of the arts, Arizona Slim, asked the great man to come up on stage and say a few words to the audience.

Slim smiled at his wife and children, then stood up with his bowtie waving in the gentle breeze of night. He strode toward the stage, still tall and erect despite his seventy-one years, carrying a carton under his arm. The audience clapped as he walked to center stage, with the bright spotlights playing on the thin tufts of white hair surrounding his mostly bald head. When the applause subsided, he took an object from the carton under his arm and raised it to the audience.

"Hello, I'm H. L. Hunt," he said, "who some people think is the world's richest man. And this here is Gastro-Majic, which I take every day, so it must be good."

And the audience sat speechless as the great man instructed his aides to pass out samples of the divine elixir among the multitudes, and then used up the rest of their intermission reading them a sermon from next week's "Life Line" broadcast. Arizona Slim had brought an opera to the citizens of Dallas, and since he was paying for it all himself, intermission was as good a time as any other to treat them all to a good, hard-hitting commercial.


Slim's curious blend of "fascist democracy," opera pageants, and antiaging compounds failed to attract a wide readership for *Alpaca*, much to Slim's disappointment. Convinced as he was that the novel contained the answers to all the ills that afflicted society, Slim decided that the masses of America should read his book whether they paid for it or not. It was simply too important to be ignored.

So, again at his own expense, he began shipping huge boxes of the book to unsuspecting citizens all over the globe. The offices of congressmen and senators in Washington, D.C., were suddenly inundated with unsolicited copies; colleges, libraries, business leaders, and the heads of foreign governments were swamped with thousands upon thousands of copies of *Alpaca*, most of them containing schedules of "Life Line" broadcasts pasted inside the cover.

Slim also wrote new lyrics for a popular song of a few years earlier, "How Much Is That Doggie in the Window?" which had been sung by a plumpish country-and-western singer named Patti Page. He staged an autograph-signing party for himself at the Cokesbury Book Store in downtown Dallas, and trotted out his pretty young daughters, Helen, June, and Swanee for the occasion. The proud father beamed at them benevolently as the girls sang their father's words to the popular tune:

> How much is that book in the
>    window?
> The one that says all the smart
>    things.
> How much is that book in the
>    window?
> I do hope to learn all it
>    brings.
> *Alpaca! Alpaca!* Fifty cents!

When all the free copies and all the patriotic advertising set to music still failed to bring the message of *Alpaca* to the masses of America, Slim finally allowed that perhaps his constitution needed a little updating to make it more palatable to a greater number of people. Maybe, just maybe, he had given too many votes to the rich people who paid all the taxes, and not enough to everybody else.

"I'm working on a sequel," Slim announced, "with an even better constitution. When my new novel is finished I will call it 'Yourtopia.'"

The young writer whose style Slim had criticized a few years before, William F. Buckley, Jr., who had gone on to write a few books of his own, finally seized the opportunity to get even with his old employer. Having had the good fortune to observe Slim up close for a number of years now, Buckley wrote in his magazine, *National Review*, "The capitalist cause would be greatly enhanced if H. L. Hunt had been a socialist."

All this business concerning political novels, operas and opera singers, and Fountain of Youth antacid concoctions eventually got the best of the Reverend Wayne Poucher.

Poucher was offended on several levels. First of all, Slim had never ceased his relentless bombardment of him with memos instructing him to improve his diction, to stop jazzing up his hymns, to praise or not to praise Jews and others with genetic disadvantages, and on how to conduct his life in general. To add insult to injury, after Poucher's attempts to convert Slim to born-again Christianity had ended in failure, the unpredictable oilman had allowed himself to be baptized by a more flamboyant and controversial minister. And now the Reverend W. A. Criswell had superseded Poucher as the predominant figure in the "Life Line" organization. Poucher could take it no longer and resigned in a huff.

When Slim informed Poucher that his services were no longer needed anyway, and that he had been carrying him on the payroll out of the goodness of his heart, Poucher decided that merely resigning was not enough retribution for the old devil. He endeavored to hit Slim where it would hurt him the most: his wallet.

Poucher contacted a number of congressmen and intimated that he had been forced to resign from "Life Line" after he learned that certain irregularities had been taking place over the years. The so-called sponsoring churches behind "Life Line," a Baptist church in Miami and a Methodist church in Trout, Louisiana, apparently did not exist at all; they were mere post office boxes, and served as front organizations for Arizona Slim's natural-food company. "Life Line" was therefore not entitled to its tax-exempt status and its second-class mailing permit. When informed of Poucher's charges, Slim replied, "I've been in court 280 times and never lost a case."

Other irregularities were revealed by Poucher, most of them having to do with the claim that "Life Line" was, in effect, an advertising conduit for HLH food products, a profit-making business. HLH Products had received millions of dollars' worth of public service time on radio and television, and that amounted to so much free advertising. When asked if HLH Products had made a profit from its exposure through "Life Line," Slim answered, "Patriotism is always profitable."

Arizona Slim opened up his considerable bankroll once more to fight Poucher's charges, and keep "Life Line" operating under status quo conditions. The power of the purse proved greater, in this instance, than the power of the pulpit. "Life Line" stayed on the air, reaching over five million American citizens through 428 stations in almost every state. And no other in all the land was as great a fan of "Life Line" as Arizona Slim himself. As he and Ruth and their children sat down to dinner each evening at six-fifteen, the radio was turned on loudly beside him so he could hear his favorite program clearly. They ate their fruit and vegetables, and washed it down with fruit juice as they listened.

After dinner they all went over to the piano for the family singalong. With his shaky tenor voice he led them in his favorite song, "Just Plain Folks":

To a mansion in the city,
Came a couple old and gray...
We are just plain folks,
Your mother and me.
Just plain folks
Like our own folks used to be.
As our presence seems to grieve you,
We will go away and leave you.
We are sadly out of place here
'Cause we're just plain folks.

# 43.

AND THEN THINGS SUDDENLY got ugly.
Until this time, Arizona Slim's strange blend of
patriotic anticommunism, quirky half-baked racism and anti-
Semitism, semiplatonic Republicanism, and paranoid dietary
concerns were all tempered with a unique brand of eccentricity which Slim had managed to elevate to the level of an art
form. His obsession with making a profit on virtually every
action he took outweighed his arcane political opinions,
which would have been dangerous in almost anyone else with
a tenth of Slim's money at his disposal. But the potential for
destructiveness had always been there nonetheless. Allies of
Arizona Slim, most notably Senator Joseph McCarthy and
some of the more outspoken members of the more virulent
right, had caused a good deal of grief for a great number of
people during the previous decade. It was only Slim's eccentricity and lack of sophistication that blunted the edge of his
political harshness with an element of human comedy.

Finally, the offsetting balance between danger and comedy
was upset. As John F. Kennedy entered his third year in
office, he had already done enough things to convince Slim
that a son of good old Joe Kennedy could indeed be a liberal.
More upsetting than anything else the president did, however, more disturbing than all his civil-rights and social-
welfare legislation was Kennedy's continuing assault on the
oil-depletion allowance. Arizona Slim could have accepted

many things; he could even have tolerated Fidel Castro's dining at the White House. But one thing he was not prepared to accept was any tinkering with the fast tax writeoff of slowly declining oil wells.

Little by little Slim stepped up his criticism of the young president on his "Life Line" broadcasts. In January 1963 John F. Kennedy announced once again that he would work to reduce the depletion allowance, and the battle took shape. Texas oilmen put pressure on the vice president, Lyndon Baines Johnson, to work behind the scenes to change the president's mind, but everyone knew that Johnson and Kennedy did not get along all that well. Theirs was strictly a political marriage of convenience.

As the flak from Texas got heavier and heavier, Kennedy decided to visit Dallas as a gesture of friendship. He enlisted the aid of John Connally, the popular governor of the state, to prepare for the visit. In the weeks preceding his arrival, "Life Line" became increasingly strident in its anti-Kennedy rhetoric. Commentators on the program accused the president of every unpatriotic crime imaginable, from circumventing the authority of Congress to being a willing puppet of international communism.

On the morning of November 22, 1963, the day of Kennedy's scheduled arrival, "Life Line" went on the air with a dire warning to the people of America. The commentator started off by talking about the "leftist plot," fomented in Washington under the current administration, to deprive the people of their right to bear arms.

"In a dictatorship," the broadcast continued, "no firearms are permitted the people, because they would then have the weapons with which to rise up against their oppressors."

Not to be outdone by his father, Slim's second-oldest son, Nelson Bunker Hunt, helped pay for a full-page ad attacking the president; it appeared in the *Dallas News* on the morning of the visit. By the time Kennedy's plane landed in Dallas, the tone for his visit had already been set by the Hunt propaganda and by the general mood that prevailed among the oilmen of Dallas.

Slowly, the presidential motorcade snaked toward downtown Dallas from the airport. The winding gray highway bordered in green curved gracefully past a dreary brick building, the Texas School Book Depository, which was located a short distance from the railroad terminal. The depository was visible from the observatory on the roof of the Mercantile Bank Building ten blocks away, the building where Slim maintained his offices on the seventh floor. With the president in his limousine were his wife, Jacqueline, and Governor Connally; secret servicemen rode on the outside, keeping guard.

As the motorcade passed the brick depository building, shots rang out and then there was bedlam. The president was hit as his wife stared on in horror beside him. Within hours he was dead, his brain destroyed by an assassin's bullet. In the aftermath of the shooting, many people were interviewed around the country and their reactions were recorded for posterity. In Washington, D.C., Senator Maurine Neuberger of Oregon faced the television cameras and stated, "H. L. Hunt has to bear a lot of the onus because of the fanatical broadcasts he sponsors. If anybody is responsible, he is."

A man named Lee Harvey Oswald was arrested for the murder of the president, but the world may never know if he was acting alone or as part of a conspiracy, or even if he was actually the one who fired the fatal bullet. As Oswald was being led to jail in handcuffs, surrounded by FBI agents, other law-enforcement officials, and dozens of reporters, with television cameras recording the scene live for viewers across the nation, a squat man with slick dark hair who looked a little like Edward G. Robinson pushed his way through the crowd and pumped some bullets into Lee Harvey Oswald.

When the police searched Jack Ruby, the man who killed

Oswald, they found two "Life Line" radio scripts in his jacket pocket.

"Where did you get these?" they asked him.

"In a sample package of HLH food at the Texas Products Show a few weeks ago," he said.

In their interrogation of Ruby, the police also learned that he had visited the office of Lamar Hunt, another of Slim's sons, a short while before the assassination. Why he was there was never made exactly clear because Jack Ruby died not too long after his own arrest.

A lot of people who might have known something about the assassination of President Kennedy died within a few years, so many questions remain unanswered. No one has ever proved in a court of law, or anywhere else for that matter, that there was any kind of a direct link between Lee Harvey Oswald and Jack Ruby and Arizona Slim. But the questions remain and the doubts will always be there.

Yes, something ugly happened in Dallas on November 22, 1963. All of a sudden, the eccentricity and quirkiness of a very rich and very successful old man seemed not so funny any more. The half-baked racism and political fanaticism emerged triumphant over the human element. The towering hypocrisy and the monstrosity of bigamous marriages and illegitimate offspring dwarfed, for the first time, the laughable inconsistencies, the dietary paranoia, the iconoclasm, and the eccentricity.

An era was over. Comedy had turned to tragedy, as it so often does. The balance had been upset. The dangerous power of money and privilege had come more sharply into focus. The potential for destruction had become reality. The old days were over and a new age had now begun.

Because something very ugly happened in Dallas that day.

# Book VII

# The Boys

# 44.

STUPID, BOY, STUPID. I can find more oil with a road map than you can with a platoon of geologists.''

All his life Nelson Bunker Hunt had been listening to comments like that from his father. And all his life Nelson Bunker Hunt, or Bunker as he was called, was determined to prove his father wrong.

Bunker infuriated Slim all the more because, in his eyes, his second-born son was not a suitable replacement for the gene-scrambled Hassie. Hassie, with all his hypersensitivity and unpredictability, had a genius for locating oil. Without making much ado about it, he just seemed to know where it would be. Bunker, on the other hand, had blown his own inheritance and part of his father's fortunes drilling one dry hole after another. His record was incredible, as though he were possessed by a devil who was out to destroy everything that Slim had built in his long rambling life.

A lesser boy would have been destroyed by his father's ceaseless insults about and denigration of his intelligence and capabilities. A more sensitive spirit might have been driven over the brink into the abyss of insanity, as was the case with Hassie whether Slim wanted to face that ugly fact or not. But Bunker was made of sterner stuff than that. He was a boy not easily discouraged, let alone destroyed. He had his father's determination to succeed, and then some. He may not have looked much like his father, nor did he seem to possess his mental dexterity, on the surface at least, but his genes were all neatly sorted inside. Bunker was a plodder with true grit, a workhorse with the stamina to survive.

From the beginning the boy had idolized his father. He worshiped the ground that Slim walked on and, unlike Hassie, did not take it personally when his father failed to spend much time with his family. He knew his father was a busy man, a great man even, who had to fulfill in life a mission that transcended the call of normal human relationships. He did not rant and rave when Slim disappeared for weeks and months at a time, as Hassie did. Nor did he fly into temper tantrums and throw things against the wall, as Hassie did. He viewed his father as a demigod, a towering larger-than-life hero possessed of greatness, and he was content to worship that image from afar. When Slim spoke, his ideas and opinions were engrafted into young Bunker's mind; his father's words were akin to divine writ, carved tablets carried down from the mountain for mortal consumption. If Bunky was a failure in his father's eyes, he would just have to pray harder for the strength to make himself into a worthy heir in his father's kingdom. No, Bunker was not easily discouraged or destroyed. He had faith in his father and himself, and that faith would help him to survive and prosper.

Despite his own lack of formal education, and his disdain for it, Slim extended the opportunity of education to his sons as long as they selected schools he approved of. Bunker went to the University of Texas in Austin right after high school. When he turned seventeen he quit college to join the navy. World War II ended a year later, and he enrolled at SMU, his father's favorite college, where he lasted out a term. Having had enough of formal education at that point, Bunker left SMU to work full-time for his father. After drilling his string of dry holes during a good part of the next decade, Slim harbored the wish that Bunker had remained at SMU a trifle longer.

Bunker's younger brother Herbert, two years his junior, took to formal education more readily. He lasted out a full four years at Washington and Lee University, which was also high up on Slim's approved list, and graduated with a degree in geology. Herbert returned home with his degree, which he held up proudly for his father's scrutiny, only to see Slim look at it scornfully and say, "That degree's going to cost us millions. You'll end up drilling wells just to prove something rather than to find oil."

Later, when alone with Bunker, to whom he was closest in age and temperament, Herbert said, "Oh, well, he works eleven or twelve hours a day. That's how he succeeded. I guess that's more important than any piece of paper."

Lamar, Arizona Slim's youngest boy by Lyda, seemed to be cut from a different mold entirely. He inherited his father's sporting genes, the ones that once led Slim to try out for a career as a professional baseball player and to entertain the notion, if only for an instant, of trying his hand at becoming the next white hope of the boxing world.

More than anything else in the world, Lamar would have loved to be an athlete. Football, baseball, basketball, Lamar tried each one, but it was early apparent that he would never become a professional in any sport. He loved them all, but football was far and away his favorite. He loved to watch the brown elliptical pigskin sail high against the blue autumn sky before dropping perfectly into the cradled arms of a receiver running full speed. He made up his mind early in life that, one way or another, he was going to be a part of this weekend pageantry which held so many of his countrymen enthralled. If he couldn't play the game himself, he would find another way to participate.

While Lamar was entertaining notions of grandeur regarding the sporting world, much to Arizona Slim's dismay, oil remained the primary concern of Bunker, Herbert, and, later, Ray—the only son from Slim's marriage to Ruth—who all were striving diligently to fill their father's considerable shoes. None among them was content to be the idle son of a rich man, enjoying the fruits of his labor as he basked in the glory of his kingdom. All were brought up to be doers and achievers on their own. Hard work, diligence, and perseverance; that was the American way, and the sons of Arizona Slim were nothing if not quintessential Americans.

Herbert had less to prove to himself or his father than Bunker did. He was quieter and more reserved than his older brother; he was more the indoor type, poring over his geological charts and helping to run the family businesses from the sanctuary of his own office. Bunker, however, had something of the competitiveness toward his father that had plagued Hassie all his life. He was more driven, more outwardly determined not necessarily to surpass his father, but to succeed dramatically on his own and prove himself worthy in Slim's eyes. From the time he was a child, he felt that he had to earn his right to live in his father's kingdom.

After his monumental failures in searching for oil in his own country and later in Pakistan, Bunker's persistence finally paid off. At his insistence, he convinced Slim that the next major discovery of oil was going to take place in the Middle East. Using contacts established by their family friend, John Connally, the governor of Texas, Bunker zeroed in on Libya. The Hunts won the right to drill for oil from the Libyan government, and then sold a fifty percent interest to British Petroleum to ensure themselves a market.

This time Bunker was right. Not only was he right, but he was so right that his strike in Libya more than made up for all the millions upon millions of dollars he had pumped into those dry holes he had been drilling all his life. Bunker drilled into the mind-boggling Sarir field, which turned out to be one of the largest proven oil reserves on earth. The field held more than six billion barrels of oil. Within a short time after Bunker built his pipeline across two hundred miles of Arabian desert, his wells started to produce a hundred thousand barrels of oil a day.

"Bunker found so much oil there," said a petroleum engineer from Texas when he learned of the discovery, "that he could give most of it away and still make money."

Bunker had finally shown his daddy that he was not a stupid boy after all. In his own plodding way, he had found more oil in one fell swoop than Hassie ever did with his genius. It took him a bit of time, but he had proven himself to be a true and proper scion in the kingdom of his father.

# 45.

A S THE BOYS TOOK OVER the management of the various family enterprises, Arizona Slim spent more and more of his time with his literary pursuits and his political activities. In the aftermath of the assassination of President John F. Kennedy, the FBI began to worry that Slim's life might be in danger because of his own role in the "Life Line" broadcasts.

"We think it advisable that you leave Dallas and go into hiding for a while," an investigator said to him.

Reluctantly, he packed his bags and told Ruth they were leaving for Baltimore to stay with some relatives. On the way there, however, Slim decided that the underground life was not for him and he would just as soon take his chances with his enemies. Against the wishes of the FBI, he traveled instead to Washington, D.C., where he checked himself and Ruth into the Mayflower Hotel. This was tantamount to setting himself up as a sitting target inside a fishbowl, and the FBI investigators went berserk when they learned of his change of plans. Again Slim yielded to their exhortations and brought Ruth back to Dallas just a few days before Christmas.

Against Slim's wishes, Dallas detectives served as his personal bodyguards, riding with him to and from his office. At night they set up a cordon around his house to protect him against any would-be revenge-seekers. Finally, Slim could no longer take this invasion of his privacy and ordered them off his property.

"Just go away and leave me alone!" he said.

"Please, sir. We'll be blamed if anything happens to you."

"No, no. It's not your responsibility. I'm not going to put up with this any more."

And so they left.

The country mourned its murdered president, slain in the prime of his life, but gradually things returned to normal. Lyndon Johnson was president now, but he wasn't long in office before Slim decided that LBJ wasn't such a good old Texas boy after all. He was pushing those communist-inspired civil-rights and social-welfare bills through Congress even faster than Kennedy did. He was even twisting arms to get them enacted into law, and nobody could twist an arm and browbeat a recalcitrant congressman or senator more persuasively than good old Lyndon. It didn't take Arizona Slim long to decide that Johnson most definitely would not be his choice in the 1964 election.

His new man of the century was another military officer, General Edwin Walker of the United States Army. General Walker had recently been recalled from Europe for passing out John Birch Society literature among the troops, and Slim decided that he was just the man to run the country as president in 1964. Most of Slim's countrymen did not share this view, however, and General Walker ran a distant last in the Democratic primaries that year. Once again, Arizona Slim had put his money on the wrong horse. He contented himself with voting for Barry Goldwater instead, even though the Goldwater forces refused to give him the time of day at the convention in San Francisco.


In his old age, Arizona Slim started to bear an uncanny resemblance to former president Herbert Hoover. Both men were big, bulky, and bald, and wore bowties and dark-blue suits that hung like sacks from their round frames. Not infrequently Arizona Slim was mistaken for the former president when out in public, and he thought it necessary to dispel that association at once.

"I did vote for the great engineer at the time," said Slim sarcastically, "but he was overrated. I remember a speech I once heard him make, back before the Second World War. It was at the Bankers Club in New York in, I think, 19 and 38. He said there wasn't goin' to be a war because the Germans were too kindly to start one and they didn't have enough money. He said that bombing planes were ineffective against ships and cities. That man talked for two hours and there wasn't a thing he said that turned out to be right."

As long as Slim was setting the record straight on Herbert Hoover, he deemed it prudent to let the world know what he thought of other presidents as well.

"Coolidge was the best there was. He led the country in its prosperity and he cut way back on the federal budget. He also got rid of the subversives and cut the national debt."

As for Roosevelt: "The communist gains during the New Deal were no surprise to me. Roosevelt didn't know any better. He never met a payroll in his life."

Nor did he think much more highly of the presidents who came after Roosevelt. "Truman was a failure but, in some ways, an improvement over Roosevelt. Eisenhower was a total disaster. He was so genial that he gave the country a terrible push toward Bolshevism without anyone being aware of what was happening. Kennedy gave away too much and he failed on Cuba. And Lyndon Johnson didn't keep his promise to name Senators James Eastland and Thomas Dodd as special advisers on communist infiltration."

How about some of the others who didn't quite make it?

"Stevenson was unspeakable and Nixon's a bad egg."

Would Barry Goldwater have made a good president?

"He ran such a bad campaign that I wonder if he would have been a good president."

Even General Edwin Walker, who was his choice, did not get off too lightly. Why did he lose?

"He was too unresponsive to my suggestions."

There was only one man who could have saved America from communist infiltration and turned the country around.

"Douglas MacArthur was the man of the century. Next to him Winston Churchill was only a phrasemaker."

As it became clearer to Slim and those associated with him that his success in backing political candidates was not about to compare with his success in the oil fields, Slim had to settle for the satisfaction of making his utopia come true on paper at least. His revised constitution was ready for publication in his new novel, which he wisely retitled, in 1967. His original choice for a title was "Yourtopia"; at the last minute he decided to go with popular fashion and called it *Alpaca Revisited* instead.

In the new version, tax exemptions would be granted to philanthropies promoting medical science, and to organizations that preached the message of personal liberty and anticommunism, such as "Life Line." There would be no withholding taxes at all on income. Everyone would automatically receive two votes, and those in the upper tax brackets would receive bonus votes for achievement until they got a maximum of five votes. To soften the blow of this graduated voting system, those over sixty-five, as well as the infirm, would be permitted to draw relief benefits to cover their necessities.

Alas, Arizona Slim's revised utopia failed to reach a larger audience than his original version. The book came out unnoticed and mostly unreviewed. A handful of his political adversaries dismissed it contemptuously as a model for a "cashocracy." No one took it seriously, including other conservative writers and commentators. Shortly after the new book was published, again at Slim's own expense, William F. Buckley, Jr. was induced to write in one of his columns,

"Hunt's eccentric understanding of public affairs gives capitalism a bad name."

No, the decade of the 1960s was not Slim's finest hour. More and more his sons were taking over the management of the oil business as Slim devoted himself to political affairs. His political activities had begun to appear somewhat anticlimactic following the assassination of Kennedy. His ideas and entanglements, once harboring the potential, at least, for power and influence, had lost whatever impact they previously enjoyed as the decade wore on. The country got more deeply involved in an unpopular war in Asia, and the mood of the country changed. Arizona Slim had cast himself in the role of a man who was out of step with his time. He was an old man outliving his usefulness.

But still he refused to quit, to get off the stage and leave it permanently for the newer generations. He concentrated his declining energies upon the one remaining obsession of his life, aside from politics, his HLH Products company. Natural foods. The elixir of life. Through them he would remain immortal.

Yet, even here he was beginning to fail. His beloved food company was starting to lose money. Of all the vast enterprises that he had brought into being, and that were prospering now, generating hundreds of millions of dollars and adding to his magical wealth, his food company, the one area left to him in his declining years, was the single drain on the family's resources.

# 46.

LAMAR MADE HIS DREAM come true.

The boy did not become a professional athlete. His prowess in the sporting arena never matched that in his dreams. As far as football was concerned, he simply was not cut from the same block of granite that football players are made from. In appearance, he looked more like a clerk in an insurance office than the kind of man that makes muggers run for their lives. But he did have something else that would enable him to succeed in the field of his choice; he had all that money his daddy had put in trust for him, and he also had inherited his father's capacity for dreaming enormous dreams and not resting until he made them come true.

If Lamar didn't have the ability to leap high in the air and snare elusive pigskins fired like rockets, he would create his own utopia, where surrogate athletes performed his heroics for him. He would start his own football league and form his own team. And then his own players, brought into being by Lamar their creator, would fulfill his ambitions as he pulled their strings from high up in his own universe. It was all so easy to do what with all that inherited money. It was better than magic.

After graduating from SMU, Lamar married a pretty Texas girl named Norma and they started a family of their own. There would be three children in all—Lamar, Sharon, and Clark. Before he was thirty years old, a time when most young married men are struggling to launch their careers and build the family nest, Lamar was on the brink of making his secret dream, his obsession, a reality. In 1959 he formed a new football league, which he called, appropriately enough, the American Football League, and appointed himself its president. The same year he also founded his own team, the Kansas City Chiefs, which completed step two of his grand design.

Now he was ready to make his creatures perform vicariously. But suddenly the dream turned into something of a nightmare. All the money in the world, it seemed, could not turn a group of well-paid athletes, talented though they were, into a coordinated and well-oiled fighting machine. From his perch on the sidelines Lamar looked on in frustration week after week while his dream players trotted onto the field, engaged the opposition in combat, and got trounced. No matter how much money he pumped into his fledgling organization, Lamar seemed unable to turn the tide in his favor.

After a few seasons of this, a reporter approached Arizona Slim one day and informed him, "Your son Lamar is losing a million dollars a year supporting that team of his. What do you think about it?"

Slim laughed and dismissed the matter lightly. "At that rate, Lamar will be broke in two hundred fifty years," he said. But that remark was for public consumption; it was to foster his own myth.

Privately, Arizona Slim had entirely different opinions on the subject. Privately, he thought his son Lamar was a fool and told him so in no ambiguous terms. "You're wasting your time and your money, boy. You're playing, not working. You're not being serious with your life."

But Lamar was undeterred. He had inherited his father's determination and strong will as well as his millions. To Lamar, football, competition, the reality of man against man in a sporting contest was the true stuff of life. It was just as real and noble as the competition that took place in his father's world of business and politics. Lamar had merely chosen a different arena to compete in.

During the next few years, as his father entered the period of his own decline with his failures in politics and later in his food business, Lamar's fortunes changed for the better. His football franchise began to prosper, and he expanded his operations into baseball, soccer, basketball, and tennis. He founded the Dallas Tornado team in the North American Soccer League, and then financed the World Championship Tennis tournament with his nephew, Al Hill, Jr., a product of his sister Margaret's marriage in 1938.

"His next move will be to buy Wimbledon and stage his own tournament," a sportswriter wrote in his column one day.

The culmination of Lamar's efforts was the 1970 Super Bowl win of the Kansas City Chiefs. A Dallas group called the Bonehead Club decided to present Lamar with an award as a result of his winning season, and because of his role in the merger of the AFL and the NFL. At the head table with Lamar were his father and other members of his family. As the master of ceremonies, Jimmy the Greek, prepared to introduce Lamar to the crowd, Lamar grabbed him by the arm then turned to Arizona Slim. "Dad, you remember Jimmy the Greek, don't you?"

The two men, who hadn't spoken to or seen each other since Slim had refused to pay his gambling debt eight years earlier, stared into each other's eyes for a long minute. Slim was eighty-one years old and garbed in a disheveled blue suit that draped across his bulky frame like an old blanket. A few tufts of white hair stuck out above his ears, but his eyes were still as blue and clear as ever.

"Jimmy the Greek," smiled Arizona Slim. "Tell me, boy. Are you still strong on the Southeastern Conference?"

Following his big strike in the Libyan oil field, Bunker decided to expand his own area of interest too. Despite Arizona Slim's harsh criticisms of his second-oldest son over the years, Bunker was more his father's son than any of the others. Physically, they were cut from different molds. Bunker was round and fleshy, whereas his father had been hard and lean throughout his youth. Bunker was nearsighted and wore thick eyeglasses, which gave him a rather porcine appearance; his father had been clear-eyed and handsome and extremely attractive to women.

But the similarities more than made up for their dissimilar physical characteristics. More than any of Slim's other children, Bunker shared his father's political and racial attitudes. He contributed heavily to Slim's "Life Line" organization and later joined the advisory board of the John Birch Society. With his father, he helped promote the George Wallace–Curtis LeMay presidential campaign in 1968, another losing effort for the aging oilman. Again like his father, he cultivated the friendship of Jews and hired them as advisers in his own organizations, but he also believed in his heart of hearts that Jews belonged to a breed entirely different from that of Christians.

"Jews are different," Bunker said on more than one occasion. "They're different like Chinese are different, you have to admit. But they're smart and cunning. I never look a gift Jew in the mouth."

Bunker was brought up to be a God-fearing Christian by his mother, a persuasion not formally adopted by Slim until he had reached his seventieth birthday, and he shared his father's aversion to alcohol. He married a Texas girl, Caroline, shortly after his aborted college career and they brought four children into the world, a paltry number by his father's standards, but respectable nonetheless.

Bunker's share of Arizona Slim's kingdom consisted of

twenty percent of Placid Oil Company, a third of Penrod Drilling, a good percentage of the family real estate holdings, and cattle and farmlands that Slim had acquired over the years. To these he added, following his success in Libya, a growing stable of thoroughbred horses—the stable would eventually become the largest stable on earth—coal mines, and a chain of pizza parlors and food franchises stretching across the country. As the oil money flowed in from his fields in Libya, and his fortune grew, Bunker's attitude toward money developed along the same lines that Slim's had.

"Money is just something that, if you want to spend it, you have it. My father never really cared about money either. It's just how you keep score in life."

To Slim, money as money was nothing. It was something to make bookkeeping easy. The true meaning of life was the risk, the challenge. Once one had money, it was sinful to become stagnant. One had to keep searching for new risks to take. Bunker adopted that philosophy more than did any of Slim's other children. He was above all a gambler and a risk-taker. He was driven to seek out new challenges and new rewards in life.

As such, he was destined to inherit his father's mantle as head of the family. The bumbling boy who earned his father's scorn a short time earlier, emerged as the ruler of the kingdom by the time the 1970s were getting under way.

# 47.

THE LOSSES SUFFERED BY HLH Products, the food company that was Slim's obsession in later years, increasingly troubled Bunker and Herbert. It was the one weak link in the family kingdom, the only part of the sprawling network of business enterprises that lost money year after year. The boys tried to convince Slim that some of his closest aides were embezzling money from the corporation, but the old man dismissed the notion with a laugh and refused to take any action to rectify the situation. But Bunker and Herbert refused to take their father's word as final. Arizona Slim was getting old and, perhaps, a trifle senile. They decided to take matters into their own hands.

Early in 1970 a Dallas policeman stopped a car that had just run a stop sign. When he pulled the car over to the curb and saw some elaborate equipment in the back seat, he grew suspicious. After searching the car thoroughly, he discovered that the strange equipment was the kind used for wiretapping. The driver of the car admitted, under questioning, that he was a private detective and had been hired by Bunker and Herbert to tap the phones of some of their father's top lieutenants. They listened in on the conversations of his private secretary, some of the aides who had been with him for thirty years and longer, their cousin Tom, and perhaps even their half brother Ray, from Slim's marriage to Ruth.

"We did it to protect dad's money," said Bunker shortly afterward. "Besides, we didn't know it was illegal."

Somehow, the official reason for the wiretapping did not ring quite true. If Bunker and Herbert suspected Slim's associates of stealing money from him, why were they tapping the phones of their relatives as well? Might it have had something to do with the fact that Arizona Slim, after all, was getting on in years, and that they were worried about attempts by other members of his extended family to get him to change the terms of his will?

"Nonsense," said Bunker. "Dad's associates stole over $50 million from him over the years."

"Not true," said one of the accused associates. "Mr. Hunt has been stealing *from himself* to avoid paying taxes. We all knew about it, but nobody said anything out of loyalty."

Amid all the squabbling and interfamily accusations, Bunker and Herbert hired a public relations man from Denver to take pictures of themselves and their wives, their stepmother Ruth, their half brother Ray, their half sisters, and their assorted mates. They were all holding hands. We're just one big happy family, the picture seemed to say. One big happy family that would never stoop so low as to spy on one another over daddy's money.

While the wiretapping case was still going on, the plot growing thicker and more fascinating each day, America's relationship with Libya was taking a decided turn for the worse. On October 4, 1972, the Libyan Oil Ministry submitted a list of demands to Bunker Hunt. Among other things, Libya demanded a fifty percent interest in the profits he was making in the Sarir field, and fifty percent of the profits he had made in his sale of part of the concession to British Petroleum.

"Bunker Hunt's concession in Libya is purely personal," said the oil minister, Izz al-din al Mabruk, "and, frankly, such personal or family concessions are against the principles of our Libyan revolution. Bunker Hunt is doing nothing at all for us, and therefore we don't need him at all. He should adhere to this agreement with us; otherwise he will lose not just fifty percent of his interest, but the whole lot."

On December 14, after considering the demands, Bunker flatly refused to go along with them. In May of the following year, Libya made good its threat and announced that it was nationalizing his company and its operations, Hunt International Petroleum Company, which was known as Concession 65. The loss of some six billion barrels of known oil reserves amounted to a seizure of about $23 billion at the prevailing prices. Colonel Moammar el Khadafy stated that he was taking the action to give the United States, as well as British Petroleum, which shared in the venture, "a slap in the face."

Well, Bunker's religion may have told him to turn the other cheek when getting slapped in such a fashion, but he was not about to accept this decision without a fight. He immediately hopped on a plane and flew from Dallas to Tripoli, where he met with Major Jalloud, Khadafy's righthand man.

"I've always been a good friend of the Arabs," Bunker pleaded his case. "I'm not British. I have no connection with Iran and British operations in the Gulf. Why am I being held up for ransom?"

Bunker's exhortations fell on deaf ears, however. Infuriated, he boarded another plane and flew over to Algiers, where he had additional oil interest and had maintained a friendly relationship with Colonel Houari Boumedienne, the Algerian premier. Boumedienne proved more receptive than Khadafy, who was regarded as something of a fanatic even by militants within the Arab world. He wasted no time in intervening for Bunker, convincing Khadafy that the American oilman had nothing but "unswerving sympathy for the Arab cause," and that he was working to further Arab interests inside the United States.

This time Khadafy was willing to listen. His real fight was with the English, he agreed; he had nothing personally against the Hunts, only against the government in Washington and its pro-Israel position. Nelson Bunker Hunt was opposed to his government's Middle East foreign policy and was working to change it. Khadafy relented, and Concession 65 was returned to Hunt International Petroleum.

Bunker Hunt was not one to turn the other cheek. He was a battler, cut from the same cloth as Arizona Slim, and this time he had won.

When the criminal charge of wiretapping finally came to court in September 1975, Bunker Hunt asserted that he was being prosecuted by the federal government because he had refused to go along with the CIA's suggestion that he place a government spy in his Libya operation so that the CIA could keep a close watch on Colonel Khadafy. "We are being persecuted for our conservative political beliefs," said Bunker.

As the trial progressed in Lubbock, Texas, Bunker insisted that he had made a deal with President Richard Nixon that he would not be prosecuted in exchange for supplying the government with a list of Al Fatah agents in the United States, and now the government was reneging on its promise. In a show of unity, their stepmother, Ruth, declared in an interview that she supported Bunker and Herbert completely.

"I'd do anything for them," she testified on the witness stand.

Had they been convicted, Bunker and Herbert could have gone to jail for up to thirty years on six counts of wiretapping, and been fined $60,000, which would have been easier for them to handle. In the end, however, the jury believed that they had been acting in their father's interests and did not willingly and knowingly violate the law. They were acquitted on all six counts. Arizona Slim's boys had emerged victorious once again.

Alas, the patriarch of the family was not around to witness his sons' victory in court. Slim's raw vegetables and fruit, his abstention from alcohol and, later, from tobacco after he determined how much money it was costing him to unpeel the wrappers, and the rivers of Gastro-Majic he had been pumping into his system over the years all may have served to keep him in robust health into the eighth decade of his life, but not even the mythical powers of Gastro-Majic could render him immortal. The body that had served him so well, in and out of bed, on the oil fields and at the poker tables, finally stopped functioning. On November 29, 1974, three months before his eighty-sixth birthday, the old man was dead.

Arizona Slim had already left the bulk of his estate to the offspring of his first family in the trusts he had set up forty years earlier. His will gave eighty percent of the shares of Hunt Oil to his wife Ruth, and it named his only son by Ruth, Ray, now thirty-one, executor. These assets amounted to some $300 million, about a tenth of what Bunker and his siblings already possessed, but it was still enough to set the members of the extended family leaping for one another's throats. It is hard to say what offended Bunker more: the size of the estate his father had willed to Ruth or the choice of Ray, who was born illegitimately, as executor.

The total Hunt kingdom included three oil companies, Hunt Oil, Placid Oil, and Hunt International; Penrod Drilling; a refinery that produced asphalt and Parade gasoline; HLH Products; over a thousand thoroughbred horses owned by Bunker; a chain of fast-food enterprises going by the name of Shakey's Pizza; cattle ranches, coal mines, farms, cotton plantations, and huge tracts of real estate scattered throughout Wyoming, Montana, Texas, Mississippi, Arkansas, Louisiana, Florida, Georgia, and other states; oil concessions in the Middle East, Alaska, and other parts of the world; and various sports teams and related interests owned by Lamar. All in all, a mind-numbing array of wealth that made up the largest single fortune owned by one family on earth.

To complicate matters even further, Frania Tye Lee and her children from her marriage to Slim stepped out of the woodwork after Slim's death and filed suits against his estate on their own. When their suit went to trial in Shreveport, Louisiana, the families agreed to settle with Frania for $7.5 million, about which Frania had second thoughts and finally turned down.

Meanwhile, Bunker and his clan announced to half brother Ray that their interests were no longer the same, and it was time to divide the kingdom into two separate entities. Bunker formed a new corporation, Hunt Energy, which was distinct from Hunt Oil, and he and Herbert moved their offices from the twenty-ninth to the twenty-fifth floor of the First National Bank Building. The relationship between the two families had been tenuous at best over the years. They tolerated each other because it was the civilized thing to do; better to put on a good front for public consumption than to air the dirty laundry before the masses.

But now the charade was over. Arizona Slim was dead. The family patriarch was resting in the earth like any mortal. Death, the great leveler, balances the scales in the end.

Another era had ended; a new one had already begun.

# Book VIII

# The Silver Bulls

# 48.

BUNKER HUNT'S FASCINATION for silver started early in life. His political philosophy, coupled with his fundamentalist Christian beliefs, had led him to the conclusion as a young man that the civilized Western world was slowly being destroyed by atheistic communism. The worldwide communist conspiracy had succeeded in stretching its menacing red tentacles across larger and larger portions of the globe, and it was only a question of time before it imposed a stranglehold on the last bastion of freedom, the United States of America.

The communist assault was being coordinated in the capitals of the Soviet Union and Red China. It was aided and abetted by those in America who had taken control of the CIA, the Trilateral Commission, and the eastern liberal establishment, which was led by the Rockefeller clan. Henry Kissinger, George Bush, and Senator Jacob Javits of New York were just a few of the prominent Americans who had allowed themselves to be used by those arch villains Nelson and David Rockefeller.

Bunker Hunt had tried to combat the communist conspiracy all his life by establishing counterorganizations that identified the enemy and preached the truth. In addition to his personal and financial support of the John Birch Society, Bunker helped establish the Campus Crusade for Christ, a theologically conservative political and religious group which includes on its advisory board cowboy singing star Roy Rogers and W. Clement Stone, one of Richard Nixon's more outspoken and well-heeled supporters in the late-1960s.

But, with all his proselytizing and political activism, Bunker Hunt knew deep down that he was fighting a losing battle. The opposition was too well organized, and had taken control of our major universities long ago. Generations of American youth in our public schools had been brainwashed with the liberal-left message from the time they were old enough to start kindergarten. The intellectual poisoning of American youth had reached such startling dimensions that Bunker frequently instructed William Bledsoe, one of his aides, "Never hire a Phi Beta Kappa. They all turn into communists."

Later, on, when confronted with this statement, Bunker amended it slightly.

"I know a lot of Phi Beta Kappas that are good conservatives," he said. "A lot of them turn into communists, though."

Because he sincerely believed that the anticommunist Christian world was losing its battle with atheistic communism and was eventually headed for extinction, Bunker started to worry more and more about his own survival and that of his family. Somewhere in this world he had to find a bedrock of stability and anchor his fortunes to it. Gold was the divine commodity, the key to salvation, for a great number of people who shared political and economic views similar to his own. Bunker flirted with the goldbug philosophy for a while but eventually turned from it. True, gold had been an anchor of stability through the ages, the one standard of true value as the world struggled through centuries of war, famine, plague, darkness, and staggering inflation. But gold was too easily manipulated for Bunker's tastes. It was too political, too readily controlled by forces beyond his sphere of influence.

No, gold would not do for him. He would have to keep searching until he found something else to which to tie his fortunes.

And then one day he found it. If not gold, why not its sister, silver? Overlooked and neglected for decades, silver had at one time been as sound a backing for paper money, and as reliable a discipline and hedge against inflation, as the more glamorous gold. Bunker put his researchers to work immediately, and what they discovered about the metal convinced him all the more that he was on the right track.

As the decade of the 1970s was getting under way, silver was selling for about $2 an ounce, down from $5 an ounce a few years earlier. World silver production was some three hundred million ounces a year, and consumption, primarily because of industrial demand, was growing steadily. Already the demand for silver had risen to five hundred million ounces a year, and the gap between production and demand was being filled mostly by sales of government supplies in the United States, Mexico, Canada, and India, and from private hoards in the Arab countries. When these supplies dwindled, Bunker's advisers told him, the shortfall between production and demand would drive the price of silver to historical highs.

Bunker Hunt needed no further convincing. The price of silver was much undervalued, he told his brother Herbert. Acting on the advice of Alvin Brodsky, who was affiliated with the investment firm of Bache, the brothers started buying futures contracts. The difference between the two Hunts and the other buyers of futures contracts was critical. When the average speculator buys a futures contract, he is hoping that the price of the commodity in question will rise in value during the life of the contract so that he can sell the contract for a profit. The Hunt brothers, however, unlike other speculators, were not interested in trading for short-term profits. They were investing for the long haul; they were thinking of Armageddon. Salvation and survival were their concern, not another few million dollars to add to their already vast supply of paper currency, which was depreciating in value every year because of inflation. With all his billions, Bunker Hunt was truly worried about going broke some day in the future.

"A billion ain't what it used to be," he remarked on more than one occasion to William Bledsoe.

He was well versed about the great German hyperinflation of 300,000 percent a year and the several trillion marks needed to buy a loaf of bread. The way things were going in the United States, it was not too farfetched to think that it could happen here. Then what good would his estimated worth of $3 to $4 billion do him when paper money became virtually worthless? No, Bunker was not merely interested in trading futures contracts for a measly few million bucks of profit in paper money. He wanted the commodity itself, salvation and survival for himself and his family in the future. Unlike other buyers of futures contracts, he wanted to take delivery of the metal.

And in December 1973 he did just that. He and his brother Herbert took their first delivery of twenty-five million ounces of silver, worth about $3 an ounce, which they had to pay for, of course. It was the beginning of their quiet and orderly purchases of the bedrock of salvation.

# 49.

WILLIAM BLEDSOE WAS HIRED by the boys in
1965 to work for Placid Oil, and soon he became
one of their most trusted lieutenants. He assisted them in just
about every area of their varied activities, buying oil leases,
managing their cotton plantations, buying up hundreds of
thousands of acres of ranch land for Bunker, and helping him
to broaden the boundaries of the kingdom to encompass
nearly four million acres of land, a hundred thousand head of
cattle, and nearly a thousand thoroughbred racehorses. He
was a soft-spoken, unassuming man, hard-working and loyal,
who completely identified his own interests with those of his
employers. As such, he was the perfect aide-de-camp and all-
round amanuensis.

In addition to his usual duties, Bledsoe became closely
involved with Bunker, Herbert, and, to a lesser extent, Lamar
when the brothers grew infatuated with silver in the early
1970s. Bunker, particularly, had taken to speculating on
soybeans, sugar, and avocados, but these were amusements for
him, diversions to satisfy the inclination for gambling he
inherited from Arizona Slim. Silver was different. Bledsoe
noticed early that Bunker's preoccupation with silver was
becoming an obsession with him. The aide could not completely understand it at first. He did notice, however, that
Bunker's monomania had also infected Herbert. Bunker had
managed to turn his younger brother into a true believer.

When the boys took delivery of the first twenty-five million ounces in 1973, Bledsoe realized that silver had suddenly become the most important thing in the world to them.

"They discuss silver all day long," said Bledsoe. "They have other interests, yes. But silver is first and prime in their minds. The strategy is determined daily whether Bunker and Herbert will buy or sell in their own names or in family or corporate names."

Early the following year, Bunker and Herbert took delivery of another huge supply of silver, bringing their total to fifty-five million ounces, or slightly less than ten percent of the known world supply. Imagine that. In no time flat the boys accumulated almost ten percent of the world's existing silver supply, and largely because of their own heavy buying, the price shot up to a shade over $6 an ounce. Now they had a unique problem. There they were, in possession of this gargantuan mountain of silver, worth around $300 million, and they had nowhere to put it. What were they to do with it now that they had taken delivery?

Hiding fifty-five million ounces of silver safely so that no one else can lay greedy hands on it is not child's play. First of all, one needs a big place to store it. Second, the place must be so secure as to be immune to war, pestilence, calamity, and social upheaval.

Only one place on earth passed that test, Bunker reasoned. One safe spot remained that respected privacy and monumental wealth, with no questions asked as to how it was acquired, and that stood aloof from all the squabbles afflicting other nations. That place was Switzerland, and somehow or other, come hell or high water, Bunker must find a way to transport his silver mountain there.

The time was early 1974, shortly before the split between Bunker and Herbert on the one hand and Slim's third family, by Ruth, on the other. Randy Kreiling, one of his brothers-in-law through that marriage, was managing one of the family's cattle ranches on a twenty-five-hundred-acre spread east of Dallas. Randy was something of a commodities expert as well as a ranch boss, and along with Alvin Brodsky, the broker from Bache, had been advising Bunker and Herbert in their silver dealings.

"Tell Randy," Bunker said to Bledsoe, "that I want to get that silver over to Switzerland the soonest. It's more important than anything else he's got to do right now. We got to get it over there as quiet as possible. He'll know how to handle it."

Randy was a good manager and knew what had to be done. He enlisted the aid of his brother Till, and they decided to hire some airplanes to carry the metal across the ocean. The planes had to be big, big enough to accommodate all the silver and people to stand guard over it twenty-four hours a day. The Kreiling brothers scouted around and chartered three 707s for the trip at a cost of about $200,000.

Next, Randy and Till required some devoted and capable men who could be trusted to safeguard the precious metal with their lives and be quiet about it. Those were the two characteristics essential for the job: ability to use a shotgun and a pistol, and devotion to the Hunt family and their interests. The Kreiling brothers knew such men; they were ranch hands and cowboys at the family's Circle K Ranch, which Randy managed.

Randy wanted to recruit the best among them, only the best, to do the job. What better way to find out who had the fastest draw and who was the surest shot than by staging a shootout? In bygone days, feudal lords had their warriors engage one another in combat to see who was the strongest, and the survivors were rewarded with money and position. Nowadays, however, things are done differently. The cowboys on the Circle K did not have to peg shots at one another to win their master's favor. Instead, they merely shot at practice targets set up away from the cattle and other domesticated beasts so as not to frighten them. When the final shot was fired and the scores tallied, the twelve winners were chosen to ride shotgun on the 707s during the journey ahead.

One by one the huge airplanes took off from Dallas, shining, appropriately, bright and silver in the moonlight. Broad swaths of tape covered the name of the charter company on the side of the planes. In the darkness of night the 707s landed at LaGuardia in New York City. As Kreiling's cowboys stood guard, shotguns in hand, armored trucks drove out to the airport from the New York Commodity Exchange warehouse in Manhattan, and security guards started to load some forty million ounces of silver into the planes. The remaining fifteen million ounces still sat in vaults across the Hudson River in New Jersey and out in Chicago. Randy had miscalculated when he chartered the 707s. He had rented three planes and recruited a dozen cowboys before realizing that this was clearly a four-plane, sixteen-cowboy job. Storage alone was costing Bunker and Herbert $3 million a year.

In Zurich the 707s were again greeted by armored trucks, these from five different banks scattered across the city. It was just as well that Randy had taken only forty million ounces of the metal with him. Switzerland, after all, is a small country. Space is limited—every mafia chieftain, South American dictator, and nervous multimillionaire on earth is hiding a hoard there—and what is available is in the high-rent category. Bunker's silver was stashed away in the vaults of the Credit Suisse Bank, the Banque Populaire Suisse, the Union Bank of Switzerland, the Swiss Bank Corporation, and Freidlager's, but not all; there wasn't room enough. At the last minute, Randy and Till had to make some hasty phone calls and locate more available vault space. Switzerland, land of lakes and mountains and contraband, virtually lay atop a sea of silver.

Meanwhile, back in Chicago, word began to circulate among the brokers and traders on the floor of the commodities exchange that *one* party had taken delivery of all that silver. Previously it was believed that thousands of individual traders all over the world had suddenly grown bullish on silver.

"*One* party?" the traders asked one another in disbelief.

"Who? Who took delivery of all that silver?"

"Some Texan named Nelson Bunker Hunt."

"Nelson Bunker Hunt? Never heard of him."

"You goddamn well better know who he is. The son of a bitch is going to corner the market."

In the spring of 1974 panic set in. One man was going to corner the world's silver supply. The price of silver was going to go sky-high. Buy, buy, the word went out to commodity exchanges in London, Switzerland, Frankfurt, and Tokyo. The value of silver has got to go to the moon. When enough people believe a thing will happen, it becomes a self-fulfilling prophecy. They act in concert, spontaneously, to make it happen.

Sure enough, the price of silver suddenly started to go up.

# 50.

AT THIS STAGE OF HIS LIFE, as he approached his fiftieth birthday, Bunker Hunt weighed in at somewhere around three hundred pounds. The chubby, nearsighted boy who had earned his father's scorn in the years right after World War II had a voracious appetite for food as well as for silver. The last time he had been relatively slim was twenty-five years earlier, when he was courting Caroline, the wholesome Texas girl who became his wife. He had gone on a diet at that time, but shortly afterward he resumed his gargantuan consumption of cheeseburgers, pie, cake, and vats upon vats of ice cream.

Despite his size, Bunker was surprisingly active physically. He enjoyed mounting his high-bred horses on his sprawling estate outside Dallas for a romp through the fields. His horses fascinated him for a variety of reasons.

"Horse racing," he explained to a friend, "is an irresistible combination of business, sport, and genetics."

Yes, it was all in the genes. The way it was with people, so it was with horses. Genes. Breeding. That's how you got superior stock.

In addition to horseback riding, Bunker made a point of getting out on the track as often as his busy schedule would allow and jogging to keep his body in condition. He was a surprisingly nimble man, with excellent stamina, for someone with three hundred pounds to lug around. He also enjoyed a vigorous game of racquetball to work up a heavy sweat.

To the traits and beliefs that Bunker had inherited from Arizona Slim, another must be added, this one touching on the eccentric. Slim was rarely seen in public without his ill-matching blue suit in his later years, and Bunker had a mania for the color brown. As he entered the middle years of his life, his business attire was invariably a rather drab and lifeless brown suit.

Nearly equaling his attachment to brown was Bunker's penchant for ice cream. His employees had long ago gotten used to passing his office on the twenty-fifth floor of the First National Bank Building in Dallas, and observing their boss, behind his paper-strewn desk, dictating reports to a battery of secretaries while he spooned ice cream from a quart container in his hand.

Bunker's younger brother Herbert was less quirky, less flamboyant in his lifestyle and personal demeanor.

"Bunker is very farsighted, very perceptive," Herbert unashamedly admitted to his associates. "He's not one to fool with details. He prefers to conceive something and then step back. I get more involved in the details."

Herbert, while occasionally running a bit to the beefy side, was more fanatical about maintaining an exercise program to stay in condition. He jogged regularly around the track that circled Bachman Lake near his home in University Park, a Dallas suburb. When he finished his daily four-mile run at six or six-thirty in the morning, he would jump into his old Mercedes and return to the white-brick house he bought for himself and his wife, Nancy, for $70,000 in 1960. After a dip in his pool to cool off, Herbert, water dripping from his bathing suit, would go into the kitchen to prepare himself a huge breakfast of cantaloupe, grapefruit, orange juice, and eggs.

His office was much tidier than Bunker's, which he described as a filing clerk's nightmare. Everything was neatly in place, and it was more traditionally furnished than his brother's—Bunker had paintings of his favorite racehorses on the walls and a $30,000 statue of a Texas Ranger in the corner. In the evenings, Herbert played tennis with Nancy or tossed a football around with one of his sons to work up an appetite for dinner.

Despite these outward differences in personality and style, or maybe because of them, Bunker and Herbert got along with each other extremely well. They complemented each other perfectly. They were two peas from the same pod, more alike deep down than appearances revealed.

With all that silver tucked away in warehouses and vaults in the United States and Switzerland, Bunker decided it was time to put phase two of his grand design on silver into operation. Now that he owned his own private silver mountain, he had to make sure that it kept growing in value, that the price of silver kept on moving in the right direction—upward. There was no point in stuffing fifty-five million ounces of silver away for a rainy day if it were going to lose value over the years.

The best way to make certain that a commodity appreciates rather than depreciates in value is to convince other people, lots of people with a great deal of money, that they too should buy that commodity. In March 1975 Bunker attempted to do just that. He told William Bledsoe to pack his suitcase, then the two of them boarded an airplane and flew to Iran. Their intermediary in Teheran was Prince Mahmoud Reza Pahlavi, the shah's brother, who had scheduled an interview with the shah upon Bunker's arrival. When their limousine pulled up at the Royal Palace, however, Prince Mahmoud informed Bunker that his brother was not available.

"He is attending to other pressing business," said the prince as diplomatically as he could. "But he did ask me to have you meet with his minister of finance, Hushang Ansary, at his villa tomorrow morning at 7:30."

Disgruntled but not defeated, Bunker returned to his hotel only to discover that the airline had lost his luggage. Here he was, the leader of one of the wealthiest families on earth, without a change of clothes or a toothbrush to his name. Bledsoe, faithful servant, was dispatched to the streets of Teheran to locate some shirts and toiletries for their meeting in the morning.

Iran is a land of lean, darkish people with fairly exotic tastes in haberdashery by Western standards, and the task of finding a suitable business shirt with a twenty-inch collar for his gargantuan boss was perhaps the most difficult one Bledsoe had ever tackled. When he rejoined Bunker at the hotel a bit later, Bledsoe opened his package to reveal a lavender frock with frilly sleeves, and some cryptic design running across the chest. Bledsoe asserted that it was the most suitable garment he could find at this late hour, but Bunker was furious. To say that it would clash with the outsized brown suit he had hanging in the closet is to strain the art of understatement.

Attired in this startling fashion, the two men set out early the following morning for their meeting with Hushang Ansary. His villa on the outskirts of Teheran was resplendent under the morning sun, a domicile fit for majesty. If ministers of finance lived this well in Iran, the shah himself must have occupied a manse worthy of the gods. Although the hour was early, the temperature had soared beyond the threshold of pain, and Bunker was perspiring profusely through his lavender shirt and brown suit.

Throughout the meeting with Ansary, the minister of finance fidgeted nervously in his chair as he stared openly at Bunker's shirt. Even Bunker's explanation of the foulup with the airline failed to mollify the man. Bunker, therefore, was at something of a disadvantage as he presented his sales pitch.

"Do you believe that you will be paying more for the price of goods next year than you are this year?" Bunker asked his host, using the same tactic Brodsky, the Bache broker, had used on him a few years earlier.

Ansary nodded in the affirmative without committing himself to words.

"Then you have to believe that the price of silver will keep on rising since it's one of the last hedges left against inflation," Bunker pressed.

"Perhaps," Ansary said softly, eyeing Bunker's chest.

"If you can convince the Pahlavi family to put one month's oil production into silver, together we can drive the price way up and ensure our assets against rampant inflation."

"You Americans are interesting people," said Ansary. "Just a few days ago I met with your secretary of state, Henry Kissinger, who tried to convince me that our best investment would be in American weapons. I find it all extremely confusing."

"My brother Herbert and I already control over fifty million ounces," Bunker continued. "That's almost ten percent of the entire world supply."

"Perhaps you would consider selling us some silver out of your private stock," Ansary teased.

"I suggest that it would be better to buy your bullion in the New York and London markets," said Bunker, growing a bit testy, "and store it in Switzerland, where we keep most of ours."

At this point in the conversation, Ansary could no longer contain himself. Fixing on Bunker's sweat-soaked Iranian shirt beneath his rumpled brown suit, a combination that offended the minister's sense of propriety, Ansary asked point-blank, in the iciest tone he could muster, "Do you mind telling me exactly how much money you made last year?"

Bunker stared at Ansary as though struck between the eyes with a sledgehammer. It was one of the few occasions in his life when he had been rendered speechless.

Clearly, this was not Nelson Bunker Hunt's finest hour.


With his luggage finally in tow, his head splitting from the thick, pervasive smog and the blasting heat, Bunker caught the next plane out of Teheran heading for parts more agreeable to his tastes; his destination was Zurich.

After a stop in Paris to check on some of his racehorses, Bunker and Bledsoe eventually set down in Zurich. Bunker was still fuming over his failed mission and the treatment he had received in Teheran, but he pulled himself together and planned his next line of attack. If the shah would not cooperate with him in his effort to corner the world's supply of silver and run up the price, perhaps King Faisal of Saudi Arabia would be more agreeable.

Bunker placed a call to Ben Freedman, an old political ally of his father's, in New York City. Freedman was a right-wing political activist from years back, and an expert on Israeli-Arab affairs who was a close friend of King Faisal. Freedman was also an anti-Zionist Jew, Arizona Slim's and Bunker's favorite kind.

"Ben, I'd like you to set up a meeting with Faisal for me," Bunker said. "I have some business I want to discuss with him."

"Listen to me now," the old man cautioned. "Everybody over there is aware of your recent presence in Iran. You have to do this just right to avoid offending anyone. If you go back right away it will look like Faisal is your second choice. Come back home now and leave from the United States to see Faisal in about two weeks. It's more respectful that way."

Freedman's suggestion made good sense to Bunker, so he agreed to fly back to Dallas with the understanding that Freedman would arrange a meeting for him with Faisal in two weeks. Bledsoe, however, was instructed to remain behind in Zurich.

"Find me some more vault space," Bunker said to him. "I got to find more room to store my silver."

Bledsoe made the rounds of the Swiss banks, presenting his business card by way of introducing himself. The card read simply:

BILL BLEDSOE
SPECIAL REPRESENTATIVE
NELSON BUNKER HUNT

Bunker's name was well known in financial circles throughout the country, and Bledsoe had no difficulty gaining access to the inner sanctums of the banks on a moment's notice. In due time he was able to locate the additional space Bunker required.

Whether or not Bunker would have been more successful on his silver crusade with King Faisal than he had been with the shah of Iran will never be known. Bunker was back in Dallas tending to family business and waiting for word from Freedman that a meeting had been arranged. He turned on his radio and heard the shocking news: an assassin's bullet had struck the monarch on March 25, 1975. The king of Saudi Arabia, the good friend of Slim's old ally Ben Freedman, was dead.

# 51.

I F BLEDSOE THOUGHT THAT he alone was concerned that Bunker was allowing the family's oil interests to slip because of his preoccupation with silver, he was wrong. Older sister Margaret, never one to hold her tongue and suppress her opinions, was opposed to her brothers' attempts to corner the silver market. So were half brother Ray, sister Caroline, and other family members with interlocking interests in the family's business empire. Lamar was the only one, other than Herbert, of course, who sympathized with Bunker's views on silver, but he was far less involved than his two older brothers.

Bunker had committed so much cash to silver purchases that on several occasions the family, with all its vast, staggering wealth, was unable to raise the money to acquire valuable oil leases. In 1975 Bunker and Herbert could not come up with half a million dollars to continue drilling in a Dutch gas field and were forced to raise the necessary funds from a German investment group. Why? Because the brothers had just spent several hundred million dollars on a new silver delivery.

In 1977 they failed to raise a similar sum to acquire an oil lease on Profit Island in Louisiana, a lease that quickly doubled in value. Fortunately for the other members of the family, the Caroline Hunt Trust Estate and the Hassie Hunt Exploration Company were solvent enough to put up the money.

To make matters even worse, the price of silver started to sag in the mid-1970s, shortly after Bunker's massive purchases. So far he and Herbert had failed to enlist the support of other like-minded investors around the world, and they were forced to keep on buying the metal themselves for no other reason than to prop up the price. Unless the brothers convinced others with millions of dollars at their disposal that it was in their best interests to start accumulating silver, they stood to lose a considerable sum on their bizarre investment.

It was inevitable that, sooner or later, given the cash crunch they had created and the mediocre performance of their silver investment to date, Bunker and Herbert would arrive at the narrow line separating them from Uncle Sam's watchdogs.

Bunker had expected the price of silver to rise to stratospheric levels by this time, and was immensely disappointed by its failure to do so. Growing more impatient by the day, he started to borrow money, using his silver as collateral, and he used the cash to speculate heavily on other commodities such as soybeans and sugar. After getting into trouble with the Commodity Futures Trading Commission for speculating beyond the three-million-bushel limit on soybeans, Bunker concentrated his energies on sugar.

The Great Western United Corporation was the largest sugar refiner in the United States, and Bunker thought it would make a splendid addition to the family kingdom. Shortly before his father's death, he invested $3 million in the company's stock only to learn soon afterward that Great Western had financial problems aplenty. Well, he reasoned, what better way to solve the company's problems than by taking it over and running it himself. So, he pumped $30 million more into Great Western stock, and that gave him sixty-one percent control of the corporation.

Now Bunker came face to face with a kind of problem different from what he had ever faced before. All the stock in the family businesses was privately held by himself, his stepmother, and assorted siblings. Private corporations are not required to file lengthy reports and financial statements each year with the federal government, and that cuts down considerably on the amount of paperwork. For the first time in his life, however, Bunker was majority owner of a corporation whose shares were owned by the general public, and Uncle Sam was breathing hard down his neck for failing to file all those disclosure papers required by law.

Compounding these thorny new legal hassles was the fact that the bottom was dropping out of the sugar market. The price of sugar suddenly started to plummet, and Great Western's fortunes fell with it, amounting to a loss of some $100 million. At this point Bunker realized that he had a potential financial disaster on his hands; he owned sixty-one percent of a time bomb that was threatening to blow up at any moment. On top of that, agents of the federal government were snooping around, checking more deeply into his affairs.

"Dad was right," sister Margaret snarled to the other members of the family. "Bunker's an idiot. He's going to drive us all into bankruptcy."

Bunker decided that maybe sugar wasn't for him after all. He had been right in the first place; silver had no place to go but up. He had grown impatient and gotten sidetracked from his main goal by fooling around with all these other commodities. The only way out of this mess was to cut his losses, take his licking like a man, and regroup for a new assault on silver. And that's exactly what he did. He sold off the rest of

Great Western's sugar contracts at huge losses, and plowed the proceeds back into silver futures once again. By early 1976 Great Western was no longer in the sugar business. All its assets were tied to silver. Later that year the company took delivery of an additional twenty million ounces of the metal.

"Get me President Marcos on the phone," Bunker said to William Bledsoe. "I'm going to make him an offer he can't refuse."

The aide did as he was told and listened as Bunker got on the extension and discussed with his friend, the president of the Philippines, one of the most fanciful schemes ever devised.

"I want to buy some sugar from you and pay for it with silver," said Bunker. "I'm willing to pay you a good price for the sugar, but there's a catch. When you buy your oil from the Saudis I want you to pay for it with the silver."

Marcos listened politely, trying to figure out in his own mind exactly what Bunker was up to with his intricate scenario. He was offering the Philippine president above-market prices for his sugar; obviously he wasn't doing this out of the goodness of his heart. There had to be something in it for Bunker on the other end of the deal, the purchase of Saudi crude oil with silver instead of with dollars and other accepted currencies. President Marcos was interested enough to invite Bunker over to discuss the matter in greater detail.

Bunker was all smiles as he hung up the phone. He came charging out of his office, rubbing his hands together vigorously and beaming broadly.

"We kill two birds with one stone this way," he said to Bledsoe. "We drive up the price of sugar by paying higher prices for it. That's good for Great Western. And we get the Ay-rabs to invest in silver indirectly by paying for it with their oil. That's good for Bunker Hunt."

Bledsoe stared at his boss in disbelief. He was mesmerized, bewitched by the immensity of it all. The plot was something straight out of James Bond. It was simple, yet diabolical. It was so crazy it could even work.

And it just might have worked like clockwork except for one huge hurdle. When Herbert Hunt went over to visit Marcos a week later, the Philippine president had bad news for him. The plan appealed to him personally, he explained, but the International Monetary Fund refused to go along with it.

"IMF lends us a great deal of money to buy crude," he said to Herbert, "and I have just been informed that they will no longer do so if we attempt to use silver as a currency. In any event, it is doubtful that the Saudis will accept the silver as a form of payment. I'm sorry, my friend."

And so, Bunker's grand design failed to fructify. It was shot down by the IMF, which, Bunker argued, was controlled by the Trilateral Commission, the Rockefellers, and the northeastern liberal establishment. Everywhere he turned, the conspiracy was there, working in concert against him. The network was vast, ubiquitous. There was no escaping its sinister web. There he was, doing his bit to save the world from the Red menace, to make the world safe for capitalism, and they wouldn't leave him alone. The communists were out to destroy every bedrock of stability and freedom left in the world. Communism was determined to undermine his security and wither away his fortune with rampant inflation.

But Bunker was not finished yet. His adversaries were tough and clever, but he would not go down without a struggle. They may have won the latest battle, but a war remained to be fought.

# 52.

W E'RE GOING TO BUY us a silver mine, the biggest silver mine in the whole country," Bunker yelled at Bledsoe. The Hunt family amanuensis had been a calm, reserved man all his life, but recently he had developed some nervous tics. This silver business was becoming a nightmare for him. On the few occasions when he attempted to divert Bunker's attention from silver to the oil business, Bunker had flown into a rage. There was just no reasoning with the man on the subject. He was possessed, a devil loose in him. Bledsoe's main concern was that Bunker was going to destroy himself and, in doing so, bring his entire family, the family Bledsoe had served so well for over a decade, to ruin with him.

The silver mine Bunker had his eye on was Big Creek Mine, just outside Kellogg, Idaho. Big Creek was owned by the Sunshine Mining Company and contained estimated reserves of thirty million ounces of silver, the largest known lode in the United States. Bunker wanted the mine badly, figuring that, as a commercial dealer in bullion, he would not be limited by the trading restrictions on the commodities exchanges. Only one thing was wrong with Bunker's plan: the company that owned the mine, Sunshine Mining, had no intentions of selling it.

Bunker was not one to be deterred by such a minor consideration. If Sunshine Mining refused to sell, why then Bunker and Herbert would have to go out and buy it behind the company's back. Sunshine Mining was a public corporation, with most of the outstanding shares in the hands of general investors. Through Great Western, the brothers started accumulating shares in Sunshine Mining, buying them in the open market. The management of Sunshine put the word out to its shareholders that it opposed this attempt by the Hunt brothers to gain control of the company. A takeover by the Hunts would not be in the best interests of the corporation, said management. Lawsuits were threatened on both sides, and in the end an agreement was struck. Great Western wound up with twenty-eight percent of Sunshine's shares for $20 million, and had an option to acquire the remaining shares for a minimum of $60 million.

All of the publicity about litigation wasn't doing Great Western any good, Bunker reasoned. In addition to its silver, its sugar refining plants, and its interest in Sunshine Mining, Great Western also owned a fast-food chain called Shakey's Pizza Parlors. The brothers decided that Great Western should get into the oil business as well, so they formed a subsidiary called the Impel Corporation to explore for oil and gas. They then changed the name of Great Western, which had become something of an albatross around their necks, to the Hunt International Resources Corporation.

The Hunt kingdom, rocked though it had been by some devastating gales, was still intact. The boundaries of the kingdom continued to broaden.


Bunker never did abandon his attempt to get the Arabs involved in his silver scheme. After his failed mission to Iran a few years earlier, followed by the assassination of King Faisal, Bunker put the plan on hold for the time being, but it was never completely out of his mind.

Early in 1978 he called his friend John Connally, the

former governor of Texas who had been in the limousine with John F. Kennedy the day when an assassin's bullet took the president's life.

"John, I understand you're a pretty good friend of Mahfouz in Saudi Arabia. Do you think you can arrange a meeting with him and some other Arab investors? I have a business proposition I want to talk over with them."

Connally was only too happy to oblige. In 1974, when Libya nationalized Bunker's oil leases, the Hunts had paid him a fee of $70,000 to help smooth out their problems. Connally's contacts among the Arabs were legendary. Sheik Khaled Ben Mahfouz, the gentleman Bunker was so anxious to meet, owned the National Commercial Bank of Saudi Arabia and had sold an interest in the bank to Connally. Well, one good turn deserves another, so John reciprocated by letting the sheik buy into the Main Bank in Houston, an establishment of which Connally also owned a piece. Another good buddy of the former governor's was Saudi investor Ghaith Pharaon, who owned a chunk of Bert Lance's National Bank of Georgia, as chance would have it. Lance had already been forced to resign his post in the Carter administration because of his questionable business dealings.

John set up the meeting Bunker requested in the Mayflower Hotel in Washington, D.C., in February 1978. Sheiks rarely travel alone, and Ben Mahfouz was no exception. He arrived with his entourage and occupied an entire floor in the hotel, with some forty personal bodyguards posted in the corridors outside his rooms. Bunker and Connally flew up together from Dallas, along with Bunker's faithful assistant, William Bledsoe. John was ushered past the platoon of bodyguards in no time flat and shown into the sheik's suite.

After making introductions all around, the men took their seats on the sofas and chairs in the living room. Connally sat across from the sheik, and Bledsoe occupied a chair alongside

Connally at Bunker's righthand side. Bunker was wearing his customary brown business suit, with a proper white American dress shirt for the occasion. No lavender lace frocks this time. Ben Mahfouz sat on Bunker's left and behind him stood a battery of financial advisers in their traditional headdress.

The men settled into their seats and prepared to discuss business. Bunker cleared his throat and made his opening pitch: "Sheik Mahfouz, do you think you will be paying more for the price of goods next year than..."

Shortly after the meeting in the Mayflower Hotel, the price of silver started to rise, apparently of its own accord. Bunker's researchers had been right six years earlier, but their timing had been off. There was a huge gap between production and demand, and sooner or later this shortfall would have to exert upward pressure on the price of the metal. Bunker had been discouraged during the recent years, waiting for market forces to take their toll, and he began to worry that he and his advisers might have miscalculated somehow. As it turned out, however, their calculations were correct; it just took the market a little longer to work in their favor than they had expected.

The sudden spurt in the price of silver was beneficial to Bunker in one way but hurt him in an area not foreseen. The benefit came from Sheik Khaled Ben Mahfouz. On his return to Saudi Arabia, the sheik was undecided about becoming involved with Bunker and his scheme to corner the world's silver market. But when he noticed that the price of silver had suddenly started to rise as though by magic, he wondered if Bunker was some kind of a clairvoyant genius who ought to be taken seriously. The man *was* an American billionaire, and a good friend of John Connally, who certainly knew his way around the financial world. Why not invest in silver? Gold was moving up strongly in value. Wasn't it logical to assume that silver would follow it?

The unexpected negative development resulted from the fact that the folk back at Sunshine Mining figured their mine was worth a lot more now, with rising silver prices, than it was when they agreed to sell it. Originally they struck a deal with Bunker and Herbert to acquire the remaining shares for a minimum of $60 million.

"The price is too low," G. Michael Boswell, the president of Sunshine, informed Bunker over the phone. "The value of the mine is worth twice that amount, maybe more."

"A deal's a deal," Bunker bellowed into the mouthpiece. "We made a bargain and that's that. Why are you trying to hold me up all of a sudden?"

"The situation's changed. We all have to adjust to new developments. That's what business is all about."

"Don't tell me about business. I'm making a tender offer for the rest of the stock and that's that," Bunker fumed, then slammed down the receiver.

"Where's Bledsoe?" he yelled at his secretary. "Get me Bledsoe! We're going after the rest of Sunshine right away."

This was a fight that Bledsoe was not looking forward to. He was already up to two bottles of Maalox a day, and his stomach still felt as though a tornado were residing there. Bledsoe had the legal staff draw up the necessary papers, and the Hunt brothers sent out letters offering to buy up the outstanding shares of Sunshine Mining for $15 a share.

Boswell reciprocated with a letter of his own, telling Sunshine's shareholders that their stock was worth much more than the Hunts' bid. He exhorted them to hold out for a better price. Boswell's letter was effective. The price of silver was mounting steadily, and most of the stockholders figured they could do better by just sitting back and letting the market drive their shares higher and higher.

Bunker wanted the company and its mine badly, but there was a limit to what he would pay for it. Conceding the battle to Boswell, he and Herbert dropped their bid for the shares and bought up the outstanding shares in Hunt International Resources instead. There was some consolation in this, at least. By owning all the stock in Hunt International Resources, they turned it into a privately held corporation. No longer would they have to comply with all those nasty government regulations on financial disclosures. Like all the other corporations and interlocking business enterprises they owned, this latest acquisition would be shielded from the penetrating eyes of Uncle Sam.

With this piece of business out of the way, the boys planned their next assault on the silver market. One way or the other, they were going to buy up most of the silver on earth. The war was just beginning.

# 53.

BUNKER'S DREAM WAS coming true. Finally, after all these years of trying to form an alliance with the Arabs and their vast resources, he saw his plan take form. On July 1, 1979, Bunker and Herbert sent one of their attorneys, Robert Guinn, to Bermuda to set up an offshore trading corporation called International Metals Investment Company. In addition to Bunker and his brother Herbert, the company's directors included two Saudi Arabians, Sheik Ali Ben Mussallam and Sheik Mohammed Aboud Al-Amoudi. The gentleman whom Bunker had met with in Washington, Sheik Khaled Ben Mahfouz, was not directly involved, but it was no doubt with his blessing that his business associates were principals in International Metals with Bunker and Herbert.

Now it was time to get down to serious business—the acquisition of a whole mountain range of silver bullion.

"If we run out of vault space," Bunker said to Bledsoe, "we'll just stick it over there next to one of them Alps. Nobody'll know the difference."

The sheiks were well connected in the Arab world, and had access to billions of dollars of investment money in addition to their own considerable fortunes. The newly formed investment company wasted no time at all. Bunker's plan was set in motion before the ink was dry on the legal forms. Using their own hoard of silver as collateral, Bunker and Herbert borrowed additional capital to buy more futures contracts.

Thus began one of the most monumental pyramiding schemes in the history of investment. The more they bought, along with their Arab partners, the more the price of silver would go up; the higher the price of silver, the more valuable their silver and their contracts would become, and the more they could borrow against them to buy additional contracts.

The scheme was foolproof just so long as the price of silver kept moving higher. With all those billions upon billions of dollars the brothers and the Arabs had behind them, there was no reason to believe that they could not continue driving up the price until... until... well, until there was no more silver left to take delivery of. Truly, Bunker was larger than life in more ways than one. He was a big man physically, yes. But he thought big too.

Through the rest of 1979, the price of silver kept advancing. Gold was roaring into the stratosphere as well, $400, $500, $600 an ounce, and silver was soaring with it, $10, $14, $17, $20 an ounce. How high could it go? There had to be a limit! Silver was heading to the moon! Bunker's plan was working so well that he decided to expand on it a bit. He created the Profit Investment Company as a subsidiary of International Metals and got more Arabs and some Brazilians in on the plan. In naming his new subsidiary, Bunker brought the Hunt myth full cycle. Arizona Slim's penchant for giving his enterprises six-letter names starting with the letter *P* reached its logical culmination in Bunker's name for the latest addition to the kingdom: *Profit Investment.*

Meanwhile, panic was setting in on the commodities exchanges. Wealthy investors all over the world had learned of Bunker's silver-buying spree, and they all wanted in on the action. Kuwaitis, Bahreinians, Lebanese, Arabs, and Brazilians all wanted a piece of the silver mountain.

"We got them all going crazy for silver now," Bunker said to Bledsoe, squinting gleefully behind his thick glasses.

Bledsoe nodded helplessly and reached for his Maalox.

A new trading syndicate was formed, this one headed by Naji Nahas, a Lebanese billionaire with financial interests all over the globe. The Commodity Exchange in New York and the Chicago Board of Trade took inventory of the silver reserves and discovered that they had only one hundred and twenty million ounces left in their warehouses. Pretty soon, if this buying mania continued, there would be no more silver left for anyone. At this point, the officials of both exchanges decided to confer with the man who started it all, Bunker Hunt.

"We're being squeezed dry," said the delegation in presenting its case. "We were wondering if you would consider selling us some of your silver so we can meet our delivery obligations to various investors."

"Sell!" Bunker roared. His whole body quivered with consternation. "Why would anybody want to sell silver for paper dollars? Paper money is worthless."

"Be that as it may, the fact remains that very shortly we will be unable to fulfill our delivery obligations. You're the only one who can help us out of this dilemma."

"I'd be a fool to sell something that's valuable and is going to get a whole lot more valuable. Besides, if I sold any of it now I'd have a terrible tax problem with all these profits. No, I think silver's still a good buy even at these high prices and I intend to keep on buying. I'll cooperate with you on the delivery part of it until you build up your reserves, but I'd have to be crazy to sell now."

The officials from the exchanges went back to their trading posts empty-handed; Bunker's promise to cooperate with them was scant consolation. The Chicago Board of Trade decided to take action immediately to protect its customers' interests and to maintain an orderly market, it said, and the board imposed tough limits on new futures contracts. From now on, it told the investing world in a statement aimed more at Bunker and his partners than at anyone else, new contracts would be limited to a maximum of three million ounces of silver at a time.

"They're not playing fair," Bunker said in a press conference which he immediately called. "They're changing the rules on me in the middle of the game. Besides," he added with a threatening glint in his eye, "there's a conflict of interest here. I have reason to believe that certain members of the exchange have taken a short position in silver and I demand a complete investigation."

Bunker's accusation struck home. According to his sources, several of the exchange's board members had formed a syndicate of their own and gone short on almost forty million ounces of silver, which meant they stood to make a profit if they could drive the price of the metal down again. In effect, Bunker was being regulated by men with a financial position in direct opposition to his own.

At the same time, Bunker was getting worried about the growing mountain of silver that he and his Saudi partners had accumulated during the recent months. He couldn't keep chartering airplanes, with cowboys on board, to fly it over to Switzerland; that was too conspicuous now that everyone knew what he was up to. But he wanted to get it out of the United States and into a safe country, as he called it, for a reason that was real in his own mind at least.

"The country's getting more and more communist by the hour," he said to Bledsoe. "It won't be long now before the government confiscates my silver like they confiscated gold back in the 1930s."

As it turned out, Bunker didn't require the services of the fastest guns in Texas to get his bullion out of the country this time around. He hit upon a scheme that was so simple it amounted to a stroke of genius. Why not, he reasoned, find some people who already have silver in Switzerland, and who wouldn't mind keeping some of it in the United States, and simply *swap* my silver for theirs? And that's exactly what he did. He located some wealthy European traders who thought the United States, by comparison with their own countries, looked pretty stable, and exchanged warehouse receipts with them. In one fell swoop, he managed to transport millions of ounces of silver into Swiss vaults without moving a single bar. It was magic.

Inexorably, the price of silver continued to soar. The buying panic, fueled by Bunker and his Saudi partners, spread increasingly among the general public. Gold was flying to historical highs as well, a result of uncontrolled inflation in the United States and other industrialized countries throughout the world. People were uncertain about the economy, about their ability to maintain their standard of living with inflation already in the high teens and inching higher, about skyrocketing interest rates, which threatened to turn the United States into the largest banana republic on earth.

When people lose confidence in the policies of their government, when they see their country's currency depreciating in value every day against other currencies, they look around for something that will maintain its value in inflationary times. They search for a bedrock, an island of stability in a chaotic and tumultuous sea. They found it first in gold and started buying it heavily, driving the price up to an all-time high of $875 an ounce by the end of 1979. And then they found it in silver, through Bunker Hunt, who was looking for the same thing they were, although on a far grander scale than his fellow mortals.

As 1979 drew to a close, the International Metals Investment Company had taken delivery of over ninety million ounces of silver, and it owned contracts on another ninety million ounces, scheduled for delivery in March of the following year. In addition to this hoard, which Bunker and Herbert owned jointly with their trading partners, the brothers had their personal treasury of fifty-five million ounces stowed primarily in Switzerland. While the world looked on in shock, the price of silver advanced at a breathtaking pace—$20, $25, $30 an ounce. At year's end, just as the world prepared to usher in a new decade, the price hit $35 an ounce.

# 54.

WE BUY SILVER. BEST PRICES OFFERED ON SILVER-
WARE AND OLD JEWELRY. BRING IN YOUR OLD
SILVER COINS. BEST PRICES IN TOWN.

Everywhere one looked in January 1980, in newspapers and magazines, in fliers distributed by coin exchanges and jewelry dealers, in advertising displays in banks and department stores, somebody was offering to pay good money for old silver. Any kind of old silver: bracelets and necklaces, watches and keychains, silverware and teapots, silver quarters and dimes, anything at all with silver in it. Someone who had the foresight to save those old silver quarters and dimes before Uncle Sam started adding copper to them—sandwich coins, they called the new ones—could have gotten 22 to 1 for them in January 1980. Imagine walking into the coin department at Macy's with $100 in old silver coins and coming away with a check for $2,200.

The lines were horrendous, ofttimes snaking around the block. People everywhere rummaged through their attics and basements, in their old storage chests, looking for those ugly old teapots their maiden aunts had left them years ago, forgotten relics nobody wanted at the time. What the hell! Silver was worth $2 an ounce way back then. Now . . . now it's worth, whew! $40, $44 an ounce and going higher. Where are the old teaspoons, the baby spoons, the anklets and identification bracelets? Hurry, hurry! Silver's going to the moon.

Not everyone was happy about this unprecedented runup in silver prices, however. Various corporations, most notably Eastman Kodak and Polaroid, which used a lot of silver in their photographic business, were taking a beating. They were forced to pay absurd prices for silver, which they could not do without, and as a result, their common stock plummeted. And jewelry dealers were equally upset; rising costs were driving the price of silver bracelets and earrings to levels many people could not afford to pay. Tiffany's, one of New York City's premier shops on Fifth Avenue, even went so far as to put ads in the *New York Times* and the *Wall Street Journal*, denouncing the "unconscionable" speculation in silver when the metal hit $50 an ounce in January.

Bunker remained undaunted through it all. "Silver's going to $200 an ounce," he told his trading partners. "Keep on buying. This is only the beginning."

At that point, with between six hundred and eight hundred million ounces of silver in existence in all the world, and only two hundred million ounces available for delivery, the Hunts and their Arab partners had taken delivery of all the available silver. The Hunt brothers controlled about a hundred million ounces. In effect, they had cornered the silver market, something that was thought almost impossible to accomplish. With silver at $50 an ounce, the paper value of their holdings came to $5 billion. Their other assets, including oil, real estate, thoroughbreds, and other collectibles, totaled approximately $9 billion. Subtracting a billion dollars that they owed at the time to the banks, brokerage firms, and other lenders, their net worth was about a comfortable $13 billion.

Putting this into a different perspective, we find that the net worth of General Motors today (calculated on a market value minus debt basis) comes to about $16 billion. Ford is worth about $4 billion, Mobil about $7 billion, RCA about $1.5 billion, and ... well, you get the idea. In January 1980, Hunt family assets exceeded those of every major corporation in the country except two—GM and AT & T. They were one of the wealthiest private entities in the world, probably the wealthiest. They gave a special meaning to the term *super rich*.

Using their growing hoard of silver as collateral again, Bunker and Herbert borrowed heavily and went on another buying spree. They had been thwarted in their attempt to acquire Sunshine Mining a couple of years earlier, so they zeroed in on another silver mining company, Goldfield Corporation, and bought $5 million worth of the company's stock. They enjoyed doing business with Bache so much that they decided to buy a 6.5 percent interest in the firm. In doing so, they failed to notify the federal government that they had acquired more than 5 percent of the company's outstanding stock, a violation of the law.

"I only bought 3.5 percent," Bunker defended. "Herbert bought the other 3 percent. Neither of us knew what the other one was doing."

Agents of the federal government declared that they had a difficult time swallowing that one whole, and they planned to launch an investigation. Undeterred, Bunker continued to borrow heavily against his silver mountain, and the brothers pumped $190 million into the Brodcaw Corporation and $100 million more into Louisiana Land and Exploration, and they took huge positions in Gulf Resources, First Chicago, and Texaco.

After silver peaked at $50 an ounce in January, 1980, it started to slip a bit, so Bunker decided to form a new investment group to raise a billion dollars or so to prop up the price. In February he and Herbert met with Sheik Mahfouz, Mohammed Ishmael, who was a partner in Mahfouz's bank, and Mario Araktingi, a Greek Arab who serves as an adviser to the Saudi Arabian royal family. At their meeting in Bunker's office in Dallas, Bunker told his partners, "There's no doubt in my mind that silver's going to $300 an ounce within the next two years. I propose that we form a new group, Gulf Precious Metals, and raise another billion dollars to buy more silver."

Before this new organization could get started, however, the price of silver started to drop considerably. From its high of $50 an ounce, it slipped down to $46, $44, $41. Someone, somewhere, was selling the hell out of the metal. Who was doing it? Where were all the sellers coming from? High interest rates had finally done the trick, some traders explained. A twenty percent prime rate, coupled with a seventeen percent return on six-month bank certificates and sixteen percent yields on three-month treasury bills, was attracting billions upon billions of investment dollars. Europeans love high interest rates since they view them as a sign of sound monetary policies.

Overnight the dollar began to strengthen against all foreign currencies. Astonishingly high interest rates in the United States, imposed in a dramatic series of increases by Paul Volcker, chairman of the Federal Reserve, renewed the attractiveness of money markets. As quickly as investors loaded up on gold during the previous six months, that's how fast they dumped their gold and used the proceeds to buy up money-market instruments in the United States. Imagine that. Without taking any risk at all, investors were able to get a seventeen percent return on their money.

As investors all over the world sold their gold, the price collapsed. From its all-time high of $875 an ounce, it dropped a dizzying $350 in a matter of weeks, all the way back to just above $500. As gold fell, so did silver. Everybody wanted to own dollars now, and dollar equivalents like treasury bills and short-term bank certificates. For the time being, at least, gold and silver had lost their shine.

The collapse of the bullion market had a devastating effect on the fortunes of the Hunt brothers. They *didn't own* their silver outright. They had borrowed heavily against it to buy more silver contracts. As they took delivery of larger and larger mountains of silver, which also kept increasing in value, they borrowed again, and did the same thing over and over again. The pyramiding scheme worked as long as silver kept rising.

But silver was falling now. All that money they had been borrowing from Bache, their broker, as well as A.G. Edwards, Merrill Lynch, and other brokerage firms they had been dealing, with had to be paid back as silver fell in value. They started getting margin calls every day as the value of their silver steadily dropped. When one gets margin calls, he can do one of two things: put up additional cash to shore up the equity in his account, or sell off his merchandise and use the proceeds to pay back his broker. Bunker refused to sell his silver.

"It's only a temporary setback," he said to his trading partners. "After it pulls back a bit, it'll start moving up again all the way to $300 an ounce."

But silver didn't stop dropping, and every day the margin calls were coming in—$10 million here, $20 million there, $30 million a few days later. All that money they had borrowed over the years, at higher and higher interest rates, had to be paid back now that their equity was dropping.

"Don't sell," Bunker instructed his partners. "We'll ride it out. Time is on our side. This selloff can't continue forever."

Bunker was in a better position than his trading partners were. He and Herbert had started buying silver at $2 and $3 an ounce; his average cost was somewhere around $14. But the

Arabs and Kuwaitis and Bahreinians didn't get aboard the bandwagon until the price of silver was pushing $20 an ounce, and they had bought tons of the metal as high as $40. They had a lot more to be concerned about than Bunker did.

Eventually, all these margin calls began to tax even the boys' monumental reserves. They were running out of cash. Silver kept falling, ignoring Bunker's insistence that it would climb to at least $300 an ounce, and by the middle of March it had plummeted to $20 an ounce. At this point, Bunker and Herbert were called upon to meet the largest margin call they had ever faced. The Bache broker located Herbert at his office in Dallas, and notified him of the catastrophic news.

"I'm afraid I've got a whopper for you this time, Herbert. You have to come with $100 million by tomorrow. There's no way we can put it off."

Herbert hesitated a moment, and then delivered what amounted to a devastating blow. "We...we don't have the money right now. We need more time to come up with it."

"But...but," the broker was flabbergasted. "But you've always met your margin calls. Do you know what this means if you fail to come up with the money?"

"We don't have it right now, I told you. I'll get back to you in a couple of days."

Herbert hung up the phone, then immediately called Bunker, who was in Paris visiting his thoroughbred horses and tending to some business.

"We got a problem, big brother," said Herbert. "Bache says we have to come up with $100 million by tomorrow. There's no way out of it."

"Damn them all!" Bunker roared, using a rare profanity. "They change the rules on us in midstream, they raise our margin requirements and lower the limits, and then they keep on hounding us for more money. They get rich on all the interest they charge us and we get it in the neck."

"What can we do? They're the house. They make the rules

we got to play by. We got to do something. There's no way out."

"Let me talk to some people over here and see what I can come up with. I'll call you back later."

Within hours after speaking to his brother, Bunker held one of the strangest press conferences in history to make a major announcement. From his offices in Paris, he announced to the world that he and some Arab partners of his were going to issue paper certificates, bonds he called them, backed by some two hundred million ounces of silver they owned. The certificates would be convertible into silver and could be redeemed at current market prices of the metal.

The financial world was stunned. What Bunker said, in effect, was that he and the Arabs were creating their own *private international currency.* They were going to issue a kind of *money* and go into competition with the United States and other leading countries of the world whose paper currencies were losing ground to inflation every year. Unlike government-issued money, which was backed by nothing but talk and empty promises, *their money* would be as good as silver. They were resurrecting the silver standard.

The purpose of this announcement was to put the world on notice that Bunker and his Arab partners were remonetizing silver, an act which would serve to stabilize the price of the metal and increase its value over the years as inflation continued to soar. But Bunker's plan backfired. Under different circumstances, it might have worked. A year earlier, before the United States had jacked up interest rates and people were starting to load up on both gold and silver, it could easily have worked. But now, with silver in a state of decline and confidence in the dollar restored once more, if only temporarily, Bunker's announcement came across as the bluff it was. Savvy investors recognized it as a signal that the Hunt brothers had run out of cash and were trying to prop up the price of silver to salvage their own position.

As trading opened the following day, the sharks struck while the silver bulls were most vulnerable. Heavy selling in silver knocked the price of the metal down $4 an ounce. That night Herbert received another call in Dallas from Bache.

"Your margin call is up to $135 million after today's session."

"How much time do we have?"

"Time? Time has run out. We need the money yesterday."

"Well, I'm afraid we just don't have it."

"Oh, my God! This means we're going to have to start selling out your silver. We've got to sell your silver and your stock positions to raise the money."

"You go ahead and do what you have to do. We got no choice. We just don't have the cash."

# 55.

O N THURSDAY, MARCH, 27, 1980, trading started
normally on the exchanges in the country. The stock
market had suffered through a tremendous crash in mid-
February, plunging 140 points in a little over a month on
extremely high volume. The Dow Jones Industrial Averages
had settled near 740 after pushing above 900 in early
February. The spectacular collapse had been attributed
primarily to record-high interest rates in the United States.
Investors sold their stocks heavily to take advantage of high-
yielding, risk-free treasury bills and six-month bank certificates.

As the third week of March rolled around, it appeared as
though the carnage was finally over and the stock market was
bottoming out. And then, suddenly, at three o'clock in the
afternoon, the last Thursday in the month, the incredible
news was flashed on newswires across the country. As brokers
sat at their desks gloomily, hoping against hope for a rally to
put some life back into the market, they stared up at the Dow
Jones ticker on the boardroom wall and read in disbelief:

HUNTS UNABLE TO MEET $100 MILLION CALL.
BACHE'S SURVIVAL THREATENED.

Immediately the telephones, quiet for nearly six weeks,
started ringing off their hooks. Telephone switchboards were

jammed with blinking red lights as callers were put on hold. The pandemonium was instantaneous. It was as though every investor in the country with an interest in the stock market had learned the news at the same time, and ran instantly to the nearest phone. Every caller who managed to get through to his broker had the same instructions.

"Sell! Sell everything right away! Get me out of the market! I'll take any price! Just get me out before I lose everything!"

Brokers couldn't get their sell orders in fast enough. "It's Wipe-Out City!" they screamed hysterically as they placed their customers' orders. "The party's over! Suicide City! Lower the windows, they're jumping out!"

The absolute madness continued for a solid thirty minutes, fueled by one new rumor after another. Everybody had a story which he heard from six people and which he passed along to ten others.

"Bache is going under. So is Shearson. Merrill Lynch and Paine Webber may follow."

It was the end of the world. The most venerable financial institutions on Wall Street were going down the tubes. Bedlam time was here. The stocks that were hit the hardest were the ones the Hunts had to sell to raise cash for their margin calls: Texaco, Louisiana Land, Gulf Resources, First Chicago. But they were not the only ones. Virtually every stock was savaged in the reckless bloodbath. Mobil, up earlier in the day, was knocked down six points in twenty-nine minutes of trading. The carnage was universal.

And then, as quickly as the panic began, it was over. At 3:30, a half hour after the news hit the wires, the market was down more than twenty-seven points in one of the most breathtaking selloffs in history. At this point, cooler heads prevailed, savvy investors realized the world was not over after all, and they rushed into the market with baskets full of money and started buying up everything at bargain basement prices.

The selloff stopped on a dime, as it were, and the market suddenly reversed itself with a vengeance. Now there was *panic buying*.

"Don't be left out! Stocks are the best buys in town! We've got specials! Bargain basement prices for blue-chip stocks!"

A great roar rose from the floor of the exchanges as the buyers took over. "The party's on again! Drive them up, drive them up! Squeeze the shorts!"

For the next thirty minutes buying continued on record volume. Investors, realizing what had happened, realizing that they had sold their stocks at lower and lower prices in a seizure of panic, wanted to get back in again all of a sudden.

"Buy back my stocks!" they screamed at their brokers. "Buy them at the market. I want my stocks back again!"

When the final gong went off at 4:00, the stock market had made back twenty-five of the twenty-seven points it lost, to end the day down a little more than two points. Imagine, down twenty-seven, then up twenty-five in the final hour of trading. Mobil, down six at 3:30, closed the session up three for the day, a rise of nine points during the last half hour. Brokers screamed with excitement as the closing buzzer sounded, throwing tons of confetti into the air before they collapsed from emotional exhaustion. The last hour of trading on March 27, 1980, had been, simultaneously, the most terrifying and most exhilarating hour of trading the market had known in many, many years.

"Shearson Loeb Rhoades has suffered no financial damage whatsoever," said Shearson's chairman, Sandy Weill, at a press conference right after the market closed. "We did some business with the Hunts a while ago, but we closed out their account with us over nine months ago. Shearson is not involved at all."

Don Regan of Merrill Lynch issued a similar statement at the same time. "We do some business with the Hunts," he said, "but they've managed to meet all their obligations to us. Merrill Lynch is not in danger. Quite the contrary. We've never been in a better financial position."

These statements served to reassure the investing public that the Day of the Beast had not yet arrived. But there was no skirting the fact that Bache had been in serious danger of going under as silver plunged to $10.80 an ounce. The firm was forced to come up with over $100 million of its own cash in order to satisfy the margin call. As assets in the account were sold off to raise cash, Bache was able to recoup most of the money.

Bunker and Herbert were unavailable for a comment in the aftermath of Bloody Thursday. Herbert was traveling on business, his secretary said, and Bunker was in Saudi Arabia conferring with his trading partners. So the press had to content itself by interviewing business associates of the brothers.

"I don't think Bunker Hunt could go broke if he wanted to," said Scott Dial, a friend of Bunker's who lived in Dallas. "He may have a little trouble getting money from point A to point B in a certain period of time, but that's all."

"No one has to run a benefit for Bunker Hunt," said Norton Waltuch, a vice president of Conti-Commodity, which traded silver contracts for Bunker, Herbert, and their partners.

As silver rallied sharply on Friday, March 28, from $10.80 to $12.00 an ounce, Bache was able to sell off more of the boys' position at higher prices. Had the value of silver continued to fall, a serious question would have arisen about Bache's remaining in business without help from other brokerage firms, and perhaps even the federal government. But because of the new buyers entering the market and gobbling up the precious metal at what they deemed rock-bottom prices, Bache would make it on its own. However, the rumblings had been felt around the banks of the Potomac, in the venerable halls of Congress. Yes, of course. There would have to be an investigation.

"It's unbelievable that these guys could disrupt the whole market," said Congressman Benjamin Rosenthal, a Democrat from New York. "I thought those days were gone."

Not everyone was unhappy with the demise of silver, however. Tiffany's, which had run newspaper ads criticizing the billionaires for their "unconscionable" speculation in the metal, immediately announced that it was "lowering prices on all silverware on our Silver Floor by increasing discounts from fifteen to twenty-five percent."

And Armand Hammer, the crusty and controversial old chairman of Occidental Petroleum Corporation, called a press conference of his own to inform the world of his sagacity.

"I went short on silver in January," he said, his eyes aglow behind thick, horn-rimmed glasses. "Last week I closed out all my short silver positions and turned a profit of $119 million."

Old Armand Hammer had never been crazy about Arizona Slim, it turned out, and now he had gained a measure of satisfaction, as well as added to his own considerable fortune, by giving Slim's boys a drubbing in the marketplace.

# 56.

"TELL ME," ASKED BUNKER'S WIFE, Caroline, in his absence, "why do people look on us as being different?"

Upon which she excused herself to leave for the airport. She had to fly to Paris, she said, to watch one of their thoroughbreds run in a race, and then she had to go to New Guinea to take care of some oil business before flying to Montreal to see another of their horses race.

"Where was Bunker?"

"Oh, he'll be home soon. He's over in Saudi Arabia talking to his partners."

Meanwhile, William Bledsoe had had enough. His stomach simply could not take any more of Bunker, Herbert, Arabs, Kuwaitis, Bahreinians, and God knows whom else. If he heard the word *silver* uttered one more time, it just might tip him over the edge into blithering lunacy. With great fanfare, and a touch of self-righteousness, he resigned from the Hunt organization, stating that he could no longer be a party to the brothers' shady financial affairs.

"Among other things," said William Bledsoe, "Bunker is anti-Semitic."

Bunker had heard this charge leveled at him before, and shortly before the collapse of silver he had responded to it by saying, "My lawyer is a Jew, my silver broker is a Jew, and I just bought into Bache. If anyone gets along better with Jews than I do, I don't know about it. They are a little different, though. Like Chinese. You have to say that."

Bledsoe carried his testimony to Washington, D.C., where he testified before the House Subcommittee on Commerce, Consumer, and Monetary Affairs conducted by Congressman Benjamin Rosenthal. Bledsoe said that he had resigned his position with the Hunts in 1979 as a protest against their "questionable business practices."

"I did not particularly endorse their manipulations, and that necessitated my leaving," he said.

Ever since he had left, he maintained, he had been subjected to all sorts of harassment by the brothers.

"Many of the other key people who have left," he continued, "have experienced harassment from private detectives, and alleged slanderous statements are made about them. The Hunts have a reputation in the oil industry of being very litigious. As some people say, they will sue at the drop of a dangling participle."

Did Bunker operate alone in his silver dealings, or did he work with his brother Herbert?

"Their silver transactions are made in concert. They work in lockstep together. They bought silver in their own names, in corporate names, in the name of 'Catfish' Smith, a pal of Bunker's, in the name of Ted Curtain, Bunker's horse trainer in Ireland, as well as in the names of their children and two sons-in-law, Albert Huddleston and Paul Flowers.

"As I see it," said Bledsoe, "the Hunts' problem in the silver market is they started believing their own information that they were putting out. They operate under the idea that you should not ever sell anything because one day it might become valuable."

Bunker and Herbert had no choice but to turn up themselves to testify before Rosenthal's committee. On the witness stand, the sons of Arizona Slim presented themselves as two wounded innocents who had been victimized by the exchanges which changed the rules on them in the middle of the game.

"We're going to sue everybody who fleeced us," said Bunker indignantly.

Is it true, the brothers were asked, that they tried to corner the silver market by acquiring billions of dollars' worth of the metal?

"We never knew how much we had," said Bunker. "A fellow who knows how much he's worth generally isn't worth very much."

Bledsoe disputed this statement of Bunker's as well.

"He's got a memory like a steel trap," he said. "Bunker knows how much money he's worth, down to the last nickel, at any given moment. He's so preoccupied with money, I've even seen him fish around in seat cushions to look for fallen change."

In the aftermath of the hearings, Paul Volcker, the chairman of the Federal Reserve, was called upon to add his own comments on the situation before a special House committee. According to Volcker, the federal government had no choice but to help the boys restructure their debt load.

"We have to do this in the broad public interest," said Chairman Volcker, "because it would prevent further reverberations in the nation's financial markets and institutions."

Incredibly enough, Volkcer was suggesting that the nation's banks get together and guarantee the sons of Arizona Slim a loan to help them out of their financial dilemma. What the hell! If they were going to do it for Chrysler, could they do any less for a couple of red-blooded American billionares?

"Aren't we really talking about retroactively refinancing the Hunts' speculative activities in the silver market?" Senator Donald Stewart of Alabama had the temerity to ask the Federal Reserve chairman.

Other members of the panel remarked that those good old boys, Herbert and Bunker, would turn out to be the main beneficiaries of their own misfortune in the silver market. Volcker prevailed, however.

"The main idea," said he, "is to restructure their debt in such a way as to get them out of silver trading permanently. This way we can be assured of orderly markets in the future."

And so a plan was drawn up whereby a consortium of banks, led by Morgan Guaranty in New York and First National Bank in Dallas, would extend a loan of $1.1 billion to Bunker and Herbert in return for certain considerations. The interest payments on this loan would amount to about half a million dollars a day. To secure the loan, the brothers had to put up a good piece of the kingdom as collateral, including: their cotton plantations in Mississippi, sixty-three million ounces of silver which they still owned in Swiss banks, coal mines in North Dakota and Montana valued at $294 million, a hundred thousand acres of land in Florida, $50 million worth of thoroughbred horses, a good portion of downtown Anchorage, Alaska, which the boys had picked up a few years before, Herbert's collection of Greek and Roman statuary, Bunker's portrait of himself and his son, and Lamar's Mercedes-Benz and Rolex watch. Under the terms of the loan, the boys would be required to sell their remaining sixty-three million ounces of silver piecemeal over the years until it was totally liquidated by 1990.

This would effectively keep them from speculating on silver again, said Volcker, and further disrupting the market.


The ink was barely dry on this agreement when Bunker announced that maybe, just maybe, they wouldn't have to sell their silver after all. On a Sunday night in April, Bunker held an auction in the barn on one of his ranches in Lexington,

Kentucky. Dressed in his usual brown business suit, high-lighted by a new bright-red necktie, Bunker mounted the lectern and told the prospective bidders, "None of the fifty-three yearling thoroughbreds being auctioned here tonight has been mortgaged as collateral on my loan. And if you don't believe me, I'll get you a letter from Peat, Marwick & Mitchell to prove it."

As the crowd applauded enthusiastically, Bunker waited politely until they finished and added, "I'm also going to give you my personal guarantee that I'll buy back twenty-five percent of any horse you buy that's later raced in America, Europe, or Canada."

The crowd started to buzz loudly after this last announcement.

"That's like giving the buyers a twenty-five percent discount," laughed Dan Baner, a horse trainer on the ranch. "For instance, if somebody was only going to bid up to $750,000 he can now bid up to a million because he knows Bunker will come in with the other $250,000. Good old Bunker. Everything he does is just another business deal to him."

"He does everything big," said Dan Midkiff, another employee, admiringly.

"I don't really know how many horses Bunker has," said Bill Taylor, the manager of the ranch.

"Bunker doesn't either," added Mary Jane Gallaher, the hostess of the occasion. "He's always moving them all around the world. He knows where to get the most money for them, whether it's from racing, selling, or breeding them."

"But the horse market is one he can't corner," said Midkiff. "Some horses will always come along and run faster than yours. That's something nobody can control."

"There are two keys to making money on horses," said Bunker as he moved into the group. "You have to sell the horses when they're fat, and you need a lot of friends around to do the buying."

The crowd became quiet as the auction began. Bunker sat to the side, jotting entries on his program as, one by one, his thoroughbreds were led to the auction block and the crowd yelled out their bids. The proceedings lasted three hours, at the end of which the auctioneer informed Bunker that he had netted $10.3 million for the evening. Bunker smiled broadly and said, "That takes care of my interest payments for the next twenty days. You wait and see. I'm going to get to keep my silver after all."

A British reporter went up to Bunker and complained out loud, "This is a farce, it's absolutely phony. Most of these buyers here are personal friends of yours."

"Bunker Hunt is the only guy I know who can make more than $3 million an hour," laughed Dan Baner, the horse trainer.

Finally, having had enough of it all, Bunker went over to his wife Caroline and said, "Come on. Let's go find an all-night hamburger stand. I hate to go to bed on an empty stomach."


A few weeks later, on May 28, 1980, Herbert testified again, this time before a House agricultural subcommittee. As far as he and Bunker were concerned, he said, there was nothing in the terms of their loan agreement that stipulated they would have to sell their remaining sixty-three million ounces of silver to satisfy their creditors.

"As long as we pay off the note," said Herbert, "we're free to hang on to our silver. And nothing says we can't buy more silver if we want to."

To drive this point home in the most direct way possible, Bunker announced shortly afterward that one of his daughters had just acquired a fifty percent interest in a New Mexico silver mine, with proven reserves of over two-and-a-half-million ounces. Bunker negotiated the terms of the agreement himself for his daughter, Ellen Hunt Flowers. The mine in question, the St. Cloud Silver Mine, would be a jointly owned venture between Ellen and Black Range Mining Corporation, a subsidiary of the Goldfield Corporation.

Oh, yes, Bunker was still as bullish as ever on silver. Come hell or high water, he was going to find a way to pay off his $1.1 billion note, and not only get to keep his hoard of silver in Switzerland, but add to it as well.

While all this was going on, new information revealed that Armand Hammer, the feisty old chairman of Occidental Petroleum, may not have been so smart after all when he bet against the Hunt boys. In September 1980 a lawsuit was filed against Hammer and Occidental Petroleum in the State District Court of Jefferson County, Colorado. The plaintiff was Congdon & Carey Ltd. No. 4, a partnership managed by Thomas E. Congdon and William J. Carey, which includes trusts for heirs of the late John Murchison, who had been one of the richest men in Dallas.

Congdon & Carey alleged that it was entitled to the $119 million profit Hammer had made for Occidental. Hammer, officials said, had tricked the firm by pledging the silver output from the Candelaria Mine in Nevada, a partnership that was forty percent owned by Congdon & Carey and sixty percent owned by Occidental, as collateral against his short position. If Hammer was wrong and silver continued to go up in value, Congdon & Carey would have shared in the loss along with Hammer and Occidental. Since Hammer had pledged mutually owned assets and manipulated them into a no-win situation, Congdon & Carey was entitled to a portion of the profits.

Hammer at first denied he had pledged any of Candelaria's

silver to offset his short position, then later admitted publicly that he had. "Their case has no merit," he said testily, as he waited for the judge's decision.

Bunker, however, did not lose any sleep over Hammer's predicament. When he learned of the unexpected complication, he broke into a broad grin and squinted merrily behind his thick glasses.

"Anybody who bets against silver," said Nelson Bunker Hunt, "has got to be crazy."

Eventually, Armand Hammer lost.

# 57.

W E'RE GOING TO TRIUMPH against international, atheistic communism yet. Just you wait and see," said Bunker.

In an effort to do just that, he sent out letters to some of the wealthiest individuals in the United States. In them he stated:

"You, together with your wife or husband if convenient, are cordially invited to be our guest at a very important meeting that could help determine the destiny of civilization. We will listen to and discuss plans...that are a critical deterrent to the avalanche of evil that is threatening to engulf the world."

The letter was sponsored by Here's Life World, a division of the Campus Crusade for Christ. Bunker's goal in sending out the letter was to raise $1 million each from a thousand of the wealthiest people in the United States—a total of $1 billion—to take the Christian gospel to every soul on earth. Cosponsors of this mission with Bunker included former president Gerald Ford, football stars Roger Staubach and Terry Bradshaw, Watergate prosecutor Leon Jaworski, former Texas governor John Connally, and businessman Cullen Davis, who was acquitted of charges that he had murdered his stepdaughter and conspired to murder the judge who presided over his divorce before he discovered Jesus.

"We raised $170 million in Houston last month," said

Bunker, "and we're going to do even better in New York and Miami in the months ahead."

While Bunker was supposedly suffering a cash squeeze because of his silver problems, James Moffatt, the headmaster of the Hill School in Pottstown, Pennsylvania, opened his mail one morning and pulled out a check for $425,000. The check was signed by Nelson Bunker Hunt, and it was the final installment on a $1.2 million gift from Bunker and Herbert.

"Bunker's quite a boy," said Headmaster Moffatt. "He may be up to his ears in silver, but he's got a heart of gold."

Bunker graduated from the prep school in 1943 and was highly impressed by the brick buildings and the ornate Gothic spires that sprawled across 187 acres in the rolling hills of eastern Pennsylvania. Hill School has remained staunchly conservative over the years, requiring its students to wear jackets and neckties to class, and successfully resisting the nationwide trend toward coeducation. As such, his high school alma mater is one of the dwindling pockets of traditionalism left in the nation that had brainwashed the minds of its youth with left-wing propaganda for decades. Or so Bunker reasoned. Could he do any less than help support it in his battle to save the world?

In Dallas, Herbert Hunt had just returned from his morning jog around Bachman Lake. He dove into his pool to cool his body, then, still wet, went into the kitchen to prepare himself a hearty breakfast.

"I do this strictly to control my weight," he said to his wife, Nancy. "I sure as hell don't do it for fun."

Nancy patted him on the stomach, then giggled as she

watched him move around the kitchen. "You're a much better cook than I am," she said. "Thank God for that."

It was Saturday morning. Herbert didn't have to go in to work today, so he spent a bit more time than usual slicing his cantaloupe and grapefruit and cooking his eggs.

"The mail is heavy again as usual," said Nancy. "Here. Do you want to take a look at your fan mail?"

Herbert glanced at the first letter, from a mining engineer.

"You may be taking a lot of flak," the letter said, "but we in the mining industry consider you heroes."

A second letter, from a professor in Maryland, was equally laudatory. "I have asked the Franklin Mint to create a silver medal honoring the Hunt brothers as a scholarship-fund-raising device. I hope your sense of humor will authorize me to have the medal struck."

But a third letter was hostile. "How could the Hunt brothers obtain such a fast bail-out when Chrysler had so much difficulty arranging one?" the writer wanted to know.

Herbert laughed and said to Nancy, "Chrysler *needed* a government guarantee. We didn't because we had the assets. The terms of our loan were very tough. We had to put up eight or nine times the amount of the loan as collateral. Even after we pay it off, we'll still have $7 billion left."

"Well, Bunker's determined not to sell off any silver," said Nancy. "Do you think you can manage without doing that?"

"We're working hard to pay it off our way. Silver's very cheap right now. When it regains its true value the world will see how right we were after all."

As Herbert and Nancy finished their breakfast together, the chimes of the front doorbell resounded throughout the house.

"Uncle Bunker's here," said David, Herbert and Nancy's seventeen-year-old son.

Sure enough, in came Bunker, a tentlike flowered sports

shirt ballooning over his brown slacks. As Herbert and Nancy got up to greet him, Bunker stormed into the kitchen and announced, "I just got back from Paris and I'm as hungry as a dog for some good Mexican food. Let's go down to Chiquita's."

"We just finished breakfast," said Herbert, smiling.

"So what. We'll jog it off later. Let's go."

Herbert, Nancy, Bunker and David piled into Bunker's mud-covered Cadillac DeVille, while Bruce, Libby, Barbara, and Doug, Herbert's older children, followed them in one of their own cars. Once ensconced at a long table in Chiquita's, Bunker proceeded to order a family-sized tray of tortillas, tacos, and enchiladas. When the food arrived, Bunker covered the Mexican specialties with a generous coating of butter and wolfed them down.

"I missed this stuff," he said, "but, to tell you the truth, one of these hot meals a month is enough for me."

"How was Paris?" Herbert asked.

"Let me tell you something about Paris," said Bunker. "When they give you a bill at the Ritz, you think you've bought the place. There's no such thing as a cheap meal over there.

"Did you see any of your horses race?" asked Nancy.

"I've got seven hundred horses left and they're all in hock. I can still do whatever I want with them, though," Bunker said, winking at his brother and sister-in-law.

Herbert laughed and commented, "I don't like to own anything that can get sick and die on me. I'd rather have something that takes a long time to rust away, like an oil rig."

"Well, getting back to more serious matters," said Bunker after a few moments of silence, "those commodity exchanges almost did a job on us, but we'll come out on top yet. They got themselves a real nice club there. The exchanges are run by the shorts, for the shorts, with the connivance of the shorts."

"They made money on us, that's for sure," said Herbert.

"Money? There are twenty-three people on the Comex," Bunker fumed, "and almost half of them went short on silver before they changed the rules on us. One guy alone, I heard, made $15 or $20 million from us. It was a sting, a scam."

"I felt like a lady who had her purse snatched and then got arrested for indecent exposure because her clothes were ripped," Herbert commiserated.

"And how about that creep Bledsoe?" asked Bunker.

"The papers built him up as one of our cronies."

"Crony, bullshit!" yelled Bunker, smashing the table with his fist. "He was just out to get our hide. Things are getting so bad in this country that if you make money you get indicted, and if you lose money you *still* get indicted."

"Well, what about the price of silver now?" asked Nancy. "It's going back up again. It's $17 an ounce and going higher."

"Seventeen dollars is nothing," said Bunker. "Right now it's worth at least $125. The ratio with gold should be no worse than five to one. Three years from now it'll be at least $200 an ounce. You just wait and see."

Nelson Bunker Hunt, nominal head of the family's multi-billion-dollar kingdom, buttered another taco and slid it down his throat.

# 58.

A FEW MILES AWAY, in a house of his own not far from his younger brothers, the oldest son of Arizona Slim sat in his bedroom attended by his permanent nurse and companion. Hassie Hunt stared down at the lake through his window and watched the midafternoon sun break into a million gold coins on the rippling surface.

Under sedation most of the time, Hassie is not nearly as violent as he used to be. Occasionally, he will tie his shoelaces together and hang his shoes around his neck to help him think a bit more clearly. Although only a short distance from his famous brothers, Hassie is as far removed from the world of silver and finance as he could be. He stares at the lake and watches the sun dance on its surface. Arizona Slim did a lot of things in his life. But he was never able to put Hassie back together.

# Bibliography

## Books

Abels, Jules. *The Rockefeller Millions: The Story of the World's Most Stupendous Fortune.* London: Frederick Muller, 1967.

Acheson, Sam Hanna. *Joe Bailey, The Last Democrat.* New York: Macmillan Co., 1932.

Adams, Frederick Upham. *The Waters Pierce Case in Texas.* St. Louis: Skinner and Kennedy, 1908.

Allen, Frederick Lewis. *Only Yesterday.* New York: Harper & Row, 1931.

Bainbridge, John. *The Super-Americans.* New York: Doubleday, 1961.

Ball, Max W. *This Fascinating Oil Business.* Indianapolis: Bobbs-Merrill, 1940

Bartley, Ernest R. *The Tidelands Oil Controversy: A Legal and Historical Analysis.* Austin: University of Texas Press, 1953.

Beach, Rex. *Flowing Gold.* New York: Harper & Bros., 1922.

Beaton, Kendall. *Enterprise in Oil: A History of Shell in the United States.* New York: Appleton-Century-Crofts, 1957.

Blair, John M. *The Control of Oil.* New York: Pantheon Books, 1977.

Boatright, Mody C. *Folklore of the Oil Industry.* Dallas: Southern Methodist University Press, 1963.

Brantley, J.E. *History of Oil Well Drilling.* Houston: Gulf Publishing Co., 1971.

Brown, Stanley. *H.L. Hunt.* Chicago: Playboy Press, 1976.

Clark, James A., and Halbouty, Michel T. *The Last Boom.* New York: Random House, 1972.

Clark, J. Stanley. *The Oil Century: From the Drake Well to the Conservation Era.* Norman: University of Oklahoma Press, 1958.

Cotner, Robert C., ed. *Texas Cities and the Great Depression.* Austin: University of Texas Memorial Museum, 1974.

Cotton, Catherine. *The Saga of Scurry.* San Antonio: Naylor Co., 1957.

Criswell, W.A. *Why I Preach That the Bible Is Literally True.* Nashville: Broadman, 1973.

Dixon, Jeane, as told to Noorbergen, Rene. *My Life and Prophecies.* New York: William Morrow & Co., 1969.

Elliott, Osborn. *Men at the Top.* New York: Harper & Bros., 1959.

Engler, Robert. *The Politics of Oil: A Study of Private Power and Democratic Directions.* Chicago: University of Chicago Press, 1967.

Fehrenbach, T.R. *Lone Star: A History of Texas and the Texans.* New York: Macmillan, 1968.

Finty, Tom, Jr. *Anti-Trust Legislation in Texas.* Dallas: A.H. Belo Co., 1916.

Flynn, John T. *God's Gold: The Story of Rockefeller and His Time.* New York: Harcourt, Brace, 1932.

Forbes, Gerald. *Flush Production: The Epic of Oil in the Gulf-Southwest.* Norman: University of Oklahoma Press, 1942.

Forster, Arnold, and Epstein, Benjamin R. *Danger on the Right.* New York: Random House, 1964.

Frantz, Joe B. *Texas: A Bicentennial History.* New York and Nashville: W.W. Norton, 1976.

Fuermann, George. *Houston: Land of the Big Rich.* Garden City: Doubleday, 1951.

Glasscock, Lucille. *A Texas Wildcatter: A Fascinating Saga of Oil.* San Antonio: Naylor Co., 1952.

Goodwyn, Frank. *Lone-Star Land.* New York: Alfred A. Knopf, 1955.

Gould, Charles N. *Covered Wagon Geologist.* Norman: University of Oklahoma Press, 1959.

Hamill, Curtis. *We Drilled Spindletop!* Houston: Privately published, 1957.

Harter, Harry. *East Texas Oil Parade.* San Antonio: Naylor Co., 1934.

Heilbroner, Robert L. *The Quest for Wealth: A Study of Acquisitive Man.* New York: Simon & Schuster, 1956.

Hicks, John D. *The Populist Revolt.* Lincoln: Bison Press, 1961.

Horlacher, James Levi. *A Year in the Oil Fields.* Lexington: Kentucky Kernel, 1929.

House, Boyce. *Oil Boom: The Story of Spindletop, Burkburnett, Mexia, Smackover, Desdemona, and Ranger.* Caldwell: Caxton Printers, 1941.

———. *Oil Field Fury.* San Antonio: Naylor Co., 1954.

Hunt, H.L. *Alpaca.* Dallas: H.L. Hunt Press, 1960.

———. *Alpaca Revisited.* Dallas: HLH Products, 1967.

———. *H.L. Hunt Early Days.* Dallas: Parade Press, 1973.

Ickes, Harold L. *The Secret Diary of Harold Ickes: The First Thousand Days, 1933–1936.* New York: Simon & Schuster, 1953.

Jones, Howard Mumford. *The Age of Energy: Varieties of American Experience, 1865–1915.* New York: Viking Press, 1971.

Kirstein, George G. *The Rich: Are They Different?* Boston: Houghton Mifflin Co., 1968.

Knight, James A. *For the Love of Money: Human Behavior and Money.* Philadelphia: J.B. Lippincott Co., 1968.

Knowles, Ruth Sheldon. *The Greatest Gamblers: The Epic of

*American Oil Exploration.* New York: McGraw-Hill Book Co., 1959.

Leven, David D. *Done in Oil: The Cavalcade of the Petroleum Industry from a Practical, Economic and Financial Standpoint.* New York: Ranger Press, 1941.

Lundberg, Ferdinand. *The Rich and the Super-Rich: A Study in the Power of Money Today.* New York: Lyle Stuart, 1968.

McDaniel, Ruel. *Some Ran Hot.* Dallas: Regional Press, 1939.

Martin, Robert L. *The City Moves West: Economic and Industrial Growth in Central West Texas.* Austin: University of Texas Press, 1969.

Miller, Max. *Speak to the Earth.* New York: Appleton-Century-Crofts, 1955.

Moore, Richard R. *West Texas After the Discovery of Oil: A Modern Frontier.* Austin: Jenkins Publishing Co., 1971.

Morison, Samuel Eliot. *The Oxford History of the American People.* New York: Bantam, 1972.

Mosley, Leonard. *Power Play.* New York: Random House, 1973.

Munn, Melvin. *Life Line Freedom Talk Digest.* Dallas: Life Line, 1968.

Myres, Samuel D. *The Permian Basin, Petroleum Empire of the Southwest: Era of Discovery, from the Beginning to the Depression.* El Paso: Permian Press, 1973.

Nevin, David. *The Texans: What They Are—And Why.* New York: William Morrow, 1968.

O'Connor, Richard. *The Oil Barons: Men of Greed and Grandeur.* Boston: Little, Brown, 1971.

Owen, Edgar Wesley. *Trek of the Oil Finders: A History of Exploration for Petroleum.* Tulsa: American Association of Petroleum Geologists, 1975.

Owens, William A. *Fever in the Earth.* New York: G.P. Putnam's Sons, 1958.

Parten, J.R. *The Texas Oil Case.* Austin: Independent Petroleum Association of Texas, 1933.

Perry, George Sessions. *Texas, a World in Itself.* New York: Whittlesey House, 1942.

Pettengill, Samuel B. *Hot Oil: The Problem of Petroleum.* New York: Economic Forum Co., 1936.

Pratt, Wallace E. *Oil in the Earth.* Lawrence: University of Kansas Press, 1943.

Rees, Goronwy. *The Multimillionaires: Six Studies in Wealth.* New York: Macmillan Co., 1961.

Richardson, Rupert Norval. *Texas: The Lone Star State.* Englewood Cliffs, N.J.: Prentice-Hall, 1958.

Rister, Carl Coke. *Oil! Titan of the Southwest.* Norman: University of Oklahoma Press, 1949.

Rogers, John William. *The Lusty Texans of Dallas.* New York: E.P. Dutton, 1960.

Snyder, Jimmy, with Mickey Hershkowitz and Steve Perkins. *Jimmy the Greek.* New York: Playboy Press, 1975.

Spratt, John S. *The Road to Spindletop: Economic Change in Texas, 1875–1901.* Dallas: Southern Methodist University Press, 1955.

Tait, Samuel W., Jr. *The Wildcatters: An Informal History of Oil-Hunting in America.* Princeton: Princeton University Press, 1946.

Tugendhat, Christopher. *Oil: The Biggest Business.* New York: G.P. Putnam's Sons, 1968.

Webb, Walter Prescott. *The Great Frontier.* Boston: Houghton Mifflin Co., 1952.

Winfrey, Dorman. *The History of Rusk County.* Waco: Texian Press, 1961.

## Articles

Arenson, Karen W. "Banks Are Negotiating Big Loan to Offset Hunt's Silver Loss." *New York Times*, April 25, 1980.

_____. "Banks Charge They Were Misled on Hunts." *New York Times*, May 31, 1980.

_____. "House Panel Votes Hunts in Contempt." *New York Times*, April 30, 1980.

_____. "Hunt-Placid Oil Partnership Set." *New York Times*, May 5, 1980.

_____. "Hunts Said to Face No Silver Deadline." *New York Times*, May 30, 1980.

_____ "Placid Borrows $1 Billion to Pay off Hunts' Debts." *New York Times*, May 28, 1980.

_____. "Silver Trade: Early Alarm Cited." *New York Times*, April 22, 1980.

_____. "10 Banks Lent Bache $233 Million." *New York Times*, May 2, 1980.

_____. "Terms for Hunt Loan Indicated." *New York Times*, April 30, 1980.

Beckner, Steve. "The Silver Trading Caper." *Reason*, June 1980.

Bernstein, Peter W. "Engelhard's Not-So-Sterling Deal with the Hunts." *Fortune*, May 19, 1980.

Buckley, Tom. "Just Plain H.L. Hunt." *Esquire*, January 1967.

Donnelly, Richard A. "Hunt for a Scapegoat." *Barron's*, March 31, 1980.

Getschow, George, and Thurow, Roger. "Big Silver Debts Force Brothers to Mortgage Most of Their Empire." *Wall Street Journal*, May 27, 1980.

Getschow, George, and Hudson, Richard L. "Hunts, Banks Seen as Main Beneficiaries of Rescue Plan That's Backed by Volcker." *Wall Street Journal*, May 5, 1980.

Helyar, John. "To Keep Prep School in Chips, 'Mr. Chips' Courts the Wealthy." *Wall Street Journal*, September 5, 1980.

Hurt, Harry, III. "Silverfinger." *Playboy*, September 1980.

Mathews, Carol. "'Billionaire' Tag De-Bunkered by Commodity Whiz." *New York Post*, May 9, 1980.

Nicholson, Tom, and Henkoff, Ronald. "The Billion-Dollar Gambler." *Newsweek*, April 7, 1980.

Paul, Bill. "Silver Gains for Occidental Upset Partners." *Wall Street Journal*, September 8, 1980.

Pauly, David, with Thomas, Rich, and Dentzer, Susan. "The Hunts Go into Hock." *Newsweek*, June 9, 1980.

Rowan, Roy. "A Hunt Crony Tells All." *Fortune*, June 30, 1980.

————. "A Talkfest with the Hunts." *Fortune*, August 11, 1980.

Sherrill, Robert G. "Portrait of a Super-Patriot." *Nation*, February 24, 1964.

"The Costly Hunt for Arctic Oil." *New York Times*, June 17, 1980.

"Ex-Aide Disputes Hunt Silver Story." *Sun-Sentinel*, June 11, 1980.

"Hunt Brothers, Family Mortgage $3.2 Billion Assets." *Wall Street Journal*, April 28, 1980.

"Hunt Oil Holdings in Canada Frozen." *New York Times*, April 24, 1980.

"Hunts Claim Family Worth $9–10 Billion." *Sun-Sentinel*, July 24, 1980.

"Hunts Released from Lawsuit." *New York Times*, July 24, 1980.

"N.B. Hunt's Daughter Buys into Silver Mine." *New York Post*, June 26, 1980.

# Index

Hunt, Lyda Bunker (Mrs. Haroldson
Lafayette, Jr.), 57-58, 59, 60, 61-63, 65,
66, 68, 71, 74, 75, 76, 89, 94, 95-96,
98, 99, 101, 102, 103-5, 119, 123, 130,
131, 132, 161, 165, 178, 181, 183, 186,
194, 257-58
Hunt, Margaret (daughter by Lyda),
61, 65, 68, 79, 96, 118-19, 181, 183,
209, 299, 327, 329
Hunt, Nancy (Mrs. William Herbert),
321, 366-67, 368, 369
Hunt, Nelson Bunker (Bunker;
Bunkie) (son by Lyda), 121, 124, 219,
227-28, 253, 282, 287-89, 290-91, 300-
301, 302-5, 307, 311-43, 345, 346-47,
348-51, 352, 355, 357, 358-63, 364,
365-66, 367-69
Hunt, Norma (Mrs. Lamar), 297
Hunt Oil Company, 190, 194, 227, 306
Hunt Production Company, 164, 177,
186, 190
Hunt, Ray (Ray-Ray) (son by Ruth),
213, 254, 290, 302, 303, 306, 307, 327
Hunt, Robert (brother), 5, 6, 13, 32, 41,
59
Hunt, Rose (sister), 5, 194
Hunt, Ruth Ray (Mrs. Haroldson
Lafayette, Jr.), 212-13, 226-27, 253,
262, 269-71, 274, 279, 292, 303, 306,
307, 316
Hunt, Sharon (daughter of Lamar), 297
Hunt, Sherman (brother), 5, 10, 13, 14,
·31, 37, 41, 164, 177, 178, 194, 216
Hunt, Swanee Ray (daughter by Ruth),
226, 277
Hunt, Waddy Thorpe (grandfather), 3
Hunt, William Herbert (son by Lyda),
130, 219, 228, 253, 289, 290, 302-3,
305, 313-17, 318, 321-22, 327-28, 331,
332, 336, 337, 338-39, 343, 345, 346,
348, 349, 351, 352, 355, 357, 358-60,
362, 366-69

Ickes, Harold, 176, 184, 214, 223
Impel Corporation, 333
Indian Jack (gambler), 69
Inland Waterways Pipeline Company,
159
International Metals Investment
Company, 338, 339, 342
International Monetary Fund (IMF),
331
Ishmael, Mohammed, 346

Jackson, Henry (Scoop), 273
Jacobson, Jake, 273

Jacoby, Oswald, 255
Jalloud, Major, 304
Javits, Jacob, 311
Jaworski, Leon, 365
Jefferson (president of U.S.), 231
Jimmy the Greek, 249-51, 299
John Birch Society, 260, 266, 293, 300,
311
Johnson, Jack, 43
Johnson, Lyndon Baines, 271, 272-73,
282, 293, 294
Johnson, Robert, 153, 155, 156, 158
Joiner, Columbus Marion (Dad), 137-
40, 141, 142, 143-45, 146-47, 149, 150-
52, 155, 156, 157-58, 163, 166, 167,
169, 170, 171, 172, 173-74, 185, 221
Jones, Bob, 155
Jones, Tom M., 143-44
Justiss, Jick, 122, 153, 155, 164
"Just Plain Folks" (song), 280
Just Right Hotel (Henderson, Tex.),
148, 161, 173

Kansas City Chiefs, 198, 199
Kefauver hearings, 250, 254
Kelliher, Tom, 176, 184
Kelly, Machine Gun, 176
Kennedy, Jacqueline, 283
Kennedy, Joe, 273, 281
Kennedy, John F., 271, 272, 273, 274,
281, 282, 283, 284, 292, 293, 294
Kerr, Jean, 259
Khadafy, Moammar el, 304-5
Kissinger, Henry, 311, 324
Kreiling, Randy, 316-17, 318
Kreiling, Till, 317, 318

Lance, Bert, 334
Landreth, Ed, 237
Lake, Pete, 127-28, 129, 147, 153, 155,
156, 157, 164, 177, 190
Laster, Ed, 144, 145-46, 151, 158, 159,
163
Latham, Sidney, 214, 215, 219, 223,
224, 229, 230, 231, 233, 234
Lathrop, F.K., 160
Lechner, Walter, 154, 225, 226
Lee (general of Confederacy), 3
Lee, Frania Tye. *See* Tye, Frania
Lee, John, 202
Lee, Robert E., 259-60
Lee, Roy, 122, 164, 188, 194
LeMay, Curtis, 300
*Life*, 223, 268
"Life Line" (radio program), 261-62,
263, 264, 273, 276, 277, 278, 279, 282,
284, 292, 295, 300